The GLENELG
COUNTRY
SCHOOL

A
Margaret Wesley
BIRTHDAY
BOOK

· *presented in honor of* ·

Jim Moxley

· *given by* ·

Mom and Dad

Baseball Eccentrics

Baseball Eccentrics

The Most Entertaining, Outrageous, and Unforgettable Characters in the Game

Bill Lee with Jim Prime

TRIUMPH
BOOKS

Library of Congress Cataloging-in-Publication Data

Lee, Bill, 1946–
    Baseball eccentrics : the most entertaining, outrageous, and
    unforgettable characters in the game / Bill Lee with Jim Prime.
        p. cm.
    Includes bibliographical references.
    ISBN-13: 978-1-57243-953-5
    ISBN-10: 1-57243-953-X
        1. Baseball players—United States—Anecdotes. 2. Baseball—
    United States—Anecdotes. I. Prime, Jim. II. Title.
    GV873.L44 2006
    796.3570922—dc22
    [B]
                                                        2006033404

This book is available in quantity at special discounts for your
group or organization. For further information, contact:

Triumph Books
542 South Dearborn Street
Suite 750
Chicago, Illinois 60605
(312) 939-3330
Fax (312) 663-3557

Printed in USA
ISBN: 978-1-57243-953-5
Design by Amy Carter
All photos courtesy of AP/Wide World Photos unless
otherwise indicated.

To all my grandkids, who are not like their parents:
Hunter, Kazden, Logan, Alayna, and the soon-to-be
named one due on the Halloween moon. You
will all be eccentric like me because your parents seem
relatively normal. Eccentricity skips a generation, or
something like that. Remember your great-grandmother
Hazel Ruth Stevenson Lee. She was a character.

—*Bill Lee*

I dedicate this book to my parents, Curtis and Elsie
Prime, who gave me my sense of humor; my sister
Margaret, who willingly or not helped me to hone it;
my children, Catherine and Jeffrey, who both endured
it and fed it; and my wife, Glenna, who shares it. I love
you all.

—*Jim Prime*

Contents

Acknowledgments

Bill and I would like to thank all those wonderful ballplayers, past and present, who made this book so much fun to write. The toughest part was having to stop writing. The well of characters seemed bottomless, and just when we thought we'd heard it all, we discovered yet another great story that begged to be told. We were constantly saying to each other, "Boy, you don't see *that* every day," to the point that it became our daily rallying cry and mantra.

We would also like to sincerely thank Triumph Books for believing in this project from the beginning and helping to bring it to fruition. In particular, thank you to Tom Bast, Kelley White, and Amy Reagan for giving us free rein to make it our book.

Thanks also to our families, who were our sounding boards as we decided which stories should stay and which should go.

And finally thank you, baseball, for being an eccentric game and a breeding ground for eccentricity. You have made both our lives infinitely richer.

A special thank you to Bill Lee. Writing this book with Bill has been an experience I'll never forget. Just when you think you've covered a subject from every possible angle, Bill comes up with a fresh perspective. It's what made him a great major league pitcher and it's what makes him a great read. I have now worked with Ted Williams and Bill, and I consider it a distinct privilege in each case. I sincerely

Acknowledgments

hope that I will see the day when Bill is inducted into the Boston
Red Sox Hall of Fame, where he belongs, and is welcomed back
into the Major League fold, where he could add so much to the
game we all love.

—Jim Prime

My relationship and collaboration with Jim Prime in writing this
book is like synergy. It's like adding molybdenum to cobalt steel,
where the tensile strength increases tenfold. That's synergy. The
whole is greater than the sum of its parts.

—Bill Lee

Introduction | # Presenting My Credentials

The opposite of eccentric is conventional, normal, average. That's why I love to be called an eccentric ballplayer. It's actually a high compliment because baseball is the most eccentric of games. In order to play it well, you have to grasp that fact. Let so-called normal people play the normal games. We're in tune with the rhythms of the game. We stop and smell the roses. (I stopped and smelled Pete Rose on the way to second one day and got tagged out, but that's another story.)

You can't play the game if you don't recognize that it offers infinite possibilities for the bizarre. Here's an example. In what other sport could I have pissed off my own manager and the opposing manager at the same time? I was pitching a game against the Chicago White Sox in a driving rain and threw 14 straight slow curveballs. During the course of that, both managers simultaneously came to the top step of their respective dugouts and started yelling at me. It was one of the most amazing things in the world. I had managed to offend them both. My manager, Eddie Kasko, thought I should mix up my pitches, and Chuck Tanner thought I was disrespecting his Chicago White Sox. Ask Tanner, he was there. He was yelling, "You son of a bitch, quit showing up my hitters!" And Kasko was saying, "You can't throw that many curveballs in a row!" I was getting it in stereo.

Bill Melton was the last out of the game. He hit a line drive off my chest, and the ball fell toward the third-base side. I went down and got it, threw underneath my arm to first base for the last out, slid in the rain across the rain-soaked infield, and lay there like in the *Shawshank Redemption*. I got a standing ovation. It was a complete-game win and in the last three innings I threw nothing but slow curveballs. Why? Because the rain was coming down in such a way that when the hitters looked up they got rain in their eyes and had to blink. I factored that into my strategy, but neither manager liked it. One hated me and the other couldn't believe his eyes. They thought I should go by the book. They both were basically saying, "You can't play the game that way," even though it worked! And they call *me* bizarre. They call *me* eccentric. Why should I do hitters a favor by throwing fastballs when I can team up with Mother Nature and gain a huge advantage?

You can't play the game the same way every day. Every day you go out and play the game and have to realize the infinite possibilities that await you. Every day is different. How many times in the run of a season do you say, "Boy, I never saw that one before?" It happens *all the time*—every day you go to the ballpark. That's what makes the game great.

Baseball is an organic game and every part depends on every other part. Baseball is the only game with no time limit. As Herb Caen put it, "The clock doesn't matter in baseball. Time stands still or moves backwards. Theoretically, one game could go on forever. Some seem to." And Roger Angell agreed when he said, "Since baseball time is measured only in outs, all you have to do is succeed utterly; keep hitting, keep the rally alive, and you have defeated time. You remain forever young."

So-called normal players lack imagination on the mound, in the field, and at the plate. They fail to see the possibilities in front of them. They think of the game in its small component parts and don't see the bigger picture. As I've said many times, specialization breeds extinction. You have to adapt or you die. Jaja Q had it right when he said, "When you think a fastball is coming, you gotta be ready to hit the curve." Nomar Garciaparra's hero was the biggest multitasker of all time: "My idol was Bugs Bunny, because I saw a cartoon of him playing ball—you know, the one where he plays every position himself with nobody else on the field but him? Now that I think of it, Bugs is still my idol. You have to love a ballplayer like that."

Charlie Finley wanted to expand the foul lines and use orange balls and even change the names of his players as if they were pro wrestlers. You can't mess with the integrity of the game like that. But as far as being unconventional goes, I mean, so what? I've had a lot of theories in my time, and one of the most radical is that facial hair does not affect pitching or hitting. If baseball owners want nice All-American lads, they should recruit at Quantico. I said that to Dennis Eckersley once and he said, "They're all muscles in their upper shoulders, they're chiseled but that's why they can't hit the high cheese."

Even the greatest basketball player in history couldn't hit his own weight playing baseball. He couldn't adjust or adapt to the game. Michael Jordan hit .202—but he did buy a bus for the Barons team. So he was a good teammate. That's a pretty good rule of thumb. When a guy buys you a bus, he stays in the lineup.

Bill Veeck was my idea of an enlightened team owner. Most aren't. Bill Terry used to say that baseball has to be a great game to survive the fools who run it. Owners expect players to fall into line and be good soldiers. It's like I told the late, great Warren Zevon—and he put it in a song—"You're supposed to sit on your ass and nod at stupid things." Some of us aren't willing to do that.

Personally, I have a problem with the term "flake." I prefer the terms "gauche" or "sinister." Flake is an egotistical, right-handed, exploitative, carnivorous, non-recycling, Republican word, but what do you expect from a northpaw world? "Flake" seems to have entered the baseball lexicon, and so it will pop up from time to time in this book. Speaking of things popping up, Rodney Scott, my teammate in Montreal, was also a good friend. We were driving somewhere one day, and I commented on the signs we were passing. "Look at that," I said. "We're driving on Route 37 and we've just left the post office where I bought some 37-cent stamps. The sign we just passed said, 'Save 37¢ on gas.' It's amazing how that number 37 is always popping up." Rodney looked at me and said, "Yeah, Bill, usually with the bases loaded."

In baseball parlance, "flake" is a rather nebulous category that includes the following: malcontents, characters, cranks, rebels, fruitcakes, nut jobs, wingnuts, whackos, space cadets, head cases, nonconformists, goofs, nutcases, free thinkers, book readers, and other subcategories of eccentrics, like geography majors and left-handed Californians. Baseball never used to go west of St. Louis, and when it finally did get opened up to the rest of the planet, Californians were not accepted. The rest of America was not prepared for guys like Steve Hovley. Hovley lived in a teepee and when he finally was forced to cut his hair, he shaved his head bald. He was definitely a minimalist. "California, the land of fruits and nuts." That's what they always said about us.

I feel compelled to submit my qualifications for writing a book on eccentrics. You be the judge. I used to play for the Alaska Goldpanners and, I'll tell you, when you're playing in permafrost and it warms up and all of a sudden your center fielder disappears, that leads to eccentricity. Oddibe McDowell, our 5'9" center fielder, couldn't afford to sink two feet.

It's actually strange because many of the people in this book also played for the Panners. Jimy Williams was the first player to come out of Alaska and play in the majors. I was number nine. We also produced Tom Seaver, Rick Monday, Sal Bando, Graig Nettles, and Jimmy Nettles.

I once danced in the opera *Euripides*, the "Orpheus in the Underworld" scene with Sarah Caldwell in my Red Sox uniform (I was in my Red Sox uniform, not Sarah). I also danced with Margaret Hamilton, the original Wicked Witch of the West from *The Wizard of Oz*. My dad always called me a prima donna, and now I have the pictures to prove it. I was the first dancer, second pitcher. Boy, I could turn a grand jeté. Not many ballplayers know what a grand jeté is. I barnstormed in the Capelle Valley in Saskatchewan in the middle of a drought when farmers were praying for rain and, as soon as I hit a home run, the skies opened up and it rained for three straight days.

I helped a Salem witch named Laurie Cabot to remove the curse of the Bambino from the Red Sox. Cabot and Paul Poirier, the noted warlock, brought me in and said some mumbo jumbo. And they were all dressed to the nines. We healed this broken bat as a symbol of the curse being over. They did their thing over the broken bat and asked that they be able to beat the Toronto Blue Jays that day. I couldn't believe my ears. What the hell kind of witchcraft only allows you to beat the Blue Jays? Ask for a World Series championship! Then they presented me with the bat. I threw it in my trunk without even looking at it. I watched the game at Fenway for a while, and Tom Brunansky hit into a double play his first time up and then hit a home run. I started to drive home, and I was listening to the radio as he hit his second homer. I got through Franconia Notch, where the old man of the mountain is, and on a 3–1 pitch Brunansky hit his third homer. When I got home, I opened the trunk, looked at the bat, and it was a Brunansky model bat! Wow, I had chills all over my body! He'd not been with the Red Sox for five days. What are the odds that they'd use his bat in the ceremony to break the spell? I still have that bat in my basement to show people they're full of shit when they say I have them in the belfry.

Sonny Siebert was the most superstitious guy I played with. He'd never cross over the double foul line. He would walk around first base or walk around home plate where it wasn't but he'd never cross the double line. (He must have been a safe driver.) Siebert was my roomie when I first came up. They always said, "Bill, you're the second most valuable player on the Red Sox because you drive Sonny Siebert to the ballpark."

I was in Hawaii with the Panners to play at an army base out of Schofield Barracks, which was in the movie *From Here to Eternity*, where Montgomery Clift played taps when his buddy died. A torrential rain came. You could hardly see center field, so I bet everybody that I'd run out to center field and do 20 pushups in my jock strap. Everyone threw in $20—the whole bullpen. The 20 pushups was the tough part.

I find nothing particularly strange about any of the above, but apparently some do. In any case, I am certified, being a member in good standing of a very exclusive group known as the Baseball Reliquary's Shrine of the Eternals. In the past people have asked why I haven't been inducted into the Red Sox Hall of Fame. My answer has always been that the only way I'm going in is posthumously and, when I do, I want to go in facedown so they can kiss my ass. Remarks like that have not helped my cause, even with a more liberal ownership team in place at Fenway. I actually love the new ownership, but old grudges die hard.

My membership in the Reliquary makes me proud, but the games I won, I didn't win with smoke and mirrors. Definitely not smoke. Ballplayers used to come up and *run* to the batter's box to hit against me. They said that their *mothers* could hit me. My response was that it just shows that talent sometimes skips a generation. The more aggressive a hitter was, the more I used that aggressiveness against him. I've always been a devotee of Paramahansa Yogananda, author of *Autobiography of a Yogi*, which I've tried to live by. (Freddie Lynn used to ask me who that guy I was always talking about was, "the one with all the vowels.") I can't hear what you're going to say before and I'm not thinking about what you're going to say in the future. It drives people crazy because I'm exhaling.

The Reliquary is much more elite than the Red Sox Hall of Fame or even the Baseball Hall of Fame. The criteria for induction are very rigid. Here is their mission statement: *The Baseball Reliquary is a nonprofit, educational organization dedicated to fostering an appreciation of American art and culture through the context of baseball history and to exploring the national pastime's unparalleled creative possibilities.* They go on to say:

> The highest honor afforded by the Baseball Reliquary
> is election to the Shrine of the Eternals. Similar to
> Cooperstown's National Baseball Hall of Fame, the

Shrine of the Eternals differs philosophically in that statistical accomplishment is not the principal criterion for election. It is believed that the election of individuals on merits other than statistics and playing ability will offer the opportunity for a deeper understanding and appreciation of baseball than has heretofore been provided by "Halls of Fame" in the more traditional and conservative institutions. Criteria for election shall be: the distinctiveness of play (good or bad); the uniqueness of character and personality; and the imprint that the individual has made on the baseball landscape. Electees, both on and off the diamond, shall have been responsible for developing baseball in one or more of the following ways: through athletic and/or business achievements; in terms of its larger cultural and sociological impact as a mass entertainment; and as an arena for the human imagination.

I love that last phrase, "arena for the human imagination," because imagination is really what a ballplayer needs. The Reliquary is a place where Dick Stuart's glove is as treasured as Brooks Robinson's (Stuart was a man who said that his dapper wardrobe added 20 points to his batting average; he obviously never listened to Wilson Pickett 'cause he couldn't pick it); where Moe Berg's passport is more fascinating than his statistics; and where Jackie Robinson's character is more important than the number of times he stole home.

When I was inducted in 2000, I was introduced by Ron Shelton. Ron is a filmmaker whose credits include *White Men Can't Jump*, *Bull Durham*, *Cobb*, and *Tin Cup*. Ron played in the Baltimore Orioles farm system in the late '60s and early '70s, so he knows about baseball and its conservative culture. His speech says a lot about the love we both have for baseball and how we try to reconcile the baseball mindset with our own radical philosophies.

During the '60s and '70s, when I played high school and college baseball in Southern California and began my professional career, I discovered I had to live in two different worlds and step back and forth between those worlds as gracefully as possible. One was the world of baseball, of sports and competition, of discipline and preparation for the sheer joy of men playing boys' games. It was a gift to be able to make your living playing a game, traveling around America by bus with your peers, and being nervous eight months a year having to perform every night, rarely with a day off. Baseball got me a college education, taught me how to read and do math. I could figure out my batting average while rounding first at the age of eight. It taught me all the things that matter: the long season, the need to take your cuts, the hope of waiting till next year. Every cliché in baseball is a religious truth.

Then there was the world of politics and social activism and literature and protest and, well…all of the things that made the '60s great. This was a world you generally didn't discuss with your baseball comrades; in fact, you wouldn't say "comrade" with a fellow baseball player. And when you tried to discuss baseball with your political colleagues, they invariably labeled you a reactionary dilettante who was a puppet symbol of free market capitalism with all its ills. So I sort of couldn't figure out what my peer group was. In fact, for decades I felt part of an unidentified political party. It's actually sort of a part conservative social values and democratically socialistic one, except when it's not, and then it is a party of liberal social values and free market political ones. You get the point—it's hard to find someone to vote for. There were few public figures during this time who stood for this marriage of values. Bill Lee was one of them. This is a marriage that seemed to make perfect sense to me: playing baseball and marching against the war in Vietnam. There were many people who had trouble with that combination. And as more and more people reject the simplistic platforms of our two major political parties, Bill Lee's organic mixture of social and political values feels more and more appropriate.

Ron admitted that he stole one of my lines to use in *Bull Durham* to illustrate the clash of conservative baseball and leftist leanings. When Crash Davis makes his way to the mound to talk to his pitcher, Nuke LaLoosh, he tries to convince him that he's throwing too hard. "Quit trying to strike everybody out," he says. "It's fascist. Throw some ground balls. It's more democratic." Sam McDowell was a fastball pitcher, but his attitude was the same. He said, "It's no fun throwing fastballs to guys who can't hit them. The real challenge is getting them out on stuff they can hit."

Enough about my credentials. All I know is that if you have Mickey McDermott, McDowell, "Bird" Fidrych, and Bill Lee in a car, who's driving? The sheriff.

The point is: anyone who doesn't fit into the tight stereotype of who belongs in the Major Leagues surely belongs in this book. They are not all lovable…or even likeable. Ty Cobb and Dock Ellis were not warm and fuzzy types. They are here because they did not conform to the norm. There are polar opposites on the baseball and human spectrum represented here. The flake is not a member of a homogeneous monolithic community. Some, like Wade Boggs, are flakes because they took the game so seriously; others, like Mickey McDermott (69 wins, 69 losses, 19 DUIs), because they didn't take it seriously enough. Mickey, by the way, was voted "most likely to be found dead in his hotel room" in high school.

There are arch-conservative eccentrics like Ted Williams and bleeding-heart liberal eccentrics like myself. Some are verbal eccentrics; others are eccentrics from the *Three Stooges* school.

They are not all witty or pithy. Prop comics and malaprops comics are everywhere. Most of the people in this book have absolutely nothing in common except the fact that they are all interesting. They are all colorful. And they make the game more interesting and colorful by giving it a human face.

So "eccentric" is not inherently pejorative. Often it is a term applied to someone who is just more intelligent, creative, thoughtful, or imaginative than most. Sometimes flakes are heroic and sometimes they are villainous, just like politicians, Methodists, and marshmallow salesmen. Is a kook a flake? Is a flake a kook? Does being a midget who batted in the majors make you a flake? Probably not, unless the midget bit the umpire's knee after a bad call. Does making the decision to put a midget into a game make you a flake? Absolutely. In other words, Eddie Gaedel was no flake, he was a fluke. Bill Veeck certainly was no fluke, he was a flake. God bless them both.

Some ballplayers are intentionally funny and work to promote that side of themselves to the public. Others have zaniness thrust upon them. Manny Ramirez, for example, had no intention of being funny when he disappeared into the Green Monster at Fenway Park to have a pee, but it turned out to be a classic case of comic relief. Turns out the urinary tract is just beyond the warning track at Fenway. When Manny makes the third out at third base and kills a rally when you're down two runs with Mike Lowell coming to the plate—then Manny's not so funny. It just proves that timing is everything in comedy...and in baseball.

Some baseball positions are more prone to attracting funny guys. I don't have the scientific data to back it up, but an inordinate number of baseball's so-called characters seem to be left-handed pitchers, like Sparky Lyle and Lefty Gomez. Relief pitchers are a significant demographic within this category. A significant number also seem to have been catchers, including Yogi Berra, Bob Uecker, Moe Berg, Joe Garagiola, and Sammy White. There must be a positive-negative charge in the pitcher-catcher battery that stimulates the synapses of both, especially with lefties. On the other hand, few are second basemen, who I tend to stay away from because they're always beating up marshmallow salesmen in elevators. (Frank Duffy excepted. He went to Stanford. Duffy was the greatest shortstop with the least amount of ability that I ever saw—until I saw David Eckstein. They both got by on guile. Butch Hobson, the third baseman, was like the bug in *Men in Black*. He had the herky-jerky thing that allowed him to throw around corners. He'd miss by 20 feet when the chips locked up on him. But I digress…)

Sometimes, a player who should be a flake isn't. Tim Wakefield comes immediately to mind. He is a brilliant practitioner of the most eccentric, unpredictable pitch of them all, the knuckleball, and yet he is as colorless as George Steinbrenner's face after another loss to Tampa Bay.

Guys with great senses of humor aren't automatically eccentric, either. Lots of guys I've known are hilarious but aren't eccentric. I was drinking with Eddie Mathews, Bob Lemons, Dick Radatz, and Gary Bell. Warren Spahn came in, and Mathews said, "Hey, Lucky, how ya doin?"

Spahn said, "Why ya callin' me Lucky?"

"I ain't callin' you Lucky—everybody else is calling you Lucky."

"Whatta you mean?" said Spahn.

Mathews said, "I'm coaching third base and every time someone hits the ball to the warnin' track, they come around second base and they say, 'That lucky hook-nosed bastard.' So your name must be Lucky. Lucky must be short for lucky hook-nosed bastard."

Spahn just grinned. "You bastard," he said.

He and Gary Peters were my heroes. I ended up rooming with Gary with the Red Sox. He knew I was his heir apparent so he used to sneak up behind me during wind sprints and try to bite my left elbow because he knew I was coming to take away his job. Both funny, but not eccentric—although Peters is close.

As a general rule anyone named Dizzy, Daffy, Ducky, or Dazzy is probably a flake. Guys called Lefty are almost always eccentric. Conversely, you immediately know that Steve Garvey is the antithesis of flakedom—his is an accountant's name, or perhaps the mild-mannered alter ego of a WASPish superhero. I once got a base hit that drove in the winning run against the Dodgers, and when I got to first, Garvey looked at me and said, "You know, Bill, I don't know if you look better with or without the beard." I thought, *Holy cow, here I just get a hit to beat you guys and you're talking about facial hair.* How anal retentive. (The bumper plates in San Diego, after it was revealed that he'd knocked up two girls, said: Steve Garvey Is Not My Padre.) They were grooming him as a Republican for Congress, but Garvey didn't want to run for Congress; he wanted to be a senator. And also, when his legendary coach at Michigan State retired, he wouldn't go to the dinner unless they paid him $20,000. It was sad. He still looks good, though. He's always looked good. Every hair in place, stone-chiseled jaw, and a twinkle in his eye.

Mookie is a pretty strange name, but Mookie Wilson wasn't known as a flake. Neither was Pokey or Pee Wee Reese. Oddibe should have been hilarious. People with bird names tend to be amusing: Birdie Tebbetts, Bird Fidrych, Hawk Harrelson. Anyone named Rube is a safe bet to be a flake. So are Mad Hungarians and Mad Russians.

Superstitious ballplayers constitute a whole subcategory of flakiness. For some of them, superstitions are just a part of their eccentric behavior; others are otherwise pretty normal, save for their bizarre rituals. Personally, I always noticed that I hit better in ballparks that had an oak tree nearby. But that's not superstition, that's cold hard fact.

Physical characteristics do not necessarily make a player an eccentric. Pete Gray, the one-armed hitter of the wartime St. Louis Browns, was a dedicated athlete who overcame adversity to play in the major leagues. More recently, Jim Abbott, who won 87 games in the majors from 1989 to 1999 (he came very close to notching a 20-win season for the 1991 California Angels, finishing with an 18–11 mark) pitched effectively—and courageously—despite having only one hand. Mordecai Peter Centennial Brown was better known to baseball fans as "Three-Fingered Brown" because the right-handed hurler had lost half of the index finger of his right hand in a corn shredder when he was a kid. In his case, the deformity actually helped his pitching. It gave him one of the most sweeping curves in pitching history because of the spin he could put on the ball. Maybe I should have chopped off a digit or two myself.

Managers are apparently chosen due to their eccentricities. Anyone who can claim disability—mental or physical—can coach in the big leagues forever. They've got a bunch of pirates out there. They've got patches, peg-legs, plates in their heads. You too can be a coach in the big leagues: just name your disability. Send us your infirm, your lame, and we'll make coaches out of them. And you wonder why baseball's gone downhill. It's hard to walk uphill when one leg is shorter than the other. You keep going in circles. Earl Weaver had anger issues and may not have been able to function in a normal society, but he was fine in baseball.

On the other hand, would Yogi Berra have been as quotable if not for that great face? As if in confirmation, Yogi pointed out, "So I'm ugly. You don't hit with your face." Well, I lost my teeth six times—and counting. Stan Williams said, "You don't play with your face. Rub some dirt in it, you'll get over it." I tell kids, "After the first four or five times, it just makes a crunching noise."

Sometimes, rarely, entire teams are funny. Perhaps no team has ever been as funny as the fledging New York Mets of the early '60s. They were the Keystone Kops with different uniforms. They became a national joke that everyone got. They arrived with all the fanfare of a Broadway comedy and were directed by Casey Stengel, who provided most of the punch lines ("Can't anyone here play this game?"). The Washington Senators ("First in war, first in peace, and last in the American League") were the butt of a gazillion jokes in the '50s, when every borderline or offending player was threatened with being deported there. The Gashouse Gang had guys named Ripper, Daffy, Dizzy, Pepper, Ducky, the Fordham Flash, Sunny Jim, Wild Bill, and Leo the Lip. How could they *not* be funny? The Oakland A's of the 1970s were an assortment of characters, including the ubiquitous Reggie Jackson, and guys like Catfish Hunter, Rollie Fingers, Vida Blue, and a mule mascot named Charlie O, which was allowed to graze on the field of play and mingle with Finley's guests at cocktail parties. Some would argue that it was owner Charlie O. Finley who contrived to create color on a team that wasn't particularly colorful. He provided monetary incentives for players to grow facial hair and change their names. Thus Jim Hunter became Catfish; to his credit, Vida Blue resisted an invitation to change his first name to "True."

Every team has their right-wing conservative Christian group—which is fine except that God now has to play favorites. I was once asked by a fundamentalist if I believed in God and I said, "Yes. God's coming soon and she's really pissed." I'm not sure if that made him happy. In 2006, the Atlanta Braves had a "Faith-Based Night." One of the *true* Braves fans said, "This is the night I go because the beer lines are short." That's great! I love that fan!

Some teams are funny for a year or two and then return to their straitlaced selves. The Yankees of the late '70s were a funny team. Yes, the Yankees, the corporate entity that has all the personality and color of whole wheat toast and are about as extroverted as Boo Radley were actually once an interesting group of characters. They had Billy Martin, Reggie Jackson, Graig Nettles, and Mickey Rivers, for starters, not to mention Sparky Lyle.

The 1934 St. Louis Cardinals were reportedly hilarious, and with the cast of characters they had—the Dean brothers, Pepper Martin, Leo Durocher, Joe Medwick, Ripper Collins—who can doubt it? Like the aforementioned Yankees, they were also very good, which goes to show that you can be funny and still win. Which leads me to another interesting question: can Hall of Famers and future Hall of Famers be flakes? Was Babe Ruth a flake? Ted Williams? Wade Boggs? Ty Cobb? You bet your ass they were.

Abbott and Costello knew that baseball is a funny and eccentric game. Their timeless "Who's on First?" routine would not work if any other sport had been used. I mean Who's at quarterback?, What's at defensive end?, and I Don't Know's a middle linebacker just doesn't make for witty banter. Not to mention I Don't Give a Darn at tight end.

Baseball should be a fertile breeding ground for eccentricity like politics is ideal for fostering corruption. Maybe it's something in the intrinsic makeup of the game. It's a sport that straight-facedly employs terms such as "screwballs," "knuckleballs," "fly balls" (think about it!), "eephus pitches," "spit balls," "bullpens," and the "suicide squeeze." It's hard to imagine Babe Ruth as a beer-swilling, womanizing jockey, even if his weight didn't make the point moot. Or Mark Fidrych as a basketball player who talked to the ball before free throws. I can't see Casey Stengel getting a lot of laughs as coach of the Green Bay Packers. Or Yogi Berra becoming the great philosopher he is as a hockey goalie. Earl Wilson—the writer, not the major league pitcher—once said about Little League baseball: "It's a nervous breakdown crammed into six innings." He also said that it was "a very good thing because it keeps the parents off the streets." In major league baseball, the breakdowns come in many forms. Gabe Paul said it best, "The great thing about baseball is that there's a crisis every game." (According to Dick Radatz and Gary Bell, Paul was the cheapest bastard they ever met.)

There are funny umpires, funny managers, and funny owners. In Baltimore they even have funny groundskeepers! The point is baseball doesn't need furry mascots to be funny. It's plenty funny all on its own, thank you very much. Having said that, there have been great baseball clowns that have livened up the game. There are fictional funny guys, too. "May Day" Malone of *Cheers* fame comes to mind. According to the documentary they made about the series, the character of Sam was based on me. They described me as an "obscure left-handed pitcher for the Red Sox." That "obscure" part hurt. There are funny announcers, too, and they fall into two categories: those who are intentionally funny and those who are unintentionally funny. The former group includes Bob Uecker, Jon Miller, Harry Caray, Vin Scully, and Ken Harrelson. The latter group has folks such as Tim McCarver, Ralph Kiner, Jerry Coleman, and Phil Rizzuto.

Are there still eccentrics in baseball? Have the flakes been replaced by flaks? I think that the game has been sanitized by agents and owners to the extent that a player is barely able to ad-lib a belch. Bill Veeck, who knows something about colorful baseball players, expressed some doubts in *The Hustler's Handbook*: "What we have are good gray ballplayers, playing a good gray game and reading the good gray *Wall Street Journal*. They have been brainwashed, dry-cleaned and dehydrated!…Wake up the echoes at the Hall of Fame and you will find that baseball's immortals were a rowdy and raucous group of men who would climb down off their plaques and go rampaging through Cooperstown, taking spoils.…Deplore it if you will, but Grover Cleveland Alexander drunk was a better pitcher than Grover Cleveland Alexander sober." Veeck is right, but it makes me wonder where the line is. If you're a great pitcher with the shakes and blowing .05 on the breathalyzer, are you better at .08 when your shakes stop and your sinker kicks in? I once beat Catfish Hunter after consuming four beers, but I wouldn't recommend it.

Veeck had a valid point though. After all, it's a different game today. All-Star Games sometimes take on the appearance of the Republican National Convention. Players have agents and several layers of PR between them and us. Instead of commenting on a controversial issue, they now "issue a statement," the way David Wells (a funny guy who wears Babe Ruth underwear) did when he was suspended in 2005. They are politically correct, sterile, and bland, or so goes the conventional wisdom. Nevertheless, the answer is a yes; they are still out there, waiting to be discovered. Like diamonds or honest politicians, they are just a bit harder to find. Jim Walewander is a flake by baseball standards because he listened to a punk rock group called The Dead Milkmen. Walewander told Chin Music: "Baseball is less conservative today than it was, but it's still very strait-laced." He was asked to elaborate. "Baseball's rural. It has its roots in farmland. Shit, they still chew tobacco."

Moe Drabowsky, the pitcher and master prankster who passed away in the spring of 2006, felt that today's game lacks the kind of spontaneous fun of his era. "Players seem to be more serious now," he once told the AP. "I would tend to believe they don't have as much fun." When Drabowsky died, *Sports Illustrated* lamented the passing of the man and his legacy of lunacy: "It feels strange that there was a time when baseball players were *expected* to be a little kooky," said *SI*. Steve Dalkowski and Drabowsky came up at the same time, but you couldn't have them both in the bullpen at the same time because if they called down to have them warm up, a polka would break out.

Some observers feel that today's players are reluctant to show the public their eccentric side because it leaves them vulnerable to accusations that they don't take the game seriously. They may have a point. Radio sports talk shows are waiting to pounce on any athlete who deviates from the norm, especially if the athlete falls short on the field of play. Also, there are very few lifers out there—guys who stick with one team throughout their career—guys like Yaz and Kirby Puckett and Tony Gwynn. Players are interchangeable. The infield for the Boston Red Sox changes 100 percent in one year. Are they still the Red Sox that fans love, or a bunch of high-paid migrant workers? Mercenaries with no loyalty to the team or knowledge of the team culture and traditions. Jerry Seinfeld refers to it as "cheering for laundry" and he has a point. Fans are cheering for the uniform because the people in it change so often. It used to be that Mickey Mantle was the New York Yankees and Ted Williams was the Boston Red Sox. Not anymore. No wonder teams don't develop eccentric ballplayers. There has to be a comfort zone for eccentrics to flourish. These guys are just visitors. Johnny Damon is a hired gun—have bat will travel. He was the bearded face of the Red Sox self-proclaimed "Idiots" and now he's a faceless Yankee. As I said earlier, no wonder opposing players are so friendly on the field. They don't think in terms of teams anymore—they think in terms of contracts and the players' union.

This is a celebration of the eccentric, a tribute to flakes past. It is also a call to today's players to loosen up and have some fun.

—Bill Lee

| # Confessions of a Cunnythumber

Pitchers are a large contributor to baseball's eccentricity. Depending on their effectiveness, or lack of same, they drive hitters to the edge of insanity or managers over the edge. They say that you have to lose your fastball if you want to learn to pitch. I was fortunate enough to not have much of one from the very beginning—and then I lost it completely.

My mother called it a game only once. Both my parents tell the story in one voice. When you have been married 67 years, that is the only way to tell a tale.

It was the summer of 1941, the halcyon days before Pearl Harbor. The date that would separate my parents for the better part of four years. My father was quietly fuming behind the wheel of the old Ford. He was trying not to show any emotion. He had gotten his pitch, he thought. But after toiling in the mound for nine innings in the late summer heat, his bat had slowed down. It was a 3–1 fastball right down the chute. He got under it and popped it up to right. (Twenty-seven years later, while leaving USC on my way to Waterloo, Iowa, of the now defunct Midwest League, I saw that my father had written on my glove, covering each finger: *Throw strikes. Keep the ball down. Don't alibi. Hustle, hustle, hustle.* His advice I now give to my sons Mike and Andy, and their sons, Hunter, Kazden, and Logan Lee.) Bill Lee Jr., my father, couldn't alibi. He had learned not to alibi from his father, Williams Francis I, who played for the Hollywood Stars on the Pacific Coast League. Besides,

1

Ring Lardner had not written *Alibi Ike* yet, so no one was listening anyway.

My grandfather used to cut the center of his glove so he could feel the ball better on his palm. He said it made his hands softer and quicker while he was turning the double play. No one got the ball quicker to first base. Not until the great "No Touch" Bill Mazeroski of the Pittsburgh Pirates.

My grandfather's job, when he was not playing second base, was opening up new Gilmore Gas stations. Their symbol was the lion, and they had given him twin male lion cubs to raise. The lions lived in the backyard of his North Hollywood home. He had them for four years, in which time they traveled together up and down the California coast and had become inseparable. When Mobil Oil took over Gilmore Gas, they felt the lion promotion did not go with their logo, which was a flying horse—apparently lions eat flying horses when they land. My grandfather ended up taking the lions to the Griffith Park Zoo under the condition that he be allowed to visit any time he wished. On his first visit, the young lions came running, pressing up against the bars, purring and rolling around on their backs so that he could reach through the bars and scratch them on their bellies. The visitors at the zoo were dumbfounded by this action.

When the time came for my grandfather to leave, he had tears in his eyes, and when he turned away, the lions started to roar. They were trying to get him to stay. The other animals at the zoo sensed the anxiety and started calling out in their own voices. Monkeys howled and birds screeched. Snakes did relatively little. You get the picture. The zookeeper came to my grandfather and told him never to come back.

My maternal grandfather played football for USC. His father was Dean of Graduate Schools for USC from 1900 to 1937. When he left there he was one of the founding fathers of the University of the Pacific in Stockton, California, on the confluence of the San Joaquin and Sacramento rivers. He had been raised along those river banks. He went to World War I as a medic and was gassed in

2

some obscure farm in France. When he returned partially disabled, his brothers set him up at a farm in Oakdale on the Stanislaus River. He became president of the Oakdale water district. On his farm he raised peaches, walnuts, and almonds (people always called baseball players from California the "boys from the land of fruits and nuts" in a derogatory fashion, but I was one in a literal sense). He had learned to fly and had a couple of planes in which he used to survey the dams along the water district. When I was eight years old, he taught me to buzz the farm doing barrel rolls and loop-de-loops, culminating with a stall coming right down over my grandma—which drove her nuts.

One day he let me fly all the way back from Donnells Reservoir. He told me to follow the river and then he fell asleep. When he woke up, I was following the wrong river and was heading for Atwater Air Force Base, about 20 miles off course. When I saw the jets in the distance, I knew I was in trouble. It would have been embarrassing to be shot down by our own guys. Other times he took me up to chase the coyotes off the pheasant fields on the Rodden ranch. He would fly under the power lines, sometimes giving me the stick while he shot at them. As you can see from my two eccentric grandfathers, the apples don't fall far from the tree. While it might better serve the purposes of this book on eccentrics if I had been raised by the wild man of Borneo and a she-wolf, my mother and father were like Ward and June Cleaver in comparison, fairly normal. Like talent, eccentricity must skip a generation.

In the old days pitchers like me were called cunnythumbers. In fact, I almost called this book *Confessions of a Cunnythumber*. Then I Googled it and all kinds of interesting things popped up. I figured that we might get more readers, if only by accident. A certain demographic would have lined up to buy it because it sounds pretty filthy—like you should be going for counseling to rid yourself of it. Welcome to Cunnythumbers Anonymous, sir. *Hello, my name is Bill Lee and I'm a cunnythumber.* Or maybe you need to go to the doctor for a shot of penicillin. *Mr. Lee, I'm afraid you have a severe case of cunnythumb. You'll need a series of injections.* Actually, the term may have its origins in marble shooting. Cunnythumbing was a way of striking the "shooter." So go and wash your mouth out with soap for anything you might have been thinking.

It's an expression for a guy who can't throw hard but is still a really good pitcher. My dad told me about a guy named Red Barrett who threw the shortest game in history—he never went to three balls on anybody, induced eight double plays, and only threw 58 pitches! He was the epitome of the classic cunnythumber. You use your thumb to either make it break away or make it break in. I have a really strong thumb. I can hitchhike like nobody else. When people ask how to get a good curveball, I say, "Well you gotta get your wrist at 90 degrees, your elbow at 90 degrees, you put a beer cap in your hand and you know how to flick it off your fingers." You actually do a rotator cuff exercise while you're throwing your breaking ball. It's called multitasking. I build up my rotator cuff and my cunnythumb simultaneously.

My father was the first to call me a cunnythumber, though he ended up calling me a lot worse. Dad was a hard-throwing pitcher. His sister, my Aunt Annabelle "Lefty" Lee, pitched in the All-American Girls Professional Baseball League, more famously known today as the league in *A League of Their Own*. She pitched the first perfect game for the league. When she was interviewed years later by Joe Garagiola, he asked her, "Annie, how did you do it?" to which she replied, "Twenty-seven up, 27 down." (A lady of few words. Her nephew can't shut up. It must be a generational thing, right?) Her uniform hangs in the Baseball Hall of Fame in Cooperstown, New York. My father and my aunt taught me how to pitch; in fact, the whole family played baseball. My grandmother broke her leg sliding into second base at the age of 47. She was trying to stretch a single into a double. She lived to be 99.

The reason I was called a cunnythumber was because I couldn't break a pane of glass—but I sure could chip the edges! Remember,

Warren Spahn said, "The two inches on the inside corner are mine, and the two inches on the outside are mine. The rest of the plate belongs to the hitter."

Like the marble shooter, I use my thumb to impart break on my ball. I use it on my curveball, I use it on my screwball. Without a thumb, you would never get the ball over the plate. Even Mordecai "Three Finger" Brown had a thumb, just not much of an index finger. I had one-half more fingers than Mordecai, but I did break my middle finger playing basketball in high school, and when I pitched it forced me to do more pronation with my index finger. That's why I started turning the ball over more and made it to the big leagues. Also, in high school I got taken out at second base when a short guy hit me straight on my knee. I ruined my right knee and missed part of the season. They put me in a barrel cast. They wanted to operate and then my dad took me to this really heavy-drinking bone doctor, who said, "Oh hell, we'll just shoot it up with cortisone and put a barrel cast on it and let it quiet down for a week." I had a torn medial meniscus my whole career, but it allowed me to land on a really light right foot—it made me fall off the mound like Bob Gibson, but it also enabled me to turn the ball over more. That's how I became the little shit-baller you see before you. I was a big guy who threw pus, as Dennis Eckersley called slow pitches. He'd say, "Boy, you can throw pus," and then he'd say, "You throw salad, I throw cheese." He called me "the salad master." He said, "You don't throw hard, Bill, but you can paint!" I said, "You mean I can paint like Rembrandt?" And he said, "Who's that? I was thinking more like Sherwin Williams." So much for East Bay culture.

In reality, it looked like I was throwing harder than I was. It was hard for hitters to adjust. That's why I had such good success. Injuries came to me as gifts, not handicaps. So now when I'm doing baseball clinics for young players and the parents ask, "How can I get my kid to turn the ball over?" I say, "Well, you take his hand, you put it on a bottle, and you crush his middle finger with a Coke bottle." Yes, it's extreme, but it works.

As I've said, my father used to tell me about a guy he played with named Charles Henry "Red" Barrett. Red was a bona fide eccentric. He was a great team man who kept the clubhouse loose with his antics.

Barrett went on to play in the major leagues for 11 years and compiled a perfectly mediocre 69–69 record. His lifetime ERA was a respectable but hardly noteworthy 3.53. But Red did something that no other major league pitcher has accomplished and I admit that it impresses the hell out of me. On August 10, 1944, while pitching for the Boston Braves, the right-hander beat the Cincinnati Reds 2–0, allowing only two singles. But that's not the thing that impresses me. The game took one hour and 15 minutes to play, a record for night games. But that's not what impresses me either; I once pitched a 58-minute, seven-inning fastball game in Quebec, but that was because everyone wanted to go for beer and both teams worked as a unit to make that happen. This is what impresses me: Barrett threw just 58 pitches, a major league record for complete games that may never be broken. What Red did at Crosley Field in Cincinnati in front of 7,783 patrons was cunnythumbing at its best. Two things are clear:

1. Carlton Fisk was not catching the game, otherwise you could add another 45 minutes.
2. The entire August 10, 1944, game could be shown on one and a half episodes of *60 Minutes* and they'd still have time for five Kotex commercials and a postgame critique by Andy Rooney.

Red was a redheaded native of Santa Barbara, California, and was one of those guys who didn't become a regular in the big leagues until wartime took away many of the game's players. He had a few cups of coffee with Cincinnati but he was 28 years of age before he finally became a regular member of the Braves in 1943.

After two years in Boston, he was traded to the St. Louis Cardinals, where he was an immediate success, winning 23 games to lead the National League. He returned to the Braves in 1947 and in 1948 was part of the legendary "Spahn and Sain and pray for rain" rotation. Red was the "pray for rain" part, but actually he contributed to the team's successful pennant drive. Although Lefty Gomez usually gets credit for saying, "I'd rather be lucky than good," it was frequently used by Barrett.

Today, when pitch counts are recorded and monitored like EKGs in the coronary care unit, that figure is astounding. One hundred pitches often signals a trip to the shower for today's starters. Red was barely more than halfway there and he had a "W" under his belt. Not surprisingly, he walked no one and struck no one out. He had perfect control that day. He used the whole team to pitch that game, and they must have swung at a lot of pitches early in the count. One thing is certain: he didn't fall behind in the count on any Reds hitter throughout the entire contest. According to Joseph J. Dittmar of the *Baseball Records Registry* he "induced 13 ground outs, five fly balls, three pop-ups in fair territory, four foul outs, and two line-drive outs."

Of all the pitches, I believe the curveball is the most misinterpreted and misunderstood. A professor at MIT once said that a curveball does not break at all—it's just an optical illusion. Dizzy Dean said in response, "Tell that scientist to go hide behind a tree and I'll optical illusion him to death." Believe me, it breaks folks. It breaks. When thrown properly with a wrist bent at 90 degrees, it will go from 12:00 to 6:00. In fact, Diego Segui could throw from 11:00 to 5:00. Most kids today throw what my father calls a "nickel curve," that's just snapping your wrist on a fastball. That will ruin your medial epachondia, and you will have a zipper on your elbow before you're fifteen years old. Orthopedic surgeons don't want you to throw breaking stuff before your elbow matures, but if you don't

I was a real cunnythumber, all right—though it's probably not what you think!

learn it early, it's hard to learn late. Besides, they're orthopedic surgeons because they can't hit a breaking ball.

Barry Zito and I both have 25¢ curveballs. Bert Blyleven, Nolan Ryan, and Camilio Pascual all had 50¢ curveballs. They threw curveballs that were called "toilet seats." A lot of hitters would buckle both knees when they first saw it. It gave the appearance that they were on the throne taking a crap. The clubhouse boys on the team would say when Bert pitched against their respective ballclubs, they had to wash the right-handed hitters' shorts twice.

The first curveball was thrown by Arthur "Candy" Cummings of Ware, Massachusetts—it must have been confusing when people said, "You're from where?" and he responded, "Yes"—of the

Brooklyn Stars Juniors. He then matriculated to the Brooklyn Excelsior club and promptly went on a road trip to the Boston area, Worcester to be exact, where he hurled his first Frisbee. It is always good to experiment on the road, where there are a lot fewer critics. It was in the spring of 1867 against Harvard that he became fully convinced he had succeeded. It was the results. The Crimson hitters were coming back to the bench convinced they had holes in their hickory. Always pick on an Ivy League team, they're oh so smart.

Cummings went on to win 16 games his first season in the National League with the third-best ERA, 1.67 (a positively Gibsonesque number, but they didn't threaten to lower the mound the next year). Cummings stood only 5'10" and weighed a hefty 120 pounds. A stiff breeze would have blown him off the hill but, fortunately, they didn't have mounds back in those days.

Candy threw his last curveball in an old-timers game in Boston in 1910 at the age of 62. A writer present claims it was Zito-like— a wide and pretty curve.

As I, Ted Williams, and all Harvard grads know, the first curve was actually thrown by Daniel Bernoulli in Basel, Switzerland, in the late 1700s. Unfortunately, Bernoulli really was in a "league of his own" since baseball was still just a glimmer in Abner Doubleday's great-grandfather's eye. A great curve breaks best as the low and high pressure converges along with drag coefficient. I call it "late-breaking news," especially for the hitter.

Then there's the fastball: the high hard one, the heater, the express, or the bully pitch (my own term for it). In the first year of *Sports Illustrated*, there was an article written by a prominent physician from Johns Hopkins University. He wrote that pitching overhand was an "unnatural act." The shoulder was not constructed to throw the ball overhand. In Van Meter, Iowa, home of "Bullet" Bob Feller, an unnatural act will get you five to life. The doctor had never met Bullet Bob. Throwing over the top for him was as natural as falling off a log. Feller pitched with his whole being, his arm was just along for the ride. That ride was over 100 mph. Have you seen a pitcher today rear back, touch the ground with his pitching hand, reach for the sky with the opposite leg, then push off the rubber and come flying down the hill? Never!

Karen Blixen (under the pseudonym Isak Dinesen) wrote *Out of Africa* and so poignantly started it, "I once had a farm in Africa." Well, I once had a fastball in America. That all came crashing down on a spring day in the Bronx. Once Nettles dropped me on my shoulder, I had to summon up all my mental powers and become Obi Wan Kenobi Lee, the cunnythumber from California. When you have a fastball you can throw by anyone, you feel invincible, but that's a delusion of grandeur. Reggie Jackson said he could time a jet; I say if that jet is up and in, you'll never catch up to it. If that jet is low and down the middle and thrown from the hand of the "acid king" Dock Ellis, then Boom! Boom! out go the lights in Tiger Stadium, a la Roy Hobbs.

Jim Palmer had a smooth, easy fastball. It would come in right at the letters with a sign saying, "Here, hit me!" You couldn't quite catch up to it. During all his years with the Baltimore Orioles, Jim never gave up a grand slam. He is in the Hall of Fame. I, on the other hand, am not. I gave up two grand slams in less than a third of an inning. That is an ERA of infinity (that is Cal Ripken or Carl Yastrzemski's number lying on its side). My amazing accomplishment that day was in not getting the loss. That was given to Lynn McGloughlin. I had come into the game in relief with the bases drunk with Tigers players and a two-run lead. I promptly threw eight straight Koufaxian fastballs by those Tiger hitters. I had a big problem with the ninth one. Bill Freehan hit it over the screen. Then three hitters later, Dick McAuliffe hit one around Pesky Pole. The end! You live by the fastball, you perish by the fastball.

Doctors say you only have so many pitches in your arm. Try and tell that to "Iron Man" Joe McGinnity. Three times in August of 1903 he pitched and won both ends of doubleheaders. How about Christy

Mathewson? He completed 36 out of 38 starts one year. Then there is Ole Hoss Radbourn. He completed 66 of 68, played 23 games in right field, two games at first base, and hit three home runs. He was on the hill 632 innings; that's a career for most people. These guys never heard anything about pitch counts.

About five years ago at an old timer's game in Fort Myers, Florida, we were heading to the game and Bob Feller was on the bus. I said to myself, *Isn't that great? He's going to the game at his age.* We all went into the clubhouse and he put on his Indians uniform, and I said, *That's great. He's going to go into the dugout.* Then he grabbed a ball and went out and warmed up. Then he went out to the hill. At 60'6" away, he threw his third fastball past Joe Walsh of the Eagles. I know you're saying to yourself, Walsh is a guitar player— well, he still had a bat in his hand, and Feller struck him out at 83 years of age.

> My eyes go misty,
> As I pen these lines to Christy;
> Oh my heart is full of heaviness today,
> May the flowers ne'er wither Matty,
> O'er the grave in Cincinnati
> Which you have chosen for your final fadeaway.
> —Ring Lardner, 1916

Lardner wrote these words the day McGraw got rid of his prodigal son and traded Christy to Cincinnati so he could manage one more year. How can you do that to the boy who lived in your house for all those years?

As a rookie in 1900, Christy Mathewson thought he could beat the seventh place Cincinnati Redlegs with just his fastball. He took a 2–0 lead into the ninth inning. When he left that inning, he was beaten 4–2. I don't care how good you are, you gotta change speeds. I learned the fadeaway from my Aunt Annabelle. I heard Christy learned it from a black player named Rube Foster. Some say Rube merely perfected it because it was said that Christy had one back in

I modeled my style after Johnny Podres, and to demonstrate the baseball gods in action, I entered the big leagues on the very day he left.

Taunton, Massachusetts. In the minors, that doesn't tarnish the story anymore. Taunton is the silver city—no pun intended.

I patterned my pitches after Johnny Podres. Believe it or not, the day that Podres was released from the Major Leagues, June 24, 1969, was the day I was called up. The gods must be crazy. The hardest pitch to drive is a ball going away from you slowly. All great pitchers learn that pitch, but don't throw it to a bad hitter, or in Eckersley's case, a no-legged hitter like Kirk Gibson. Guys with big upper body strength can reach over and pull it out of the ballpark. Hendu Henderson did it to Donnie Moore. He's not around to tell the story.

When I was young and first starting to pitch, my dad said, "You have got to learn the change-up, and, son, you only throw it to good hitters. Bad hitters are bad because they can't catch up to your fastball. Don't speed up a bad hitter's bat." As pitchers get older and hurt their arms, they rely more and more on guile and changing speeds. There was a cerebral pitcher in 1952 named Elwin Charles "Preacher" Roe. It was the season after he was 23–3. After he hurt his arm, he said he had three pitches: "Ma change, ma' change off ma' change, and ma' change off ma' change." I bet you five acres in Craftsbury he taught Johnny Podres. The greatest change I ever saw was Stu Miller's, the diminutive right-hander for the Giants. The pitch was synonymous with him. At Candlestick Park one day, while in his windup, the wind actually blew him off the mound. (It used to blow the hands off the clock, too. Herb Caen said that the clock doesn't matter in baseball. Well, Candlestick was the only place where time not only stood still but moved backward when the wind blew the big hand counterclockwise.) Stu would come at you with an arm and a body going 90. He would snap his head, and the ball would come out at 62. Then, when the hitter would start his swing, the ball would know to slow down to 52. I don't know how he did it! Right when you were about to hit it, the ball knew to slow down to 52 mph. How did it do that? He would tie 6'8" Frank Howard into knots. Like Preacher Roe before him, he would change off his change and then change again.

It's not easy to make Frank Howard look weak, but Miller did. He would get him out on his front foot all day long. If Frank did hit it, he could cue it and it would just spin in front of home plate, boring a hole down to China. It was the most amazing sight—little Stu Miller throwing to Howard—David versus Goliath. Now the great change-ups belong to Greg Maddux and Tom Glavine.

My pitches were slow and even my fastball traveled within the speed limit on most state highways. In fact, I did ads for the Massachusetts Highway Department when the speed limit was lowered to 55 mph, urging them to drive the same speed as my fastball. There are a couple of other pitchers who had less than impressive speedballs. One was "Handsome" Jack Kramer. Mickey

McDermott claimed that "When Handsome Jack threw his fastball, three birds shit on it before it reached home plate." Now that's slow. But not to be outdone, Brooklyn Dodgers finesse pitcher "Preacher" Roe said that he knew it was time to retire when he faced Stan Musial in a game in St. Louis. At the time, Musial was the best hitter the National League had to offer. Preacher wound up and unleashed what he thought would be an overpowering fastball. The pitch got away from him and headed for Musial's head. Roe claims he had time to yell "Look out!" three times before it got to home plate. That's slow, too. I remember when Stu Miller threw change-ups to Frank Howard. Howard had time to clutch three times and he still swung too soon. By the way, I once saw Miller called for a balk when he blew off the mound in Candlestick Park.

As far as the screwball goes, that can belong to almost any pitcher. Tug McGraw had a good one and even inspired a nationally syndicated cartoon called Scroogie. Hoss Radbourn died of syphilis at the age of 42. He would go to the hill every other day, rain or shine, but it was not the clap of thunder that killed him. Henry Chadwick, the man who gave us the press box and the box score, said there were only two problems with ballplayers, "wine and women." Radbourn was said to have one hand on a whiskey and the other arm around a lady of easy virtue. (I once got the crabs in Baltimore. I had gone to Obrycki's restaurant where crabs were selling for three dollars apiece. I said I must be a millionaire.) Back in the old days, I bet they wished penicillin had been invented sooner. Enough said.

When young kids try to throw their first curveballs, they are actually just cutting a fastball, which actually becomes a slider. That's hard on the elbow. I didn't throw my first slider until I was a senior in college, and that was in the College World Series. I never hurt my elbow throwing a curve. When I think of slider, I think of Steve Carlton. He comes at you hard, everything is hard. His two-seamer away, his four-seamer up and in, then here comes the slider down and in on the right-handers, you just can't lay off it. Hardly a strike, it starts down the middle and ends up at your ankles. When he's ahead of you, here it comes and he leaves it for Bob Boone and Tim McCarver to dig it out.

Bob Gibson was another mean one, always coming at you hard, burying that two-seam sinker in on your hands. His slider was more like a Frisbee, from 2:00 to 8:00 on the dial. After he pounded you in with that sinker, that heavy sinker down on your hands, here comes the Frisbee. You would give just a little, that front hip would open up, then your left shoulder would follow, your head and eyes would be right behind, and the rest is history. I can still see George Scott striking out for the final out of the World Series, Gibson's third complete game, and that slider was a hanger. Scott pulled off it. The key to a good slider is getting on top of it, making sure it goes down as much as away. Making it a good eight mph slower than your fastball. You sell fastball to the hitter and when you throw a slider, he swings over it and ahead of it. If you hang it, you get a new one from the umpire. They have lots.

When I was eight years old, my mother came into my room and there were clothes strewn all over the floor. She asked me why I didn't hang them up and I said, "I don't like hangers." And, to this very day, I don't like hangers. Hanging curveballs, hanging sliders, hanging change-ups. I hate them all. Hangers used to end up over the Green Monster or well up into the seats at Montreal's Big O. So to review: I use *pronation* to turn the ball over. I use *supination* to throw my cutter. Then there is Red Sox Nation. Two of the three can get someone out. The third is a shameless method of promoting a ballclub. I was a card-carrying Communist but I still don't have a Red Sox Nation card. Damnation!

My entire philosophy of baseball and pitching revolves around the fact that I wanted to throw ground ball outs. It's much more democratic than the fastball and the strikeout because it gets everyone involved, like any good democracy. Everyone is equal. I threw a slider away and it was a ground ball to shortstop. I threw a slider *hard* away and it was a ground ball to second. Then a hitter comes up and ducks his shoulder in and drives the ball to the right–center-field corner and then I walk the next guy. Runners on first and second and then you should throw your cross-seam fastball. And I didn't have one. That's why democracy doesn't always work. That's when the manager has to pull a coup and you need to revert to a dictatorship.

As I said, my mother called it a game only once. When she did, my father turned to her and said, "Today I would have traded you for a base hit."

He set a new standard for efficiency on the mound. The runner-up for brevity—67 pitches—was in 1915. Mac Davis, a writer of the day, referred to Barrett's pitch as a "mystifying nothing-ball." That's typical. It's the fastball pitchers who get the respect. But fielders love pitchers like Barrett because they keep them in the game. Apparently, he wanted the sign as soon as he got the ball back from the catcher. That's how you stay in the rhythm of the game.

Baseball parks each have their own distinct personalities and eccentricities. Some are bland and boring, others are exciting and volatile. They almost seem to invite strange and bizarre happenings. Fenway Park in Boston has more quirks than your weird uncle Fred with the 17 cats. Wrigley Field in Chicago has ivy-covered walls and a billygoat curse. Bill Madlock once said, "Hitting in Candlestick is like trying to hit a cotton ball while wearing an overcoat." And Jim Wohlford said, "The only difference between Candlestick and San Quentin is that at Candlestick they let you go home at night." Art Spander chimed in with, "An extra-innings night game at Candlestick Park is baseball's answer to cryogenics." Even Yankee Stadium in New York has its weird side. Yes, Yankee Stadium: there are ghosts there too numerous to mention—when a ball was hit to center field past his outfielder and toward Monument Park, Yankees manager Casey Stengel yelled: "Ruth, Gehrig, Huggins—someone throw that darned ball in here now!"

Two | # The Philosophers

By its very nature, the game of baseball lends itself to discussion, analysis, and speculation, not to mention gossip, backbiting, name-calling, shouting matches, and bullshit. Unlike basketball or hockey, where nonstop action tends to preclude anecdotes and small talk, or football, where bursts of action are followed by brief, focused committee meetings called huddles, the pace of baseball allows the art of conversation to flourish. Between pitches, radio broadcasters have ample time to reminisce about shooting doves down in Georgia, as Dizzy Dean often did.

Narrative historian Bruce Catton once observed, "Say this much for big-league baseball—it is beyond question the greatest conversation piece ever invented in America." Desert anarchist Edward Abbey pointed out that "Baseball is a slow, sluggish game, with frequent and trivial interruptions, offering the spectator many opportunities to reflect at leisure upon the situation on the field: this is what a fan loves most about the game."

Catton and Abbey were both right on, but they didn't go far enough. It's not just the spectators who converse. Catchers and hitters can catch up on current events as they go about their duties. Umpires often join in. Singles hitters can stop at first base for a leisurely chat. In fact, my theory is the more power a hitter has, the less articulate he is due to lack of practice. If you think of the baseball diamond as an office, first base is the water cooler, second base is the copier where conversations are slightly more hurried, and third base is the elevator at quitting time where players are silently focused on getting home. Home-run hitters have few verbal skills and usually communicate in grunts.

And then there are the sermons on the mound, which I know something about. Meetings at the mound can often be mini-Radisson round tables of wit and erudition as the pitcher, catcher, manager, and members of the infield all join in. This is where Lefty "Goofy" Gomez, about to face Jimmie Foxx, was asked by his manager what he wanted to throw. "I don't wanna throw him nothing; maybe he'll get tired of waiting and leave." This is where Baltimore manager Earl Weaver and ace pitcher Jim Palmer had heated debates. Weaver and umpire Ron Luciano often met here for swearing summits. In fact, so did Weaver and every umpire around. This is where Don Zimmer and I often met to discuss hemorrhoid ointments, bussing, and other issues of the day.

One day Zimmer had banished me to the bullpen for something or other, and we were playing Anaheim. They had a little left-handed mini second baseman coming up with a runner at second base. Zimmer didn't want to walk the hitter because he was weak. He had Ramon Hernandez warming up in the bullpen. Finally, he goes out to the mound and he calls in Ramon. Well, Ramon had a really bad upset stomach and he was in the shitter—and he wasn't comin' out anytime soon. So Zimmer kept signaling for the left-hander and no one came. I hadn't even warmed up, but I took my jacket off, jumped over the fence, and ran in. He said, "I didn't call for you." I said, "Give me the ball, this guy couldn't hit me in his best day." We argued for awhile but finally I convinced him. I threw two pitches, he hit a ground ball to second and we were out of the inning. It just goes to show that sometimes real diarrhea trumps the verbal kind.

Dick Williams always took his glasses off when he came to the mound. I asked him why and he said that it was because if he got into a fight, he wouldn't get glass in his eye. Once, he came to the mound to take the pitcher out and all that was there was the ball sitting on the rubber. The pitcher had walked around the other way

18

and gone to the dugout. Boy, he was furious. One-person mound conferences are never good.

I had a two-run lead once while pitching at Comiskey in Chicago. There was a runner at first base after the lead-off hitter got on in the ninth. Here came Zimmer. He was going to take me out. He already had a right-hander going in the pen. The White Sox had Buddy Bradford coming up—a right-handed pinch-hitter. I said, "I know I can get Bradford to hit into a double play." I actually talked Zimmer out of taking me out. I threw a first pitch sinker right down the middle and he hit a ground ball—a perfect double play. Now there were two outs with nobody on and we still had a two-run lead. Then Richie Allen came up. I threw him a change-up off the plate away, to get him out on his front foot, and he flicked his bat at it—just kinda casually flicked it—and the ball flew by my left ear so close that I tried to catch it, then the second baseman tried to catch it. It ended up in the upper deck at Comiskey, rattling around like a pinball machine. I never saw anything like it! I ended up winning 4–3.

In July of 2002, there were two mound meetings of note. In the first, Montreal Expos starting pitcher Tony Armas Jr. was guilty of premature evacuation as he stormed off the mound before manager Frank Robinson had even reached the hill. Robinson, a veteran of the old school and one of the toughest, most hard-nosed guys in baseball, was not impressed. He marched Armas back to the mound to wait until the call went out to the bullpen. After all, Robinson was the same guy who was fed up that his ballplayers couldn't do it, so he put himself in the lineup as a pinch-hitter and hit a home run against the Red Sox, winning the ballgame in the ninth inning. He was *tough*, man! When he was league president, you didn't see players socializing. He didn't believe in it as a player or as president. Now all of a sudden, with interleague play and everything, these guys are all dating. They don't have meetings anymore, they date. It's *Brokeback Mountain* out there.

In the second incident, Milwaukee Brewers manager Jerry Royster went to the mound to take out reliever Mike DeJean. DeJean refused to turn over the ball and screeched in Royster's face for an embarrassingly long time before finally marching off in a snit. After he'd had a chance to cool off, he said, "I am not the raving lunatic that I looked like the other night." There was a similar incident recently between Toronto pitcher Ted Lilly and manager John Gibbons. They decided to have a heated discussion in front of 50,000 observers.

In the outfield, geography makes conversation somewhat more difficult, but shouted conversations still take place, and hand signals add another dimension to the art of communication.

If the baseball diamond is a great place for social interaction, the dugout and bullpen are even more so. The aptly named bullpen is the scene of countless bull sessions. In early innings, the conversation is light, but the good humor and playful exchanges give way to more serious exchanges as the game progresses. Relief pitchers become less talkative and more grave at the prospect of being summoned into action. Gallows humor is very popular. By the seventh inning, the place has been transformed into a monastery operating under a vow of silence.

The late actor Paul Gleason (of *Breakfast Club* and *Die Hard* fame) used to play in the Red Sox farm system. "I think the dugout alone should be anointed as a shrine in the pantheon of baseball lore," he said. He recalled Ted Williams "striding back and forth," repeating over and over, "Hips before hands!" He remembered Casey Stengel mumbling some timeless philosophy to himself. The dugout is now a place where players seem to talk only to each other. It used to be a pit from which insults and invective were hurled at the opposition. These monologists were called "bench jockeys." They were not politically correct. If you were black or had a harelip or were bald or bowlegged, you were fair game. They would loudly point out any perceived differences or shortcomings, be they physical or mental. References to race were not taboo. Babe Ruth got taunted because he looked like he just *might* have some un-WASPish features.

Sometimes the bench jockeys were funny. In a game between the Detroit Tigers and the Red Sox, Ted Williams was at the plate in what for mortal ballplayers would have been a textbook bunting situation—except that Ted Williams almost never bunted, and when he did it was front-page news. Hank Greenberg was playing first for the Tigers and pitcher Jim Bagby, who had a cleft palate, was in the dugout offering advice to Greenberg, who had moved down the line to field the possible bunt. "You better move back, Hank," he advised. Greenberg stood his ground. "Hank, you'd better move back." Still no retreat by the future Hall of Famer. "Hank, if you don't want to look like me and talk like me, you'd better move back!"

The baseball clubhouse is like any neighborhood, with neighbors exchanging banter across the fence, only this neighborhood is fully integrated. Natives of some poor village in the Dominican Republic are living and dressing next door to affluent white guys from Idaho. It makes for some great cultural exchanges. The funny thing is the white guys always end up sounding a little more black—never the other way around. Luis Tiant, from Cuba, taught us all to talk in the Boston clubhouse—and George Scott, from another foreign land—Mississippi—was his English teacher.

All in all, it's little wonder that this environment has cultivated so many baseball philosophers.

Satchel Paige

Satchel Paige was one of the best. I always sort of fancied myself as a left-handed Satchel Paige. We each loved baseball, we each barnstormed well after we turned 50, we both were widely quoted, we both got by on our smarts. "Nobody likes the ball low and away, but that's where they'll get it from me," said Satch. And to that, I say, "Ditto!" And we both put baseball in its proper perspective. (Someone once pointed out that Satch was black and I'm white. My response was, "I'm white?")

Paul Gleason was a friend of Jack Kerouac and Greg Corso, real philosophers of the so-called "beat generation." When I ran for president of the United States on the Rhinoceros Party ticket, we ran our campaign out of Kerouac's bar in Lowell, Massachusetts. It was called Johnny's Bench. When he was a batboy for the Brooklyn

Dodgers, Gleason encountered Satchel Paige in the visitors' dressing room late one afternoon after a spring game was long over and the players had all gone home. He recalled it years later: "I got the feeling that nothing bothered Satchel Paige....I was the last one leaving when the grand old man strolled into the clubhouse. Earlier, the St. Louis Browns' coaches were looking for him. He was AWOL. 'Where you been, Satch?' 'The fish were bitin',' he said. I said, 'Everybody was worried. They didn't know where you were. Marty Marion says you might be sick.' He said, 'Naw, I thought it was a night game. Everybody's gone, huh? I was over on the Tamiami Trail all day, fishin' off the banks of the canal.'"

Satch then took Gleason to his car and showed off five big fat catfish, each in excess of 10 pounds. He asked, "What time's the game tomorrow?" and when told that it was a night game, he said, "Well, I can make that...and I'm gonna get me some more catfish, too." I can just see Zimmer blow an artery if I had pulled that one. Actually, down in Florida at spring training, whenever the snook were biting, Yaz mysteriously had a bad back. They put a bag plaster on him and he'd be gone and then he'd come back about two days later with snook for everybody. It just goes to show, if you're the *grande fromage*, you can do anything you want in spring training. Of course, Yaz is now a recluse. He and Fisk are like the Greta Garbos of baseball—they want to be left alone.

Adrian "Cap" Anson may have been the original flake. Anson was the third baseman for the original Chicago White Stockings of the National League, later to become the Chicago Cubs. The team played its first game on April 25, 1876, and Anson was in the lineup. He remained there for 22 seasons. Anson played into his forties, and some Chicago writers started to suggest in print that it was time he hung them up—names like "Grandpa" and "Pops" started to appear in newspaper articles about him. These statements hurt Anson, and he decided to make a statement of his own. He hobbled onto the diamond one afternoon wearing a grey wig and sporting a Methuselah-style beard. Just to ensure everyone got the point, Cap proceeded to play all nine innings in this get-up. The writers relented, and Anson went on to play another five years of major league baseball, becoming the first ballplayer to accumulate 3,000 hits.

Was Anson like Methuselah? All I know is, I served with Methuselah, I knew Methuselah, Methuselah was a friend of mine, and, Mr. Anson, you're no Methuselah! When I played with Yaz, the true Methuselah—although Methuselah was a sharper dresser and probably not as cheap—the writers counted him out many times, too. He survived for 23 seasons, which is what happens when you wear the sign of infinity on your back. Like Anson, Yaz also gathered over 3,000 hits (3,419) and he also added over 400 homers (452). So much for writers' expertise.

Leroy Satchel Paige entered the major leagues in 1948 as a 42-year-old rookie who had quite possibly been the best pitcher in America long before that debut. His reputation in the Negro Leagues was legendary. His feats were almost supernatural, but there are enough cold hard facts to indicate that he was much more than a legend. He once won 21 straight games. He compiled a record of 31–4 in 1933. He pitched 64 consecutive scoreless innings. At the age of 59, in 1965, he pitched three scoreless innings for Charlie Finley's Kansas City Athletics. No less an authority than Joe DiMaggio endorsed Paige as "the best and fastest pitcher I've ever faced." Paige boasted that "if I had been pitching to Ruth and Gehrig, you could knock a few points off those big, fat lifetime batting averages."

In 1939 Satchel Paige and other stars were convinced to play ball in the Dominican Republic. President Trujillo, the dictator, was said to be personally involved in the recruitment. There were armed guards everywhere, and the rumor was that if Trujillo's team did not win, there would be repercussions. Talk about pressure! Fans were yelling threats throughout the games. They won the pennant on the last day of the season, and Paige was the starter. "The more they yelled, the harder I threw," recalled Satch. In the next day's newspaper, the team manager downplayed any claims of physical threats, claiming that "baseball is spiritual in every way, as indulged in by the Latin races." Paige agreed, sort of: "I am saving the clipping because I am thinking that if he is right and baseball is spiritual as it is played there, old Satchel could be a spirit right now if we didn't win that big game."

Paige was like the fast gun who comes into town full of bravado and then backs it all up. It took a visionary and fellow showman like Bill Veeck to recognize Paige's untapped big-league potential. In 1948 Veeck's Cleveland Indians were in the midst of a tight pennant race when he brought in Paige. Veeck's confidence in the aging star was rewarded as Paige helped the Indians capture the AL pennant.

Although it is thought that Paige was born in 1906, this is basically an educated guess. Whenever he was quizzed about his age, he would refuse to answer the question. "Age is a question of mind over matter," he offered. "If you don't mind, it doesn't matter." That's the philosophy I live by every day. All I need is my reprieve from death—a daily dose of Advil. The last two times I used it, I hit for the cycle the first time and went 4-for-4 the second time. I once pitched 54 innings in three days in Landisburg, Pennsylvania. I would take three Advil and a beer, have a nap in a rocking chair on the field, and then go and pitch the next ballgame. People asked how I did it and I said, "Talk to the Advil people." (Note to the Advil people: I should be doing commercials for you. Call me.)

How can today's fans begin to understand the phenomenon that was Satchel Paige? There are no players in the modern game who even come close. The best we can do is to suggest that he had the charisma of Luis Tiant, the fastball of Roger Clemens, and the powers of exaggeration of Muhammad Ali. He was a showman, but a showman who could back it up. Paige was the lifeblood of the

Negro Leagues and singlehandedly sold out ballparks every time he pitched. Unfortunately, statistics in the Negro Leagues were maintained sporadically, at best. Nevertheless, anecdotal evidence suggests that Paige may have won well in excess of 1,500 games and crafted more than 300 shutouts. I'm 59, and I know I'm up to 800 wins and I've got 700 more to go before I sleep. It makes my arm ache just to think about it. Pass the Advil.

As a member of the legendary Kansas City Monarchs, he led his team to four straight Negro American League championships as well as a Negro World Series title in 1942. Such was the extent of his fame that even white baseball fans were hearing the buzz about his mound achievements. Casey Stengel described him in glowing terms. "Satchel Paige threw the ball as far from the bat and as close to the plate as possible," he said. When major league barnstormers like Bob Feller and others matched up with Paige's teams, they came away shaking their heads and eager to return to Major League competition. "Nobody ever stopped Joe DiMaggio as cold as he did," recalled Bob Feller, who barnstormed with Paige annually starting in 1937. "I've seen Satch walk a man *deliberately* to get at DiMaggio." I would have done that, too—if it was *Vince* DiMaggio. However, I will say that I've had people in fantasy camps sit down in the infield and the outfield when I struck out a guy because he was hitting on the other players' wives and I wanted him so bad. (Of course, he was a 60-year-old insurance salesman from Bangor, but still…)

Paige's wisdom has now entered the folklore of America. By the time Satchel was allowed to pitch in the Major Leagues, he was like the aging star of a minstrel show, well past his prime. He still gave the audience glimpses of the greatness that was once overwhelming. The Negro Leagues star was a genuine, one-of-a-kind original. His appearance added to the legend. He was 6'3" with size-12, triple-A shoes, but weighed about 145 pounds. He walked with a loosey-goosey gait that invited laughter. He featured his famous "hesitation pitch" and others called Little and Tom Long, Hurry-Up Ball, Midnight Creeper, Four-Day Rider, Nothin', Bee Ball, The Barber, the Two-Hump Blooper, and the Jump-Ball. His barnstorming appearances were sometimes promoted with the following extraordinary promise: "Satchel Paige, World's Greatest Pitcher. Guaranteed to Strike Out the First Nine Men."

I could have roomed with Satch and impressed the heck out of him. Satchel claimed that his roommate, Cool Papa Bell, was so fast he could turn out the light in his hotel room and be in bed asleep before it got dark. Sure, that sounds impressive, but sometimes I was passed out before I even got back to my room. (I was in Cleveland once and we came across some guys smoking these big hooters in a van. Well, we started smoking them and, when I went back to my hotel, I never made it out of the elevator. I had these beautiful leather boots and when I finally got to my room, I laid in bed and it took me twenty minutes to try to get the zippers down. I was thinking, *Wow!*)

Incidentally, Satch also said of Cool Papa: "One time he hit a line drive right past my ear. I turned around and saw the ball hit him in the ass sliding into second base."

During the 1948 pennant drive, the 42-year-old Paige was a key reliever for the Cleveland Indians. He brought his timeless wisdom to the team and imparted it whenever possible. Rookie pitcher Mike Garcia was the recipient of one such seminar in a game against the heavy-hitting Boston Red Sox at Fenway Park. Since Paige had pitched the night before, it looked like it might well be the rookie's first exposure to big-league hitters.

The score was knotted at 0–0 and as the legend and the kid warmed up alongside each other in the bottom of the ninth, Paige kept up a steady stream of advice designed to calm the nerves of the rookie. "Don't worry kid," he drawled. "These Red Sox hitters are overrated. They're just human beings, after all." No sooner were the words out of his mouth than Boston pinch-hitter Billy Goodman beat out a drag bunt to put a runner on first. "Pure luck," Satch assured his young student as lead-off man Dom DiMaggio came to the plate. "DiMaggio is certainly not the hitter his brother is," he said reassuringly. "No, sir, this is Dominic, not Joe." The 5'9", 160-pound DiMaggio promptly slapped the first pitch to center field.

Runners were now at first and second with no one out, and all eyes were on Cleveland manager Lou Boudreau to see if he would send out a call to the bullpen. No signal was forthcoming. Johnny Pesky was next up. Satchel was positively dismissive of the needle-nosed Red Sox shortstop. "Pesky's nothing more than a banjo hitter. All you have to do is pitch him around the knees and he's gone." Pesky lined the second pitch past the pitcher and up the middle to load the bases.

There was a pause in the steady stream of advice from Paige. Both pitchers paused in their pitching and watched as Ted Williams strode to the plate, squeezing the bat as if trying to extract water. The Fenway faithful were going crazy. Lou Boudreau walked to the mound and signaled for Paige. Garcia felt like a man granted a last-minute reprieve from the electric chair. He turned to his mentor and awaited further words of optimism, but Satch remained quiet. With a deep sigh, he began the long trek to the pitcher's mound, pausing only to cast his eyes skyward and address the rookie one last time. "One last thing, son," he said in reverential tones. "When you're playing the Red Sox, put your trust in the good Lord."

Paige is one of the most quoted of baseball's philosophers. His oft-quoted rules for living a long and happy life are always worth repeating. They first appeared in 1953 in *Collier's* magazine and were repeated in Paige's autobiography:

1. "Avoid fried meats which angry up the blood." (I guarantee you Satchel ate a lot of fried foods. He can speak about it firsthand.)
2. "If your stomach disputes you, lie down and pacify it with cool thoughts." (His stomach was always disputing him because of the fried foods. That's why he had to lie down.)
3. "Keep the juices flowing by jangling around gently as you move." (He had to jangle a lot to keep those fried foods moving through his system before they stuck to the insides of his arteries.)
4. "Go very light on the vices, such as carrying on in society — the social ramble ain't restful." (He saw and heard the cock crow more than once in his lifetime, I'll guarantee you that.)

5. "Avoid running at all times." (Don't lose your legs. Once you lose your legs they put you in the home and don't let you out. Keep your legs at all cost. It's better to lose your faculties than your legs.)
6. "And don't look back—something might be gaining on you."

When I look back, I see Nettles and Zimmer and they're both losing ground. But I'm sure the way Satch drove, there was no one who was going to catch him anyway. Anyone who could pitch a game in Kansas City and then throw the nightcap in Chicago definitely went through a few speed traps. He was once driving up the central valley of California and they didn't catch him until he got to Oakland. He drove like he pitched in his early days—at 120.

Satch also advised, "Just take the ball and throw it where you want to. Throw strikes. Home plate don't move." Satch used to warm up throwing to a pack of Lucky Strikes. The catcher would put down the Lucky Strikes and he wouldn't throw it over the red part. That's why they called them lucky strikes. It's also where the term "throwing smoke" originated (not really, but I want to add to Satch's legend).

Some other Paige pearls of wisdom:

- "I ain't ever had a job, I just always played baseball."
- "I don't generally like running. I believe in training by rising gently up and down from the bench."
- "I never rush myself. See, they can't start the game without me."
- "I use my single windup, my double windup, my triple windup, my hesitation windup, my no windup. I also use my step-n-pitch-it, my submariner, my sidearmer, and my bat dodger. Man's got to do what he's got to do."
- "If a man can beat you, walk him."
- "It's funny what a few no-hitters do for a body."
- "My feet ain't got nothing to do with my nickname, but when folks get it in their heads that a feller's got big feet, soon the feet start looking big."

Satchel Paige was one of the greatest baseball philosophers ever. Here relaxing in the bullpen, he once said he got most of his training in by rising slowly up and down from the bench.

- "One time I snuck a ball on with me and when I went to winding up, I threw one of them balls to first and one to second. I was so smooth I picked off both runners and fanned the batter without that ump or the other team even knowing it."
- "The only change is that baseball has turned Paige from a second-class citizen to a second-class immortal."

- "There never was a man on earth who pitched as much as me. But the more I pitched, the stronger my arm would get."
- "When a batter swings and I see his knees move, I can tell just what his weaknesses are—then I just put the ball where I know he can't hit it." (The other day, I did my double hesitation, I did my double windup with my over-the-top movement, and I threw two innings, struck out four, and gave up an 0–2 base hit with a ball over the guy's head, and I could hear Satchel saying, "Man, he shouldn't have been swinging at that pitch. Cause I guarantee he had to have given up some hits.")
- "Ain't no man can avoid being born average, but there ain't no man got to be common."
- "I never threw an illegal pitch. The trouble is, once in a while I would toss one that ain't never been seen by this generation."
- "They said I was the greatest pitcher they ever saw...I couldn't understand why they couldn't give me no justice."
- "Don't pray when it rains if you don't pray when the sun shines."
- "How old would you be if you didn't know how old you are?"
- "Money and women. They're two of the strongest things in the world. The things you do for a woman you wouldn't do for anything else. Same with money."
- "Work like you don't need the money. Love like you've never been hurt. Dance like nobody's watching." (That is the greatest advice ever written. Sheer poetry. So great psychologically.)
- "You win a few, you lose a few. Some get rained out. But you got to dress for all of them."
- "My pitching philosophy is simple; you gotta keep the ball off the fat part of the bat."
- "Mother always told me, if you tell a lie, always rehearse it. If it don't sound good to you, it won't sound good to no one else."

When his truncated Major League career was over, Satch's record stood at 28–31 and his ERA a very respectable 3.29. It was just enough to make fans wonder just what they had missed—what they had been cheated out of. The press once went to Buck O'Neil,

30

another guy who didn't get to play in the Major Leagues, and they asked him, "Buck, isn't it sad you didn't get to play against the best?" His answer was perfect: "Maybe I did." Well, Satchel finally received some delayed justice in 1971, when he was elected to the Hall of Fame. But as far as playing against the best goes, maybe he did.

Oil Can Boyd

If they ever make a movie about Satch, I've always said that Oil Can Boyd has to play the lead role. The Can playing Satch! It's a natural. He's Satchel incarnate, at least in his appearance. He came into a tough situation in Boston. He was touted as a young Satchel Paige, and everyone expected him to be all funny and lovable. He was an angry man. He said that "after all these years of trying to emancipate us, you haven't come very far." He saw that inequality in Boston. One thing about the Can, though—geography was not his forte. He was pitching in Cleveland one spring and it started to snow. "What do you expect when you build a ballpark on the ocean?" he said.

Steve Hovley

Steve Hovley was a California free spirit and graduate of Stanford University who went on to play with the Seattle Pilots in 1969. The most amazing thing of all was that good old conservative Stanford—the "Harvard of the West Coast"—produced a guy like Steve.

He possessed good speed and was a decent hitter who was often used as a pinch-hitter. He caught the attention of the media when he let his hair grow and refused to cut it—he said that he didn't want to discriminate against any individual hairs. He ran afoul of Pilots management, not for using steroids or corking his bat; his crimes were his long hair and—wait for it—reading Dostoyevsky. He was as out of place as those three old fishwives in the Monty Python skit who used to discuss philosophy.

Hovley once observed, "To a pitcher, a base hit is the perfect example of negative feedback." Jim Bouton, who immortalized not only Hovley but the entire cast of the Seattle Pilots in his classic book *Ball Four,* says of Hovley, "Hovley became a plumber, just like any other former Major Leaguer who went to Stanford and read Dostoyevsky in the clubhouse."

Dizzy Dean

If Hovley was a sublime eccentric, Dizzy Dean was definitely ridiculous. It might not have happened, but I like to think it did. If it didn't, it should have. Jay Hanna "Dizzy" Dean and Pee Wee Reese were broadcasting a game on CBS TV. Around the fifth inning, one team pulled off a very slick double play. Pee Wee says, "Wow, Diz, what do you think of that?" Dean replied, "Sorry, partner, I wasn't really watching the game. For the last two innings I've been watching this young couple down the third baseline. I think I've finally figured out their system. He kisses her on the strikes and she kisses him on the balls."

I can't imagine that kind of exchange on network radio or TV today. McCarver and Buck blush and wash their mouths out every time they have to say, "The batter has two balls on him."

Dean, the announcer, was an affront to the English language. He reported that a runner had "slud into third." And on another occasion two runners had "returned to their respectable bases." He cautioned the radio audience, "Don't fail to miss tomorrow's game." But when a teacher pointed out that he should improve his grammar, he replied, "A lot of people who don't say 'ain't,' ain't workin'." During World War II, Dean was calling a game that was rain-delayed. Because of wartime restrictions on reporting such information, he was unable to give the cause for the delay. Instead he said, "I can't tell you what it's doin', folks, but if you'll stick your head out the window, you'll find out." Another version has the game underway and him saying, "I ain't allowed to say what the weather's like. But that ain't sweat what is runnin' down the pitcher's face."

As an announcer, Diz often had difficulty with players' names. When Ed Hanyzewski joined the Chicago Cubs, Dean's challenge was the broadcasting equivalent of facing Babe Ruth with the bases loaded. "I like to broke my jaw try' to pronounce that one," he admitted. "I said his name by holdin' my nose and sneeze."

Writer Tom Meany described Dizzy as "a combination of Paul Bunyan, Baron Munchausen, and Will Rogers." I would like to officially add Foghorn Leghorn to the mix. Dizzy and his brother Daffy were the leaders of the Gas House Gang, also known as the St. Louis Cardinals of the 1930s. "Me and Paul," as Ole Diz called the Dean team, were the heart and soul for the 1934 championship team. On September 21 of that year, the Cardinals played a double-header against Casey Stengel's Dodgers. Both were key games in the tight pennant race. Dizzy won the first game, a laugher, 13–0. His brother toed the rubber in the second contest and remarkably pitched a no-hitter. Dizzy's postgame reaction? "Shucks, Paul, if I'd a knowed you wuz gonna pitch a no-hitter, I'd a throwed one myself."

Early in the 1934 season, he boasted, "Me 'n' Paul will win 45 games." It turned out that he was being uncharacteristically modest. Paul won 19 games and Dizzy an incredible 30. "Who won the pennant?" he asked rhetorically after the regular season, before answering, "Me and Paul. Who's gonna win the World Series? Me and Paul." And who could argue with him? He and Paul were on the mound in all four Series wins against the Detroit Tigers.

In the fourth game of the '34 Series against the Tigers, Diz was inserted as a pinch-runner for Virgil Davis. This move elicited huge cheers from the partisan crowd at Sportsman's Park in St. Louis, since Dean was the most popular guy on the team. The same crowd grew deathly silent just moments later when Dean, going into second on a force play, inexplicably jumped high in the air just as Tigers shortstop Billy Rogell was throwing to complete the double play. The ball hit Dean square in the forehead, and he went down like a pole-axed mule. The ball ricocheted into right field, and Leo Durocher scored from third to tie the game 4–4. Dizzy was carried from the field on a stretcher. His only comment before being taken to the hospital was, "They didn't get Pepper [Martin], too, did they?" At the hospital, Paul took over the role of family spokesperson. He

Dizzy Dean was more of a philosopher when he was conscious. Here he's shown out cold after taking a line drive to the head.

told reporters, "Diz'll probably pitch tomorrow. He warn't hurt that much. Just hit on the haid."

Joe Williams of the Scripps-Howard newspaper chain asked, "Was he unconscious when you helped carry him from the field?"

"Oh, no," replied Paul. "Diz warn't unconscious at all. Was talkin' all the time, in fact."

"What was he saying?" asked Williams.

"Nuthin," replied Paul. "Just talkin'."

That exchange spoke volumes about Dizzy Dean.

On another occasion, Dean was struck in the head by a line drive off the bat of Burgess Whitehead. The headlines in the next day's paper shouted: X-Rays of Dean's Head Reveal Nothing.

Dean loved to hear the sound of his own voice and had something to say even when he had nothing to say. If he spoke to three different reporters after a game, he often gave them three different versions of what had happened. "I give 'em each a scoop...so that their bosses can't bawl the three of 'em out for gettin' the same story."

There is no question that Dean cultivated the southern "poor boy" image and made it his trademark. He sang "The Wabash Cannonball" during TV broadcasts and spoke of "huntin' doves down in Georgia." When he was asked about his second-grade education, he explained, "If I'd a gone to third grade, I'd a passed my old man." During his time in the army, Dean was assigned duty shoveling manure for an officer's wife's garden. The officer asked when he might expect the job to be started. "Soon, sir," he replied. "You're number two on my shit-list."

There is also little doubt that Dean was a braggart, but some people can own this characteristic and make it an asset rather than a liability. When he was first scouted by the St. Louis Cardinals, the right-handed Dean claims that they thought he was a southpaw. According to him, the scout found him in the backwoods of Arkansas killing squirrels with rocks thrown with his left hand. Later, when the scout discovered that the prospect was actually a righty, Dean explained. "I throw so hard with my right arm," he said, "that I squash up them squirrels somethin' terrible, and they ain't fit eatin' then. If I'm just huntin' for fun, I do throw right-handed, but when I'm out rustlin' up our grub, I dasn't throw thataway. I gotta throw left-handed."

After he reached the majors, the hyperbole continued. He once put a block of ice on home plate and, when asked why, said it was to cool down his fastball. He told the Boston Braves team, "Tell you what I'm gonna do, fellas. We won't use no signs today, and I'll throw nuthin' but fastballs—honest." He was true to his word and pitched a shutout. Is it bragging when you carry through with your boast? At a minor league game in which the club president was in attendance, Dean threw a masterful 12–1 victory and then went to the president's box and apologized for giving up the single run to "them bums." The brash prospect then encountered the club president again, this time in the lobby of a hotel at 2:00 in the morning. "Well, I guess you and me'll get the devil for this," he said. "But I won't say nuthin' about it if you don't."

One moment of humility came in a game against Mel Ott of the New York Giants. Ott had doubled off Dean in the early innings when he came up again in the ninth with the score tied and two out. Frankie Frisch, the St. Louis manager, came to the mound and insisted that Diz walk Ott intentionally, even though there was a runner on first. Naturally, Dean objected. He was much too prideful for such cowardice. "That's an insult to my pitching," he pleaded. "I can get him out. He only has one hit against me today." Against his better instincts, Frisch gave in. "Okay," he said, "I'll give you two pitches. If you get behind 2-and-0, you got to walk him." Dean agreed. His first pitch was a ball. His second was blasted to the furthest reaches of the ballpark for a home run. As Ott rounded third on the walk-off homer, he passed Dean, who was on his way to the showers. "Ottie," Dean said, "a fellow like you can take all the fun out of pitching."

Another slightly humbling moment came in the seventh game of the 1934 World Series between the Cardinals and the Detroit Tigers. Dizzy was the starting pitcher for the Gas House Gang, and his matchups with slugging star Hank Greenberg were the marquee event of the Series. The first time up, Dean struck him out with heaters in tight and just above his wrists. The next time up, Dean wanted more of a challenge. Leo Durocher described what happened years later:

> I was watching from short to catch the signs from our catcher, Bill Delancey, so I would know which way to move when the ball was pitched. I saw Diz shake off Bill a couple of times and then beckon him out to the mound. I knew what was coming. Dean, with our big lead, was going to experiment. Frankie Frisch, our manager, came over from second base to the mound, and I moved in from short to be in on the conference. Dean turned to Frisch and, as innocent as a child, said, "Where did you say this guy Greenberg's strength was, Frankie?" Frisch almost exploded. Here we were a couple of innings away from the pot of gold and Dean was starting to clown around.

"You know well enough where his strength is," roared Frisch. "You've been doing alright with him. Just don't pitch him high and outside where he can get the fat part of the bat against the ball."

"I don't think he can hit *me* high and outside," said Dean slyly. Frisch threw up his hands in disgust and went back to his position. Diz pitched high and outside, and Greenberg almost took his cap off with a line single to center. Dean turned to Frisch and winked. "You're right," he said, "that's where his strength is."

The next time up, Dean decided to play it straight and struck Greenberg out for the second time—on a pitch high and tight.

There was a time when a St. Louis nightclub owner struck a bet with Dean. Dizzy had boasted that the next day he would strike out Vince DiMaggio every time he batted. Even if you allow that Vince was not the hitter that brothers Joe and Dominic were, this was a tall order. The amount of the bet was pocket change at best, but Dean's pride was at stake. He struck Vince out the first three times he faced him. The fourth and last time DiMaggio was to bat, he quickly got ahead of the hitter 0–2 in the count. On the third delivery, the batter reached out and hit a high foul behind the plate, an easy play for catcher Bruce Ogrodowski. The rookie catcher settled under the ball and waited for it to land in his waiting glove. Suddenly, Dean was off the mound in a flash and yelling in the catcher's face, "Drop the ball! Drop the ball! Damn it, if you want to catch me again, DROP IT!" Not wishing to question the strange ways of the major leagues, the startled rookie did just that. Cardinals manager Frankie Frisch shot up from his place on the bench and hit his head on the cement dugout roof. Before he could go to the mound to question his bizarre action, Dean strode back to the mound and unleashed a blazing fastball that struck out DiMaggio. Such was the ego of Dizzy Dean.

Dean once wrote a book—a thought that must have had English teachers jumping off bridges. It was called *The Dizzy Dean Dictionary and What's What in Baseball.* His foreword (spelled "Forward" by Dean) explains why he decided to take pen to paper: "The trouble is, I figured, that there ain't no good expert source where you kin look up some of them words....I mean the real technical words that's used by the players and has growed right out of baseball." Somewhere along the line Dean's dictionary became Dean's Diatribe. His first chapter, titled "Who's the Greatest Pitcher in the World?" sets the tone for the ones to come: "Anybody who's ever had the privilege of seein' me play ball knows that I am the greatest pitcher in the world. And them that ain't been fortunate enough to have a gander at Ol' Diz in action can look at the records."

Chapter Two is "Who's Got the Greatest Throwing Arm in the World?" Chapter Three is "Who's the Greatest Hitter in the World?" and contains the humble line: "The fact that I am such a great pitcher overshadows my wonderful work with the willow when I step up to the plate....I once made a home run on a bunt." Chapter Four is "Who's the Greatest Runner in the World?"

When Dean was inducted into the Hall of Fame, he said that he wanted to thank God for "giving him a good right arm, a strong back, and a weak mind." He certainly had the first two in spades, but there was nothing weak about the mind of this master showman.

Jimy Williams

If Satchel and Diz were the masters of the homespun school of philosophy, manager Jimy Williams is an adherent of the abstract. He is the king of the cryptic, the nabob of the nonsensical non sequitur. While managing the Boston Red Sox, Williams had a gift for using postgame press conferences as a kind of dumping ground for leftover words. Maybe that's why his first name is missing a consonant. He likes words, but he doesn't treat them with a whole lot of respect. (Sort of like George W.) Williams's forays into the English language during pre- and postgame press conferences resulted in something that has become known throughout New England as "Jimywocky." For example, he once said, "If a frog had wings, he wouldn't bump his booty." When he was asked about whether a ball hit by Manny Ramirez was fair or foul, he replied, "I'm not the ball. I think the ball is the only one who knows." He explained that "I let my eyes evaluate what I see."

Commenting on whether the 1999 season had been a surprise, he offered this perspective on the craft of writing: "I don't know about that. Surprise or all those other adjectives, or what do you use, adverbs? Prepositions? I like gerunds. I went to high school with a guy named Gerand Thornquist. His dad drove a bus for Greyhound. He was almost the valedictorian. You'd have to be with a name like that."

After a game in which Red Sox reliever Tomo Ohka was throwing his fastball well, he observed, "He had some giddy-up. How do you say giddy-up in Japanese? 'Hi-ho, Silver?'"

When reporters asked if they could see him earlier in the day, he responded, "As long as I've got my cup on." He was asked to comment on the tearing down of Seattle's Kingdome: "One less racquetball court." During an interview, he was asked about the state of his pitching rotation: "It's in Ohio, and Friday, it'll be in Boston." And once he complained about the way games dragged on when my friend Carlton Fisk was catching for the Chicago White Sox. "These guys play like they get paid by the hour," he said.

When he was grilled about when his base runners should steal, he explained, "The runners dictate it. The catcher dictates it. The score dictates it. The situation dictates it. But I'm not a dictator, whatever that means." When he took over as manager of Houston, and was asked about what he thought of Enron Field, he countered with, "What position does he play?"

Summing up, Jimy Williams is a man of many words, some of them quite interesting. Let's let him describe himself: "I guess, you know, when I was a little kid, I liked to play marbles. You know, everybody has different games they like to play. I liked to play marbles. A lot of people think I've lost mine. I don't know. I still got them at home in a big brandy snifter. I really do." Wow! A manager with a sense of humor. If this catches on, there could be anarchy.

Of course, you have to remember Williams's roots in small-town America and cut him some slack. He is from Arroyo Grande,

California. "It's about three miles past Resume Speed," according to Jimy. You know, I think I played there once.

As Jimy said, "In retrospect, you are always looking back."

Ken MacKenzie was a southpaw pitcher who toiled for the Mets under Casey Stengel. He was also one of the few Ivy Leaguers to play in the majors, having graduated from Yale. Sitting on the bench one day he seemed to be second-guessing his career choice. "Do you realize," he whined, "that I am the lowest paid member of the Yale Class of '59?" Always anxious to help, the Old Perfessor weighed in with, "Yes, but with the highest earned run average."

Casey Stengel

I could have played for Casey Stengel and I'll tell you why. He understood pitchers. He said, "Left-handers have more enthusiasm for life. They sleep on the wrong side of the bed and their heads get more stagnant on that side." That is sound science from the man they called "the Old Perfessor." He earned the title. Players gathered around him in the manner that students might once have sat at the feet of Socrates. Physically, Stengel was a cross between Einstein and Yoda, and he possessed about the same command of the intricacies of the English language. The former player and manager has become synonymous with baseball humor and a kind of convoluted wisdom. And no wonder: all of his wisdom was imparted in Stengelese and, when uttering this weird and wonderful tongue, everything he said seemed exotic and profound. One of the very best examples of Stengelese is this: "Good pitching can stop good hitting every time, and vice versa." It's very profound. He also told young hopefuls at the Mets' initial spring training: "Alright men, everybody line up alphabetically, according to height." Welcome to the major leagues.

But Stengel was wise, make no mistake. You don't last as long as he did in baseball and not acquire wisdom. He shared this piece of managerial advice with his younger colleagues: "The secret of managing is to keep the guys who hate you away from the guys who are undecided." He knew that it took more than early curfews to make a team. "Sure, some of my players drink whiskey," he said. "In my experience, I've discovered that the ones who drink milkshakes don't win many ballgames."

He was a master of subtlety when dealing with his players. He once called Bob Cerv into his office and said, "Nobody knows this yet, but one of us has been traded to Kansas City." When infielder Jerry Lumpe was hitting sharp line drives all over the park in batting practice, Stengel quipped, "That's Lumpe. He's a great hitter until I play him." Similarly, after alleged good field–no hit catcher Chris Cannizzaro committed two errors in one game, he not only heaped scorn on him, but he didn't even get his name right. "He's a remarkable catcher, that Canzeroni," he said. "He's the only defensive catcher in the game who can't catch." Nevertheless, he was occasionally supportive of his talent. Well, sort of. "See that fella Greg Goossen over there?" he asked a reporter. "He's 20 years old and in 10 years, he's got a chance to be a star in this game. Now see that fella over there? He's 20 years old, too. In 10 years he's got a chance to be 30."

Contrast these put-downs with his comments about the indispensable Tommy Henrich: "I don't want you to sit in a draft. Don't slip and fall in the shower—and under no circumstances should you eat fish, because them bones can kill you. Drive carefully, and stay in the slow lane, and sit quietly in the clubhouse until the game begins. I cannot let anything happen to you!"

Despite his success as a player, Casey remained humble. "I was such a dangerous hitter," he recalled, "I even got intentional walks in batting practice." And managing made him even more humble. After the Yankees won the 1958 World Series, he generously allowed that "I couldn't have done it without my players."

The trials and tribulations that came with managing the expansion New York Mets, the worst team in baseball, brought out the best and worst in the Old Perfessor. One thing for sure, he would not have made it as a motivational speaker. One day when the true horridness of his Mets team hit him full force, he admitted, "You look up and down the bench and you have to say to yourself, 'Can't anybody here play this game?'" New York fans came out to watch his team, if only to see firsthand if they were as bad as Casey said they were. He piqued New Yorkers' interest by claiming that "the only thing worse than a Mets game is a Mets doubleheader." When the Mets faced the powerful Cincinnati Reds, Casey looked across the diamond and mused, "Take a look at their bench. It's made of pure mahogany. Now look at ours—driftwood."

Even when he was at the helm of the mighty Yankees, he was a realist. "Right now we're playing bad every place," he said. "We're not hitting, we're not pitching, and we're not fielding too good." And then he added, "And judging from what I read in the newspapers, the Yankees writers are in a slump, too."

Casey was perhaps the only man who addressed the U.S. Senate and made less sense than they do. On July 8, 1958, the Yankees manager appeared before Senator Estes Kefauver's Senate Anti-Trust and Monopoly Subcommittee. His testimony before the Kefauver hearings represents the funniest comedy monologue this side of Johnny Carson. Mickey Mantle and Ted Williams, who also testified, were in stitches throughout the proceedings. Here is a very brief excerpt from the actual transcripts of the session. Space restrictions prevent us from reprinting the 7,500-word masterpiece in its entirety, and that's a shame, akin to editing the Gettysburg Address or the preamble to the Constitution.

> Mr. Stengel: Well, I started in professional ball in 1910. I have been in professional ball, I would say, for forty-eight years. I have been employed by numerous ballclubs in the majors and in the minor leagues. I started in the minor leagues with Kansas City. I played as low as class D ball, which was at Shelbyville, Kentucky, and also class C ball, and class A ball, and I have advanced in baseball as a ballplayer.

I had many years that I was not so successful as a ballplayer, as it is a game of skill. And then I was no doubt discharged by baseball in which I had to go back to the minor leagues as a manager, and after being in the minor leagues as a manager, I became a major league manager in several cities and was discharged, we call it "discharged," because there is no question I had to leave. (Laughter.)

Much more followed, and then:

If I have been in baseball for forty-eight years there must be some good in it. I was capable and strong enough at one time to do any kind of work but I came back to baseball and I have been in baseball ever since. I have been up and down the ladder. I know there are some things in baseball, thirty-five to fifty years ago, that are better now than they were in those days. In those days, my goodness, you could not transfer a ballclub in the minor leagues, class D, class C ball, class A ball. How could you transfer a ballclub when you did not have a highway? How could you transfer a ballclub when the railroads then would take you to a town you got off and then you had to wait and sit up five hours to go to another ballclub?

How could you run baseball then without night ball? You had to have night ball to improve the proceeds to play larger salaries and I went to work, the first year I received $135 a month. I thought that was amazing. I had to put away enough money to go to dental college. I found out it was not better in dentistry, I stayed in baseball.

Any other questions you would like to ask me? I want to let you know that as to the legislative end of baseball, you men will have to consider that what you are here for. I am a bench manager. I will speak about anything from the playing end—in the major or minor leagues—and do anything I can to help you.

Casey then launches into a lengthy diatribe in which he addresses everything but the question. When he pauses to take a breath, Senator Kefauver breaks in:

Senator Kefauver: Mr. Stengel, I am not sure that I made my question clear. (Laughter.)

Mr. Stengel: Yes, sir. Well that is all right. I am not sure I am going to answer yours perfectly, either. (Laughter.)

When Stengel's hilarious 45-minute lecture was finished, Mickey Mantle was next. A tough act to follow, to say the least, but Mantle was equal to the task. Mickey was sworn in, and his testimony began.

Senator Kefauver: "Mr. Mantle, do you have any observations with reference to the applicability of the antitrust laws to baseball?"

Mr. Mantle: "My views are about the same as Casey's."

Contrast Casey's appearance before the Senate with that of Rafael Palmeiro, et al, and ask yourself: Who was speaking the real gibberish? Trying to define Stengelese is like trying to dissect a joke to discover why it's funny. It doesn't work. Sure it's rambling and sure it's ambiguous and vague. And it certainly ignores most of the conventions of good English; almost everything is left dangling, including the listener. But Stengelese is a thing of beauty and it speaks best when it speaks for itself. Here is another example: "That feller runs splendid but he needs a little help at the plate, which coming from the country chasing rabbits all winter give him strong legs, although he broke one falling out of a tree, which shows you

Casey Stengel (left) was the "Old Perfessor" himself, and people would try to get near him to hear his next nugget of wisdom. Yogi Berra (right), on the other hand, was more of an "accidental philosopher."

can't tell, and when a curveball comes, he waves at it and if the pitchers don't throw curves you have no pitching staff, so how is a manager going to know whether to tell boys to fall out of trees and break legs so he can run fast even if he can't hit a curveball?"

Stengel's battles of wits with umpires are legendary. When an umpire rejected his appeal to call a game because it was too dark to continue, Stengel emphasized his point by using a flashlight to relay signals to his pitcher. When calls were going against him in a game umpired by Beans Reardon, Stengel swooned and fell to the ground in an apparent dead faint. Reardon, wise to Stengel's tricks, promptly lay down beside him. "When I peeked out outta one eye and saw Reardon on the ground, too," said Stengel, "I knew I was licked."

Stengel was still confounding questioners as late as 1969, when he replied to a question from Frank Brady of the *Philadelphia Bulletin* about introducing a livelier ball.

"They already lived up the ball! It's too fast for the pitcher, he'd say, and the infielder, too, and there is a problem if you would like to bunt, which most do. The pitcher is liable to get hurt and the infielder, too, and I would say you could say there will be more hitting because the ball gets down there faster and it goes through because you can't get there to catch the ball which you would have."

After the Mets had completed a rare-as-plutonium doubleheader sweep in Milwaukee, Stengel and his team flew to Houston, arriving at 7:00 AM. The manager wolfed down a quick breakfast and announced that he was going to bed and didn't want to be disturbed. "If anybody comes looking for me," he said, "tell 'em I'm being embalmed."

Yogi Berra

Yogi Berra is quoted as often as Stengel, maybe more so. But there aren't really a lot of similarities between the two. I consider Yogi to be an accidental philosopher. Most of his quotable comments were unintentional.

Many children used to think that Yogi Berra was named after the Hanna-Barbera cartoon bear instead of the other way around. It's not such a silly notion. Think about it. Was it the bear or the Berra who said, "If you come to a fork in the road, take it"? When asked what time it was, who responded, "You mean now?" And was it the Berra or the bear who said, "I'm gonna get that pic-a-nic basket!" Okay, that one was the Bear. The rest were from the mouth of the Hall of Fame catcher for the New York Yankees. Both were lovable despite their utter contempt for the English language. One called Jellystone home and one Yankee Stadium. One continually tried to outfox Ranger Smith, the other helped to bamboozle American League batters. One had a friend named Boo Boo; the other never heard a boo in his entire career.

The strike zone to Yogi Berra was little more than a suggestion, an imaginary line as meaningless as that separating the US and Canada on the map. He was the best bad-ball hitter in the history of the game (although Vladimir Guerrero is making a concerted effort to replace him). When players like Ted Williams lectured him about patience and proper thinking at the plate, he'd just laugh and say, "How can anyone think and hit at the same time?"

Yogi first arrived at the Yankees camp straight from the Navy and sporting a sailor suit. Years later he asked coach Frank Crosetti if he remembered that day. "Sure," said Crosetti. "I bet you didn't think I looked like a ballplayer," said Berra. "You didn't even look much like a sailor," said Crosetti.

Yogi once received a check from a friend made out to "bearer." He showed it to some Yankees teammates. "I've known this guy for twenty years and he can't even spell my name." Yogi was reportedly even funny as a kid. When a friend asked how he liked school, he responded, "Closed." When his major league roommate Bobby Brown was working his way through medical school, Yogi looked up from his favorite TV show to see Brown finally close the cover on his medical text. Yogi asked him, "How did it come out?" When he received a message in the Yankees clubhouse that his wife would be late in picking him up because she was going to see *Dr. Zhivago*, he was concerned. "What's wrong now?" he asked the messenger.

Yogi was the master of the malapropism, and his humor lay in the fact that he was not trying to be funny. In that way, he was the antithesis of fellow catcher Bob Uecker, whose humor was very sharp but very intentional. It didn't hurt that Berra had an old St. Louis friend and neighbor named Joe Garagiola to record, chronicle, and perhaps occasionally invent his verbal gems and help make him a legend. His claim that "I didn't say all the things I said" is almost certainly true. And not everything Yogi said was a classic. He could actually be quite a boring interview and, as a philosopher of the common man, he's hardly a Mark Twain. Writer Jack Mann once said that Yogi's standard answer to every question was, "Huh? How the hell should I know?" This scarcely competes with the Algonquin Round Table for wit. Bill Veeck thought that Yogi was a "completely manufactured product." When Casey Stengel was managing the Mets and Yogi Berra was at the helm of the Yankees, Veeck had this to say about the battle for the hearts and minds of

New Yorkers. "Pitting Yogi against Stengel was the worst mismatch in history. No boxing commissions would have allowed it. He is a case study of this country's unlimited ability to gull itself and be gulled." He went on to say, "Every time Yogi hiccupped, he was answered by gales of laughter. 'Boy,' you said to yourself, 'nobody can hiccup as funny as that Yogi.'"

But there was enough evidence to suggest that Yogi said enough of the things he is credited with saying to confirm his credentials as a genuine baseball flake. Many of them have made their way into our everyday lives. Many make sense. Some are even profound. Who among us hasn't quoted Yogi's "This is like déjà vu all over again"? or "You can observe a lot just by watching"? (A notion, by the way, with which Sherlock Holmes would have agreed, having explained the difference to Watson on many occasions.) When he said "It gets late early out there," he was referring to the way in which the late afternoon sun became a problem in Yankee Stadium's left field. Even though the math may be questionable, his assertion that "Baseball is 90 percent mental, the other half is physical," is a truism, as is "You give 100 percent in the first half of the game, and if that isn't enough in the second half you give what's left." Yogi drew a fine distinction when he said, "Slump? I ain't in no slump. I just ain't hitting." And an even finer one when he said, "If the fans don't want to come out to the ball park, you can't stop them."

Not everything he said was as easy to defend. "I knew I was going to take the wrong train, so I left early," is the kind of paradoxical statement that hurts the listener's brain. So is "No one ever goes there anymore. It's too crowded." When asked if a young hitter had exceeded his expectations, Yogi replied, "Oh, he's done more than that." When asked if master base stealer Rickey Henderson would be able to run on his own as the situation dictated, he said, "He can run anytime he wants. I'm giving him the red light." In spring training the Yankees trainer asked what hat size he took. "I don't know," said Yogi. "I'm not in shape yet." And finally, when Yogi's wife inquired whether her husband wanted to be buried in his hometown of St. Louis, his current home state of New Jersey, or New York, where he made his fame and fortune, Yogi replied, "Surprise me." But he was discriminating. When some teammates invited him to watch a stag movie with them, he replied, "Who's starring in it?"

When he came out of retirement to become Warren Spahn's personal catcher, he was asked if they represented the oldest battery in baseball history. "I don't know if we're the oldest, but we're definitely the ugliest," he said.

On the occasion of his being honored with Yogi Berra Appreciation Day in his home town of St. Louis, Yogi spoke from his heart. "I want to thank you for making this day necessary," he said. On behalf of baseball fans everywhere, and English teachers around the world, I'd like to thank Yogi for being necessary, too.

Joe Garagiola

It's hard to mention Yogi without talking about Joe Garagiola in the very next breath. He was to Yogi what Watson was to Sherlock Holmes. Joe Garagiola and Yogi were both from a part of St. Louis known as "The Hill." Garagiola actually showed more promise than Yogi, although it was Yogi who became the legend.

Garagiola saw the funny side of baseball. Catchers who hit .257 with no power have to if they want to survive. Catchers have the perfect position to observe all that goes on in a ballpark. They have the best seat in the house. And Garagiola was a great observer.

He once observed: "One thing you learned as a Cubs fan: when you bought your ticket, you could count on seeing the bottom of the ninth."

And: "I went through baseball as 'a player to be named later.'"

And: "Nolan Ryan is pitching much better now that he has his curveball straightened out."

And especially: "Baseball is a game of race, creed, and color. The race is to first base. The creed is the rules of the game. The color, well, the home team wears white uniforms and the visiting team wears gray."

Moe Berg

Yogi and Garagiola were both catchers, and so it's only fitting to add a third catching philosopher to their ranks. I am proud to be a member of the Baseball Reliquary with Moe Berg and to have been inducted in the same year. We would have made a hell of a battery. Albert Kilchesty, the Baseball Reliquary's archivist/historian, spoke to the audience before Moe Berg was inducted into the Shrine of the Eternals. He referred to his previous year's address:

> I spoke at some length about the difference between baseball fact and baseball fiction and the precarious position that the Baseball Reliquary occupies between these two poles. It isn't at all surprising to me, then, that I have been asked to introduce our first inductee this year. After all, Morris "Moe" Berg made a career out of blurring the distinctions between fact and fiction in his personal life. Additionally, his wide-ranging inter-ests, his esoteric and encyclopedic knowledge, and his unlikely career as a catcher and a spy make Berg, at least in my opinion, the quintessential Reliquarian. To paraphrase another writer speaking about another American original: if Moe Berg hadn't really existed, it would be necessary for us to invent him. Thankfully Moe Berg did exist, for I doubt that even the most imaginative and talented among us would be able to conjure a character as inscrutable, enigmatic, and con-tradictory as Berg. In fact, being asked to introduce Moe Berg, I feel as though I have been asked to explain the Sphinx or to describe the meaning of Mona Lisa's smile in less than two minutes.

They call catcher's equipment the "tools of ignorance," but as a catcher Moe Berg was considered the brainiest man to have played the game of baseball. He graduated with his B.A. magna cum laude from Princeton in 1923. While there he studied Latin,

Greek, French, Spanish, Italian, German, and Sanskrit. He played shortstop for the Tigers and he and his second baseman used to communicate in Latin when there was a runner on second. There are so many languages in today's game that consecutive translation is needed when there's a meeting at the mound. It's like the Tower of Babel to some but I like to think of it as the United Nations.

Moe later studied at the Sorbonne in Paris and Heidelberg in Germany. He finished second at Columbia Law School. He reportedly read ten newspapers a day—and I'm not just talking about the comics. Incidentally, that's the same number of Boston newspapers that Ted Williams used to wrap his fish and line the bottom of his bird cage. Moe's apartment had stacks of books and magazines strewn about everywhere. He used to talk of these piles as if they were living entities. He thought that if someone else read them, the stacks would die. And they got on my buddy Bird Fidrych for talking to balls! Dom DiMaggio was dismissed as his roommate because Dom allowed players to scatter Berg's stacks around the floor. Even Casey Stengel called Berg "the strangest man to ever play baseball."

Author Nicholas Dawidoff, in his book *The Catcher Was a Spy*, points out, "He was many things ballplayers are not supposed to be: educated, intelligent, cosmopolitan, well-spoken, Jewish, and slow-footed." Wow, what a scouting report. No wonder he was a third-string catcher. In fact, Berg supposedly inspired—if that's the right term—the infamous phrase, "Good field, no hit." He managed only six homers as a major leaguer, and his lifetime average was .243. It has been said of Moe Berg that "he could speak a dozen languages and couldn't hit in any of them." It's true that his batting average was closer to his IQ than most players, and despite what Ted Williams used to tell me, it makes you wonder just how smart you have to be to be a good hitter. His teammate Buck Crouse expressed it best: "Moe, I don't care how many of them damn degrees you got, they ain't never learned you to hit the curve."

This all goes to show you what a freak Moe Berg was in the game of baseball and how he was viewed as a result. Baseball likes and even encourages mediocrity in everything except on the field of play. They don't want a player to stand out. Players with ideas scare the hell out of owners, managers, and other players.

So with all that he had to offer the world, why did Moe want to be a ballplayer? "I'd rather be a ballplayer than a justice of the U.S. Supreme Court," he once said. Based on some of the judges that have been appointed lately, he was probably overqualified anyway.

He once made a great comment about a teammate of mine, George Scott. He said: "I believe there are fortunes to be made by the contractors who replace the walls he will tear down by the force of the baseballs he will hit." No wonder he's been called the "erudite eccentric." Compare that to what Luis Tiant said about George: "Boomer, you can be anything you want to be in the jungle." Boomer brightened up and said, "Yeah?" Tiant said, "Except the hunter." Tiant was the greatest teammate. Actually I guess they're both pretty pithy. Berg did his best to steer teammates away from profanity by pointing out that it showed a lack of vocabulary. "Have you ever employed a polysyllable?" he once asked a player. There is no record of the reply, but if I know ballplayers, it was probably, "I don't know no Polly and I don't have to pay for it." It's like the old joke about the old ballplayer who decided to visit Harvard and asked directions from a passing English professor. "Where's Harvard Yard at?" he said. The prof corrected him, "You should never end a sentence with a preposition." "Where's Harvard Yard at, asshole?" the player said.

As a catcher, Berg was apparently a pretty good pitch-caller and could use psychology when needed. That's important, especially where young pitchers are involved. You don't go out and try to use that stuff on Bob Gibson—Gibson once told visiting catcher Tim McCarver to get the hell back behind the plate because all he knew about pitching was that "you can't hit it."

Berg once wrote a primer on pitching for *Atlantic Monthly* called "Pitchers and Catchers." He uses French and Latin phrases, almost insuring that no ballplayer would ever benefit from it. I like what he said: "Baseball men agree with the philosopher that perfection—which means a pennant to them—is attainable only through a proper combination of opposites."

While managing the infamous "Daffiness Boys" Brooklyn Dodgers (their opening-day war cry being "Wait until next year!"), Casey had a player called Frenchy Bordagaray, a colorful figure who was a perfect foil for Casey. Frenchy was on second base and was absentmindedly tapping his foot on the bag between pitches. A throw from the pitcher to second baseman Billy Jurges resulted in him being called out by the umpire. Casey charged from the dugout, chin thrust out and battle-ready. As the second-base umpire saw him coming, he retreated to left field. Meanwhile, as Stengel passed second base in hot pursuit, he passed Frenchy at the pitcher's mound. "Outa the corner of my mouth, I says to him, 'You were safe, weren't you?' " He was momentarily stopped in his tracks when Frenchy answered, "Nope, I was out."

"I'm stuck, see," Casey recalled years later. "But I gotta go through with the act." He tried to maintain his outrage all the way out to the umpire's retreat. He placed his hands on his hips, threw his cap disgustedly to the ground, and appeared to be giving the umpire both barrels. In reality, he was saying, "What did you say he was?" The umpire replied that he was out. "So I reach down and pick up my cap and walked away," he said. "But when I gets to the bench, I really tear into Bordagaray. 'I saw your foot on the bag,' I tells him. 'How could Jurges tag you out?' So Frenchy explains. 'It was this way, Case,' he says. 'I'm standing near second base, doing a tap dance. I guess he tagged me out between taps.' "

Sometimes two flakes can say the same thing and from the mouth of one it sounds stupid, while the other guy sounds profound. It's like when a great control pitcher gets the benefit of the doubt on a pitch on the corner. Here's an example: Casey Stengel, from the school of hard knocks, once said, "Good hitting will beat good pitching every time, and vice versa." He was laughed at, and his comments were considered nonsensical. Meanwhile a scholar like Moe Berg, who graduated from an Ivy League college, said virtually the same thing in his primer: "Good fielding and pitching, without hitting, or vice versa, is like Ben Franklin's half pair of scissors—ineffectual." Casey, all I can say is, "You could look it up."

Berg makes reference to the "2:00 hitter" who can hit like Ted Williams in batting practice but can't hit at all when the game starts. He explains how to throw a knuckleball and a forkball and other trick pitches to plant doubts in the hitter's mind and—I kid you not, he really says this—"to fool the hitter, there's the rub." God, that sounds so much more profound than when Zimmer told me to "throw strikes."

Berg goes on to say that the catcher must be able to "cock his arm from any position, throw fast and accurately to the bases, field bunts like an infielder, and catch foul balls like an outfielder. He must be adept at catching a ball from any angle, and almost simultaneously tagging a runner at home plate." He ends up by calling the catcher "the Cerberus of baseball." I love it! I love the image of the catcher being the "hound of Hades" who guards the gates of Hell. (This image is repeated throughout literature, right down to *Harry Potter and the Sorcerer's Stone*. Only in J. K. Rowling's version, the creature that guards the gate is called "Fluffy." Somehow that name just doesn't intimidate base runners trying to score from third.)

New York columnist John Kieran recorded some of Berg's movements over a short period of time. On one occasion he was spotted attending lectures on Goethe's *Faust* at Princeton. (Note: That's not to be confused with the feeble-minded Faust you will encounter later in this book.) On another, he met with Albert Einstein to discuss Professor Archibald Henderson's theories on "the internal bisector problem in Euclidean geometry." According to Dawidoff's book, "Professor Berg has had [this] on his mind since he read Professor Henderson's monograph in the bullpen during a double-header between the Red Sox and Detroit Tigers in Detroit one day late last summer." I'd like to be able to say that this is pretty much the life of all ballplayers away from the field, but unfortunately I can't. The closest I can come is the time we went to see the "yak man" when the circus came to Braintree.

Berg read books such as *An Enquiry Concerning Human Understanding*, by David Hume. Today's ballplayers scan the latest adventures of Harry Potter and consider that pretty deep.

Berg's circle of friends was eclectic. He hobnobbed with Einstein and then went on jaunts with Al Schacht, the "Clown Prince of Baseball." After seeing Berg's library, which extended to every room of his house, Schacht delivered his thoughts. "No wonder he can't hit a curveball," said Schacht. "A guy who read half of these ought to be stone blind."

But we haven't talked about Berg's chief claim to fame. Spying has been going on in baseball since the game began. We covertly obtain secrets from the enemy all the time. It's called "stealing signs." Berg took the concept to a whole other level. I've never seen this degree of skullduggery and espionage on a ballfield—among owners, sure, but never among ballplayers. (Well, I once had a mole in the Commissioner's office. I met her poolside at a motel we were staying at. And believe it or not, she had a little mole, too, but the statute of limitations hasn't run out on that one yet so I'd better shut up. Suffice it to say she fed me information that helped the Player's Association.)

Spying is all about disguises and trickery and when you think about it, what better alter ego for a spy than being a third-string catcher? Like James Bond, who claimed to be "a cunning linguist" (I think 007 may have slipped one of those suggestive double entendres in on us there), Berg was able to make trips to Japan as part of Major League All-Star squads. If Tojo had really been paying attention, he might have wondered why Babe Ruth and Lou Gehrig had a lowly .250 hitter in their midst.

Berg was an Office of Strategic Services (OSS) undercover agent who had orders to kill theoretical physicist Werner Heisenberg if it looked like Germany was about to build a nuclear bomb. The Manhattan Project had President Truman nervous, and Berg was sent to Zurich outfitted with a gun and a cyanide pill to gather information on Heisenberg. I've often wished I had those two things when the bases were loaded with nobody out. Moe determined that Germany was not on the brink of developing such a weapon, and so the third-string catcher did not become a double-naught spy. With little more than a double-naught batting average, the only thing he had the ability to kill was rallies. Nevertheless, Moe is the only person to have entries in both the Baseball Encyclopedia *and* the Encyclopedia of Espionage.

I was lucky enough to be a battery mate for two Hall of Famers in Carlton Fisk and Gary Carter. I'm quite sure that neither of them was a spy. They were too good at hitting. Hall of Famers don't make good spies. They draw too much attention to themselves.

Were they smart? Neither was a Rhodes Scholar. Fisk is a friend who's turned into a surly son-of-a-bitch. Like all catchers, he was nasty. They say that Will Rogers never met a man he didn't like. Well, he obviously never met Jerry Grote. I didn't like the way Fisk showed me up by throwing the ball back to the mound faster than I had pitched it. He was tough, probably because he was the runt of the litter in the Fisk family. He had the toughness to be a spy—the spy who gloved me. As for Carter, he brought way too much attention to himself to be a spy. He'd have to tell everyone within earshot about his plans. He'd be announcing it all in post-game interviews. He'd have used it as the text for his acceptance speech in Cooperstown. He'd name names.

Fisk and Carter were exact opposites. Fisk was methodical, slow, reluctant to put down a finger. Carter was ADD. He was all over the place. He was quick as a cat, never let the ball get by him, and if he did he ran right after it. Fisk was plodding, like Berg, and method-ical, like Berg. When Fisk gets on his deathbed, he'll be there for three years. Carter could probably be a spy because people would probably say, "There's no way this guy's a spy." He's like cow manure, he's all over the place. Fisk *looks* like he's spying because he's so slow and methodical. Trouble is, he could be sleeping.

Still, there was only one Moe Berg. Albert Kilchesty said it best on the day we were inducted into the Shrine of the Eternals:

> In the figure of Moe Berg, we find a very comfortable
> and near-perfect fusion of what we artist types like to

call high and low culture. He could converse as easily with diplomats, scholars, and nuclear physicists as with unschooled teammates, hack sportswriters, and fans. He could handle a fastball from Lefty Grove as well as a difficult assignment from OSS chief "Wild Bill" Donovan. There is no either/or quality to Moe Berg's life, nothing that indicates that he had to pursue one vocation rather than another. He was not afflicted with the disease of the specialist. Berg was a scholar and a lawyer; a linguist and a radio show personality; a convivial conversationalist and an utter cipher; an intensely private man and a citizen of the world; a third-string catcher and, if you choose to believe all the reports, a first-rate atomic spy.

Perhaps the weirdest Moe Berg fact of all came when Moe contemplated writing his memoirs. His coauthor was ready to proceed until he discovered that the biography was not about Moe of *Three Stooges* fame! But all fans of baseball and espionage know he was no stooge. Quite the opposite, in fact. This man was more likely to hang out with Pussy Galore and Moneypenny than Larry and Curly. Or, as he might have explained to his potential coauthor: "The name's Berg...Moe Berg."

Dan Quisenberry

Dan Quisenberry was a submarine pitcher, giving some credence to the theory that the odder the pitch, the odder the pitcher. Quisenberry delivered his quips the same way he delivered pitches—with practiced delivery and from an unexpected angle. He once said, "I found a delivery in my flaw," which is pretty funny but also true. The more unusual the delivery, the harder it is for the batter to pick up.

As a college senior at La Verne College in California, he pitched 194 innings. Apparently, all that work caused him to drop his arm for self-preservation—like any animal, he adapted. He evolved. As a submariner, his pitch was naturally the sinker. "Without my flawed delivery, I wouldn't have made it to the major leagues," he explained.

Not only was he a submariner, but Quiz was also a reliever. I've always claimed that Tibetan priests would make ideal relief pitchers. If they have the mental discipline to sit naked in the snow at 20,000 feet and generate enough heat to melt the snow for 15 feet around them, they are good candidates. Put that same Tibetan priest on the mound with a baseball in his hands and it doesn't matter how tight the situation is. He can use his power of concentration to make the ball disappear and then materialize 60'6" in the catcher's mitt. That's pretty much what a relief pitcher needs to do. Quisenberry didn't claim to be a Tibetan priest, though; he put it less romantically. "I'm just a garbage man. I come into a game and clean up other people's messes." He added, "It helps to be stupid if you're a relief pitcher. Relievers have to get into a zone of their own. I just hope I'm stupid enough."

A published poet, he was a man with a ready wit and the eloquence and timing to deliver the punch line. He once said, "A manager uses a relief pitcher like a six-shooter, he fires until it's empty then takes the gun and throws it at the villain." Now that's funny *and* accurate. He also observed, "Natural grass is a wonderful thing for little bugs and sinkerball pitchers." And another zinger from the Quiz show: "Our fielders have to catch a lot of balls, or at least deflect them to someone who can." He described his friend and teammate, pitcher Renie Martin, as follows: "Some pitchers throw to spots, Renie throws to planets."

His teammates joined in the spirit of the Quiz. When he was making pregame use of the portable john in the Boston bullpen, teammate Jamie Quirk set fire to newspapers and smoked him out. He was literally caught with his pants down as he scrambled to safety in front of the assembled Fenway throng.

Quisenberry was wise enough to know that baseball is just a game. But the main target of his zings was himself. "Reggie Jackson hit one off me that's still burrowing its way to Los Angeles." And this,

"I lull them into a false sense of security by letting them watch me pitch. If overconfidence can cause the Roman Empire to fall, I ought to be able to get a ground ball." And, "I want to thank all the pitchers who couldn't go nine innings, and manager Dick Howser, who wouldn't let them go."

He knew the agony of defeat: "Once I tried to drown myself with a shower nozzle after I gave up a homer in the ninth. I found out you can't." But he learned to be philosophical—as all relievers, Democrats, and residents of death row must to survive. He rationalized the difference between an effective sinker and a dud. "The batter still hits a grounder. But in this case the first bounce is 360 feet away."

Quisenberry did something that is very radical in baseball. He read books. He read le Carre and Hemingway. He followed the stock market and could discuss the drug issue in baseball and world issues. Baseball did not define him.

I mean this isn't just baseball funny, it's David Letterman funny.

- "I've seen the future and it's much like the present, only longer."
- "Most pitchers fear losing their fastball and, since I don't have one, the only thing I have to fear is fear itself."

Quisenberry had the soul of a poet, and it would be unfair to leave the impression that he was merely a master of the one-liner. His baseball philosophy appeals to me. "I just want to boil everything down to a simple game of catch," he once said. "The people who play catch the best will win." He was first and foremost a humanitarian. He believed in Christianity intertwined with politics, brotherhood, peace and hunger. He founded an organization known as the Quiz Relief Fund, with proceeds going to a community food network known as Harvesters. Here is his poem "Baseball Cards":

> I look back
> At who I thought I was
> Or used to be

Now, trying to be funny
I tell folks
I used to be famous
I used to be good
They say
We thought you were bigger
I say
I was

The Umpires

Since they always get the last word anyway, let's give the umpires the final word here. Their official vocabulary is limited to "Strike," "Safe," "Out," and a few other monosyllabic words. But some felt no such restrictions. There are countless colorful umpires from the past, and they all had their unique style. Some had tact and some didn't.

Clarence Rowland once called Babe Ruth out on a close play at second base. Ruth was furious. He leaped to his feet and charged toward the umpire, intent on inflicting grievous bodily harm. Before he could act on his intentions, Rowland disarmed him with the following: "What a shame I had to call you out, Babe, after such a beautiful slide. It was the best slide I ever saw." Babe actually thanked Rowland before retreating to the dugout.

Bill "Lord" Byron was a singing National League umpire in the early part of the century. He used to announce his calls in verse when the mood struck him. The louder and more obnoxious the batter, the more likely he was to serenade him. He'd say, "It cut the middle of the plate. You missed because you swung too late." I can just see some of today's hitters after that call. Or this one: "You'll have to learn before you're older. You can't hit the ball with your bat on your shoulder."

Johnny Evers, the second baseman of Tinker-to-Evers-to-Chance fame, got a second-base solo from Byron after being called out on a failed steal attempt. Not only did Evers loudly protest the call but he also held his nose to show the umpire and the entire ballpark that it stunk. With an infuriating calm, Byron chanted, "It's a difference of opinion, difference of opinion; that's all I have to say."

Evers was an unappreciative audience, and his profanity-strewn critique of Byron's umpiring talents was anything but poetic. The Lord was unshaken. He did an encore to the tune of "In the Shade of the Old Apple Tree":

> Go sit down with the other men.
> If you don't it will cost you ten.
> If you don't go away,
> It will cost you your pay
> While mine will go on, don't you see?

Byron was more than a songbird. He sometimes livened up the game by changing the rules to suit his calls. In one game, the Baltimore Orioles had the bases loaded with two men out and a chance to break the game wide open. However, the next batter hit a sky-high pop-up down the first-base line in foul territory. Jack Dunn, the Orioles' first-base coach, decided to try to outfox the first baseman by yelling, "Back off! I got it! I got it!" The first baseman did just that, allowing the ball to drop unmolested and presumably giving the batter a second life. It was not to be. Byron immediately called the batter out. When the Orioles loudly protested and demanded an explanation, Byron cited "interference." Dunn was incensed. "What do you mean interference?" he asked. "I didn't come near the first baseman or the ball!" "I mean vocal interference," explained Byron.

Emmett Ashford was a regular Dapper Dan. He wore gold or diamond cuff links and dressed to the nines, but he was old and slow-footed like my cat Rupert. He had the same wondering look on his face that Rupert has, like he was born six days after the rest of the litter.

There was also Bill Klem, my personal favorite. He's already in the Hall of Fame in Cooperstown, but I think he should be inducted into the Baseball Reliquary Shrine of the Eternals. Pam Postema is the only ump in there, thus far.

Klem was a wise man. They called him the Old Arbitrator, and he had the respect of all ballplayers. He once said, "An angry player can't argue with the back of an umpire who is walking away." Many umpires never learn that lesson. They want to be the center of attention when they should really be anonymous. "The best-umpired game is the game in which the fans cannot recall the umpires who worked it," Klem said.

On the other hand, he was colorful and flamboyant. When someone anticipated a strike call, he'd say, "It ain't nothin' 'til I call it." He stood up to batters and demanded their respect. When someone showed him irrefutable photographic evidence of a call he had gotten wrong, he replied, "Gentleman, he was out because I said he was out." Of course, like all umpires, he gave the benefit of the doubt to the great hitters. He told one irate pitcher, "Son, when you pitch a strike, Mr. [Rogers] Hornsby will let you know." Man, that's cold!

He once said, "Baseball is more than a game to me, it's a religion." That's what I like about him. Of course, he didn't like to be shown up by managers. "The most cowardly thing in the world is blaming mistakes upon the umpires," he said. "Too many managers strut around on the field trying to manage the umpires instead of their teams."

He umpired in 18 different World Series from 1905 to 1941 before being named the chief of National League umpires. He helped to pioneer the arm signals for "safe," "out," and "strike" that have become part of the game. He also pioneered the chest protector. Here are some other classic Byronisms:

- "Fix your eye on the ball from the moment the pitcher holds it in his glove. Follow it as he throws to the plate and stay with it until the play is completed. Action takes place only where the ball goes."
- "I told the umpires to walk back at least 35 feet from home plate. That reduced the arguments."

- "That guy in a twenty-five cent bleacher seat is as much entitled to know a call as the guy in the boxes. He can see my arm signal even if he can't hear my voice."
- "There are 154 games in a season and you can find 154 reasons why your team should have won every one of them."
- "Your job is to umpire for the ball and not the player."

Three | **Ranters and Ravers**

Impassioned speeches are part of American history. They represent significant milestones in our social and political development. Abe Lincoln, Franklin Roosevelt, Martin Luther King, John F. Kennedy, Ronald Reagan, and other great communicators galvanized the American public with their eloquence. They are emotional, both in their telling and in the impact they had on their audiences. They influenced large numbers of people in a very positive way and changed the world in the process. There is a sub-genre of the great American speech that is exclusive to baseball. I will call it the Great American Baseball Rant. The rant can be a thing of beauty if it is well delivered. Joe Schultz, manager of the Seattle Pilots, delivered most of his using only two words: "shitf*ck" and "f*ckshit." But Schultz wasn't intense or mean enough to be a first-rate ranter.

Of course, the audience has to be receptive in order for the rant to be effective. Johnny Pesky, who once managed the Red Sox and is much too nice to be a classic ranter, was giving a much-needed talk about team morale to his troops. The main reason for the talk was Dick Stuart, who was to team chemistry what Fox News is to fair and balanced reporting. Stuart was inevitably late for every team meeting and often didn't show up until just before game time. This infuriated Pesky, the ultimate team player. Ironically, but fittingly, Stuart was also late for the meeting on morale. When he did arrive, he burst through the door and strutted to the center of the clubhouse like a male model working the runway in Paris. When he had everyone's attention, he did a perfect pirouette and announced, "Here he is, tastefully attired in a black suede jacket from the Stanley Blacker spring collection. He is sporting blue velvet trousers, and his shoes are by Florsheim. The silk handkerchief that adorns his breast pocket and adds just a touch of devil-may-care flair is by Christian Dior." So much for team morale. The entire clubhouse was reduced to chaos, and any message about team play over individualism was lost in the laughter. Even Pesky was in stitches.

There have been many classic rants, but I like to think of the ones that follow as exemplary. The practitioners are at the top of their form, and we should look on their speeches as the essential canon of the category. Please note how the orators use colorful and descriptive language to make their points.

Tommy Lasorda

I hesitated to include Tommy Lasorda in this book. Many of us remember those huggy-kissy Dodger teams managed by Lasorda in the '70s, and many of us cringe at the memory. (My close personal friend, Yankee Graig Nettles, once said that the key to beating the Dodgers was "to keep them from hugging each other too much.") I remember him hanging out with Frank, Sammy, Joey, and other rat pack wannabes, and I cringe some more. I mean, what's rebellious about hanging out with celebrities and dropping names like Manny drops fly balls? Johnny Carson recognized the Hollywood atmosphere of Lasorda's Dodger Stadium love-in when he asked, "Whoever heard of a game being called because of bad karma?" It all seemed rather tacky to me.

But I also remember a game at a Marine base in San Diego when I was playing for USC and my dad was sitting with Lasorda. I think we were playing Utah. We were staying in Quonset huts and all of us decided we wanted to stay in school if only because we wanted to stay out of the service. All of these Marine recruits were marching behind the playing field, running the obstacle course, climbing in full gear, and all that. I think I was facing George

Theodore, and I had him 0–2 and tried to sneak a 78 mph fastball by him. I believe in Einstein's theory of relativity because I thought that my fastball was fast, so it's all relative. Anyway, Theodore hit the pitch over the left-field fence where the Marines were sweating and training in the sun. One Marine retrieved the ball and threw it to our left fielder and it made its way back to me. The next hitter hit the next pitch for another homer in the same spot. The same Marine threw it to our left fielder Bill Brown, and it came back to me again. Same ball, two homers. I stepped off the mound to the left and threw the ball as hard as I could between home plate and first. It was the parade square where all the Marines were marching around. The ball hit the pavement and rolled for three-quarters of a mile. It was like watching your dog run away from home on the Kansas plains. You can watch him run away for three days. Lasorda turned to my dad and said, "Don't worry. He'll make it to the big leagues." That was pretty astute of him under the circumstances.

And then I remember The Tirade. That one press conference proved that, above all the phoniness and celebrity hype, Lasorda loved baseball, loved his Dodgers, and loved winning. He was not a phony after all. He really did "bleed Dodger blue" (that corporate phrase was another thing about Lasorda that used to make me cringe). He also swore until the air was blue.

My epiphany came on May 14, 1978. The remarkable diatribe was prompted by a seemingly innocent question from a member of the working press, one Paul Olden to be exact. The Dodgers had just lost to the Chicago Cubs by a score of 10–7 in fifteen innings, and Cubs slugger Dave "King Kong" Kingman had connected for three monstrous home runs. Olden asked for Lasorda's opinion of Kingman's performance. Here is his response. (Caution: If there are children present, please avert their eyes.)

What's my opinion of Kingman's performance? What the f*ck do you think is my opinion of it? I think it was F*CKING HORSESHIT. Put that in, I don't f*cking care. Opinion of his performance? Jesus Christ, he beat us with three f*cking home runs! What the f*ck do you mean, "What is my opinion of his performance?" How could you ask me a question like that, "What is my opinion of his performance?" Shit, he hit three home runs! F*ck. I'm f*cking pissed off to lose the f*cking game. And you ask me my opinion of his performance! Shit. That's a tough question to ask me, isn't it? "What is my opinion of his performance?"

There's more, but I think you get the idea. I'm embarrassed to admit that up to that point I had questioned the man's managing credentials and his ability to put baseball in its proper perspective.

Lasorda dropped a few other gems as a manager. When he was asked in 1984 about Kurt Bevacqua's hitting abilities, he threw political correctness aside and gave his opinion: "[Kurt] Bevacqua couldn't hit water if he fell out of a f*cking boat!" When starting pitcher Don Sutton gave up a towering first-pitch homer on Opening Day, Lasorda went to the mound and told him, "I know they want us to send the first pitch from Opening Day to the Hall of Fame, but I thought we'd just mail it to them, not send it direct." Pitchers just love it when managers are supportive like that.

Lasorda was a spiritual man who had some definite ideas of right and wrong, good and evil: "I leave you with a saying in this country; if you don't pull for the Dodgers, there's a good chance you may not get into heaven." Which was consistent with this statement: "I bleed Dodger blue and when I die, I'm going to the big Dodger in the sky." I bled a lot of Red Sox red and Expos red, and when I get to heaven I expect the Big Guy will be wearing umpire's gear.

But just as I was starting to warm up to this two-time National League Manager of the Year, he goes all Maya Angelou on me by spouting touchy-feely stuff like this: "Managing is like holding a dove in your hand. Squeeze too hard and you kill it, not hard enough and it flies away." Or, "The difference between the impossible and the possible lies in a man's determination." Or, "About the only problem with success is that it does not teach you how to deal with failure." Gag me with a rosin bag! And then I think back to his reasoned response to Paul Olden's innocent question and I know he belongs.

I might have had trouble playing for Lasorda. During the 1978 season, the year he managed the Dodgers to the National League flag, he went a bit fine-crazy. He fined players for practically anything. The weirdest fining incident was when he fined Tommy John, Charlie Hough, Burt Hooton, and Bill Russell $50 each for arriving at the ballpark a half hour past Tommy's deadline for being in uniform. The players protested to Lasorda, thinking they had a pretty valid excuse for being tardy. It seems that the three players had been driven to the ballpark by a guy named Tommy Lasorda, who insisted on stopping at donut shops and other eateries on the way to Dodger Stadium. Lasorda listened patiently to their explanation and then informed them that the fine would not be rescinded. His rationale? "When you have to be somewhere at a certain time, you should go with someone who is reliable."

Earl Weaver

Often rants and raves are practiced by managers and umpires. Occasionally, baseball personalities are pretty bland on their own, but when they are paired with certain other people, the sparks fly. George Burns needed Gracie Allen, Jerry Lewis needed Dean Martin, and Earl Weaver needed umpire Ron Luciano. Come to think of it, any umpire was a potential vaudeville pairing when Weaver stormed from the dugout, so let's call the act Weaver and the Umpires. Umpire Marty Springstead bitterly claimed that "that midget can barely see over the top of the dugout steps and he claims he can see the pitches." Continuing with the midget theme, his colleague in blue Steve Palermo said, "Weaver is a militant midget. He just uses umpires as props in his circus act." And of course Luciano noticed that he was vertically challenged, too. "He's about 3'1"," he once claimed. "I tell him to keep his nose off my kneecap." He also offered some less-than-sincere concern: "Can you imagine going through life and never seeing a parade?"

Jim Evans said that Weaver was "the Son of Sam of baseball" because of the way he disregarded the laws of baseball. Not to be out-done, Nick Bremigan referred to him as the "Ayatollah of the '80s."

Not that they'd wish him any real harm...oh, I take that back. "I've never seen him do anything funny," said Larry Barnett. "No, I take that back. I once saw him slip and fall coming out of the dugout. That was funny."

Well, it turns out that Weaver isn't really that funny. He was just nasty, as in: "His out signals looked like a spastic trying to hitch a ride on the L.A. freeway." Springstead spoke for the entire umpir-ing fraternity of the day when he said, "He never shuts up. The way to test a Timex watch would be to strap it to Earl Weaver's tongue."

Earl Weaver has such an acid tongue that his teeth were in danger of dissolving. And he was equally mean-spirited toward players. He claimed that he had given pitcher Dave McNally "more chances than my first wife." He was always arguing—often with his own pitchers, and sometimes with opposing pitchers. He once accused Don Sutton of doctoring the baseball with a "foreign substance." Sutton stood his ground. "That's not true at all," he said patriotically. "The label says that this here jar of Vaseline was made right here in the United States."

I never used to complain when I pitched against Sutton. Every ball I got when we played against each other was scuffed. I'd just match him pitch for pitch as long as his balls were left in the game. If he was scuffing the balls up with sandpaper, I was glad to use those same balls for my own purposes. I'd turn them over and throw them in the other direction. I never complained. I'd say "Shoot, that doesn't bother me."

Here Earl Weaver is during a pre-taping taping of Manager's Corner with Earl Weaver. Even though the tape was a put-on, it gives you some idea of what umpire Ron Luciano and pitcher Jim Palmer had to endure from the "malignant midget."

> **Q:** Bill Whitehouse: [This caller] from Frederick, Maryland, wants to know why you and the Orioles don't go out and get some more team speed.

The fiery Earl Weaver had a tendency to really flip his lid when something set him off.

A: Team speed, for chrissake? You get those f*ckin' goddamned little fleas on the f*ckin' bases getting picked off, trying to steal, getting thrown out, taking runs away from you. I get those f*ckin' big cocksuckers who can hit the f*ckin' ball out of the f*ckin' ballpark and can't make any goddamned mistakes.

Q: Well, certainly this show is going to go down in history, Earl. Gary Elliott of Washington, D.C., wanted to know why you don't use Terry Crowley as the designated hitter all the time.

A: Well, Terry Crowley's lucky he's in f*ckin' base-ball, for chrissake. He was released by the Cincinnati Reds, he was released by the f*cking, goddamned Atlanta Braves. We saw that Terry Crowley could sit on his f*cking ass for eight innings and enjoy watchin' the baseball game just like any other fan and has the ability to get up there and break one open in the f*ckin' ninth, so if this cocksucker would mind his own business and let me manage the f*ckin' team, we'd be a lot better off.

Q: Well, certainly you've made your opinions known on the fans' questions about baseball, but let's get to something else. Alice Sweet from Norfork wants to know the best time to put in a tomato plant.

A: Alice Sweet oughta be worried about where the f*ck her next lay is comin' from rather than where her next goddamn tomato plant is coming from. If she'd get her f*ckin' ass out to the f*ckin' bars at night and go hustlin' around the goddamn street, she might get a prick stuck in her once in awhile....I don't under-stand where these questions are coming from, Tom. That's about it for Manager's Corner. Go f*ck yourself and then f*ck with your show comin' up next on the Baltimore Orioles Baseball f*ckin' Network.

Ron Luciano

But what about the other partner in the act? We've heard from Abbott, now it's Costello's turn. Ron Luciano was about as eccentric as an umpire can be. From 1968 to 1980 he used his major league stage to perform and was the antithesis of those umpires who felt that a well-umpired game was one in which they were anonymous. Luciano was flamboyant and craved the spotlight. He was a gentle giant who played on the line for Syracuse University. Instead of thumbing a runner out at first base on a close call, he would pump his arm multiple times or gun him down with his index finger. His

Ron Luciano (far right) was a ranter and a raver and probably the most flamboyant umpire the game has ever had.

fights with Weaver were the most well-known, but many managers objected to his antics. He was criticized for not taking the game seriously enough. He once admitted, "I never called a balk in my life because I didn't understand the rule." While this was doubtlessly said for comic effect—he was actually a very good umpire—the impression bothered managers.

After he retired from umpiring, he expressed dismay at the way the game had changed: "When I started, the game was played by nine tough competitors on grass, in graceful ballparks. But while I was trying to answer the daily Quiz-O-Gram on the exploding scoreboard, a revolution was taking place around me. By the time I finished, there were ten men on each side, the game was played indoors on plastic, and I had to spend half my time watching out for a man dressed in a chicken suit who kept trying to kiss me."

Sadly, Luciano died at the age of 57. He was found in his garage in Endicott, New York, and it is believed he died of carbon monoxide poisoning, an apparent suicide.

Don Zimmer

Don Zimmer and I go way back, of course. Our relationship is like *The Simpsons'* Itchy and Scratchy. I apparently caused his ass to itch, and he scratched it all to rat shit. Well, until he discovered the Preparation H, at least. Zimmer is a baseball lifer. He is a baseball man through and through. He lives and breathes the game and has spent his entire life as a player, coach, and manager. He came out of the Brooklyn Dodgers system as a third baseman and was indoctrinated with that organization's old-school philosophy of hard work and respect for the game.

Zimmer was hit in the head by a pitch while playing for the Dodgers and has a plate in his head as a result. Naturally, players were sympathetic. Once when Graig Nettles was getting nothing but static on his clubhouse radio, he turned to Zimmer and said, "It must be you, Zim. The plate in your head is messing up my radio." If I had said that, I'd have been pitching in Pawtucket later that day.

He loved to bet the horses, and his favorite line was, "I sure hope I break even today, I could use the money."

We've had our disagreements, but one thing I would never deny is his passion to win. I remember that he was critical of Dwight Evans, one of the best right fielders in Red Sox history. He said, "Next to Jim Rice, he's the strongest guy on the team, maybe in all of baseball, but he's got the balls of a female cow."

Here he is at full throttle after a ballgame, possibly before he discovered the soothing relief that Preparation H can bring. The diatribe begins when another reporter asks him about the performance of opposing pitcher Goose Gossage:

> I don't want to f*ckin' talk no more about f*ckin' Goose Gossage, for chrissakes. What do I want to talk about Goose Gossage for? That's the only f*ckin' question I've been asked since the f*ckin' game's been over. He went in and got the job done—what more do you want me to say about Goose Gossage? Go ask Roger Craig what a f*ckin' great job he did. I

Don Zimmer is probably best known for his baseball mishaps: the steel plate inserted into his head after taking a pitch to the noggin; his classic "encounter" with Pedro Martinez; and yet another ball—this time a foul ball—catching him on the head, after which he donned this WWII helmet for protection.

got my own 10 pitchers. I ain't got Goose Gossage. The guy went in and done a great job, whattaya want me to say? I know what the f*ck you want me to say...everyone here wants me to say somethin' bad about Goose Gossage, and I ain't gonna do it. I know what it's all about. I know exactly what the f*ck's goin' on here. And it ain't never gonna happen because I ain't never gonna say anything bad about Goose Gossage. That's what you…I won't say everybody, but I know six out of seven of them that come in here that's all that they want me to say—somethin' bad about Goose Gossage. Here's a f*ckin' guy who's been one of the great pitchers of baseball and I'm gonna say somethin' bad about him? I was a .230 hitter all my life. How the hell am I gonna say somethin' bad about him? But that's what some people want me to say and I'm too f*ckin' smart for that. I ain't fallin' for that, Jack.

Lee Elia

In April of 1983 Lee Elia, then manager of the Chicago Cubs, delivered the rant of ages. In fact, it was the Gettysburg Address of rants. The Cubs had just lost to the Los Angeles Dodgers at Wrigley Field, and Elia was not happy with the Chicago fans:

> F*ck those f*ckin' fans who come out here and say they're Cubs fans that are supposed to be behind you, rippin' every f*ckin' thing you do. I'll tell you one f*ckin' thing, I hope we get f*ckin' hotter than shit, just to stuff it up them 3,000 f*ckin' people that show up every f*ckin' day, because if they're the real Chicago f*ckin' fans, they can kiss my f*ckin' ass right downtown and print it!
>
> They're really, really behind you around here…my f*ckin' ass. What the f*ck am I supposed to do, go out there and let my f*ckin' players get destroyed every day and be quiet about it? For the f*ckin' nickel-dime people that show up? The motherf*ckers don't even work. That's why they're out at the f*ckin' game. They oughta go out and get a f*ckin' job and find out what

it's like to go out and earn a f*ckin' living. Eighty-five percent of the f*ckin' world is working. The other 15 come out here. A f*ckin' playground for the cock-suckers. Rip them motherf*ckers. Rip them f*ckin' cocksuckers like the f*ckin' players. We got guys bustin' their f*ckin' ass, and them f*ckin' people boo. And that's the Cubs? My f*ckin' ass.

They talk about the great f*ckin' support the players get around here. I haven't seen it this f*ckin' year....

The name of the game is "Hit the ball, catch the ball, and get the f*ckin' job done." Right now, we have more losses than we have wins. The f*ckin' changes that have gone on in the Cubs organization are multi-fold. Alright, they don't show because we're 5 and 14...and unfortunately, that's the criteria of them dumb 15 motherf*ckin' percent that come out to day baseball. The other 85 percent are earning a living. I tell you, it'll take more than a 5 and 13 or 5 and 14 to destroy the makeup of this club. I guarantee you that. There's some f*ckin' pros out there that wanna f*ckin' play this game. But you're stuck in a f*ckin' stigma of the f*ckin' Dodgers and the Phillies and the Cardinals and all that cheap shit....It's unbe-lievable. It really is. It's a disheartening f*ckin' situa-tion we're in right now. 5 and 14 doesn't negate all that work. We got 143 f*ckin' games left.

What I'm tryin' to say is don't rip them f*ckin' guys out there. Rip me. If you wanna rip somebody, rip my f*ckin' ass. But don't rip them f*ckin' guys 'cause they're givin' everything they can give....

And once we hit that f*ckin' groove it'll flow, and it will flow, the talent's there. I don't know how to make it any clearer to you. I'm frustrated, I'll guaran-tee I'm frustrated. It'd be different if I walked in this room every day at 8:30 and saw a bunch of guys that didn't give a shit. They give a shit and it's a tough National League East, it's a tough National League period.

Amazing, isn't it? Even though he seemed to lose steam at the end, it was still pretty impressive. One of the amazing features of this rant is that he was calling anyone who came out to Cubs games—they were all day games at the time, as Wrigley had yet to install lights—stupid and lazy for doing so. My question is this: if they weren't supposed to go to day games, and there were no night games, on what particular occasions (aside from Saturday and Sunday) were they supposed to attend games? Little wonder he was gone by August.

Leo Durocher

Leo Durocher was often not a very nice man, which was probably all right with him since he famously claimed, in reference to Mel Ott's New York Giants, that "nice guys finish last." Durocher's humor was served up hard-boiled with a side order of cruelty. He once got into a heated argument with umpire George Magerkurth, and when the ump threatened to "bend down and bite your head off," Durocher shot back, "If you do, you'll have more brains in your stomach than in your head." He sounded like Billy Martin with a better writer.

Durocher was kind of the Tommy Lasorda of his day. He loved to hang around with celebrities like actor George Raft. He married actress Laraine Day.

On the field, Leo the Lip, as he was called, made many enemies with his aggressive style of play and abrasive manner. He said, "I'd trip my mother as she rounded third if it meant saving a run." As a member of the St. Louis Cardinals, the infamous Gas House Gang—one of the most colorful teams ever to play in the big leagues—Durocher was in his element, along with Pepper Martin, Dizzy Dean, and Dizzy's brother Paul. When the Cards won the 1934 pennant on the final day of the season, fans looked forward to a classic World Series against the American League's Detroit Tigers. It did not disappoint. The Series went to seven games before a champion was declared. Dizzy started for the Cardinals and struck out Hank Greenberg three times as the Cardinals won 11–0.

As a manager, he was just as tough. In fact, the Lip is the only manager to have his own players strike against him. In 1943 Durocher was quoted in the newspapers as saying that Bobo Newsom had been suspended because he had criticized catcher Bob Bragan. He tried to portray himself as a hero coming to the defense of a young player against a veteran. In actual fact, the suspension was due to a heated argument with Leo himself. The next day his players organized a protest in the Ebbets Field clubhouse. The ringleaders were Dixie Walker and Arky Vaughan. They demanded that Leo retract his claim and reveal the real reason for Newsom's suspension. Finally, the Dodgers players were persuaded to end their job action and take the field—all but Arky Vaughan. The next day the front page had only two stories: the Allies had landed in Sicily, and the Dodgers had gone on strike against Leo the Lip. Bobo Newsom was sent to the St. Louis Browns soon after.

The Lip is exemplary of a sub-genre of baseball comics known as bench jockeys. The practice was once widespread and was in its heyday at the time of Durocher. He seemed to take great delight in ridiculing opposing players. Even Babe Ruth, or maybe especially Babe Ruth, was a favorite target. The bench jockey has all but disappeared in recent years. Sure, there are still outbreaks, such as the shouting match that erupted between the White Sox and Houston Astros benches during the 2005 World Series. But that wasn't really bench-jockeying in its purest form. The bench jockey was more personal in his attacks, with race, religion, and physical characteristics fair game for the perpetrators. Durocher raised—or lowered—the practice to an art form.

On July 15, 1942, the Dodgers were playing the Chicago Cubs at Wrigley Field. At the time, the Cubbies were so far behind in the pennant race (18½ games back) that they represented no threat to anyone, let alone the first-place Dodgers. But for Leo, bench-jockeying was a sport unto itself. He was like the "sportsman" who hunts moose for the thrill of the kill and then leaves the carcass to rot. Of course, with the hapless Cubs, a better analogy might be shooting fish in a barrel. In any case, Leo and his chorus of hecklers started their barrage in the first inning and didn't stop. Despite the verbal abuse, Chicago managed to stay focused and clung to a 5–2 lead going into the fifth inning. And then the hecklers turned their venom on Cubs reliever Hi Bithorn.

Van Lingle Mungo was a great pitcher for the Brooklyn Dodgers. Only his off-field behavior and violent temper kept him from enjoying a Hall of Fame–caliber career. On one particular day, notoriously weak-fielding Long Tom Winsett had made an egregious outfield error, costing Mungo a sure win. The pitcher completely lost it, ranting and raving and questioning Winsett's ancestry. Usually players cool down as quickly as they heat up. Not Van Lingle Mungo. He walked several blocks to a telegraph office, fuming all the way, and sent the following wire to his wife: "Pack your bags and come to Brooklyn, honey. If Winsett can play the outfield in the big leagues, it's a cinch you can, too."

Not one to turn the other cheek, the pitcher lost his composure and his control. He walked the first two batters he faced and the dugout sharks smelled blood. He then unleashed a wild pitch that brought jeers from his tormentors. Another base on balls, a fielder's choice, and a base hit later, the Dodgers had scored three runs. Yet another walk raised his blood pressure and the decibels from the Dodgers dugout. Hi had lost his cool and the lead. Finally, the Chicago manager walked to the mound to make a pitching change. Seeing him approach, Bithorn decided to make one last throw. He charged toward the enemy bench with murder in his eye and unleashed his best fastball at Durocher. Sadly, he missed, giving Leo one last opening: "You couldn't hit the strike zone and you can't hit me either," he crowed. (If it had been me, I'd have used my foot to test his cup.)

Leo also loved to bait umpires. On one occasion he got into a classic confrontation with home plate umpire Beans Reardon. Bill Nicholson of the Chicago Cubs had hit a drive down the first-base line that Reardon called fair. Durocher gave his vocabulary a workout and called Beans every name in the book, questioning his eyesight one minute and his ancestry the next. Leo was not a stupid man, and when it looked as if Beans was about to throw him out of the game, he turned on his heels and walked back toward his dugout. He couldn't resist one last parting shot and it was delivered with his retreating back to the umpire. The umpire couldn't hear what Leo had said, but he strongly suspected it wasn't complimentary. He called time and went to the Dodger bench.

"What did you just call me?" he demanded.

"What's the matter, didn't you hear me?" Leo shouted back.

"No," admitted the umpire.

"Well then," said the Lip, "guess what I called you. You've had lots of practice. You've been guessing all afternoon anyway."

He also had a classic confrontation with legendary arbiter Jocko Conlan when he was a coach under Walt Alston in Los Angeles. Durocher's Dodgers were in the fourth inning of a game with the Pittsburgh Pirates at the L.A. Coliseum when L.A. first-sacker Norm Larker lofted a ball down the first-base line. The ball landed fair and then bounced foul. Conlan called it a foul ball. Durocher charged onto the field and insisted that Pirates catcher Hal Smith touched the ball and deflected it into foul territory. When Durocher finally returned to the dugout, he continued to rant and rave and punctuated his tirade by throwing a towel in Jocko's direction. The umpire jerked his thumb to indicate that Leo was gone from the game. The coach threw additional paraphernalia onto the field and then advanced upon the umpire. The confrontation that followed made little old ladies cover their ears and children scurry for the aisles. The Lip kicked dirt on Jocko's trousers. Jocko tried to reciprocate but missed and kicked Leo in the shins. Leo kicked back, striking Conlan in the shins. It took the rest of the umpiring team to separate the two. After the dust had settled and the game was over, Durocher admitted to the media that he had gotten the worse of the exchange. After all, Conlan had steel-toed shoes and was protected by shin guards. "When he kicked me, it was steel on bone. When I kicked back, I almost broke my toe on his shin guards. I finally realized that it wasn't a fair fight."

Ted Williams

Ted Williams might have been the most foul-mouthed ranter in baseball history. He was an articulate and even poetic speaker when he wanted to be, but when he lost his temper, the air quickly turned a dirty shade of blue. Ted had many targets, including ungrateful, front-running fans, whom he occasionally spat at or made obscene gestures to. But his choicest attacks were reserved for the media—in particular, Boston writers. Paul Gleason recalled talking with Ted on the bench before a 1960 game at Fenway Park. The opposing team was taking batting practice, and he and Gleason were discussing their swings, comparing the relative merits of California and Florida weather. In other words—small talk. At this point in his career—he would retire at the end of the season—he was not talking to reporters much. Desperate for stories on the biggest name in Boston sports history, the competitive writers had to get quotes secondhand, if at all. A choice Ted Williams quote would sell significant numbers of papers.

On this day, three writers were sitting on the far end of the bench, pretending they were observing the action on the field. Ted noticed that they were edging closer to him, trying to pick up a few phrases. Suddenly he exploded in a voice that was a mixture of John Wayne and General Patton. Ted talked in CAPITAL LETTERS, by the way, screaming, "I SEE YOU SONS OF BITCHES! GET THE HELL OUT OF HERE! I AIN'T TALKIN' TO YOU! THIS AIN'T NONE OF YOUR F*CKIN' BUSINESS. GET THE HELL OUT OF HERE, YOU MOTHERF*CKERS! GET YOUR ASSES OUT OF HERE!"

On another occasion, it was Paul Gleason himself who bore the brunt of a verbal assault from Terrible Ted. It happened when the young hopeful Red Sox minor leaguer was foolish enough to tell Ted that he felt that Paul Waner's approach to hitting was better suited to his natural style. Specifically, Ted believed in a slight upper cut swing, while Waner preached that you should swing down on the ball. It was a classic disagreement between two Hall of Fame hitters. "You've got to swing up, damn it!" said Ted his voice rising. Gleason, little more than a fresh kid, continued to promote Waner. Finally Ted lost it: "Ah, f*ck Paul Waner! What does he know?" And then the funny side of Ted came out, as if he knew that he was sometimes a caricature of himself. He began a controlled diatribe that was as playful as it was sincere. "You've gotta realize," said Gleason years later, "that here he was talking to a baseball bum—an out-of-work minor league wash-out hitter talking to a future Hall of Famer.

"Oh, okay," he yelled. "You're right! I'm wrong! You're definitely right and I'm definitely wrong! I've been wrong all these years! Oh no, hey, you're right! You've hit a lot of home runs! I've been wrong all these years, man! I'm glad you set me straight on that, Paul, ya f*ckin' punk!"

Now that's funny. It's funny because it's Ted Williams, the greatest hitter who ever lived, and it's funny because he was having fun. He wasn't trying to destroy a young player. He was bonding with a young player.

Dummy Taylor

Let's give the last word on ranters and ravers to Dummy Taylor, and that last word is ____! (He couldn't talk, get it?)

Dummy Taylor was what used to be known as a "deaf-mute" back in those politically incorrect days when he pitched for the National League's New York Giants in the early part of the twentieth century (1900–1908). He won 116 games in his career and led the Giants to the National League pennant with 21 victories in 1904.

The fact that he couldn't hear or speak didn't prevent Taylor from expressing himself in no uncertain terms, especially to umpires.

Of course, he used sign language to communicate his thoughts, something I admit to doing on occasion, too. But Luther Haden Taylor was a bit more subtle than the one-finger salute. He used to hurl abuse from the mound when he disagreed with calls. He even became a practiced bench jockey. Umpires were reluctant to toss him from games because they couldn't prove what he was "saying," and they feared that the sympathies of the crowd would be with the poor, unfortunate pitcher.

The sound of silence is the sound of one hand clapping…whatever that means.

Four | Hotfoots and Hotdogs

Eccentric behavior in baseball is more often lowbrow than high-brow. There are more hotfoots and pies in the face than witty comebacks of the sort engaged in by Frasier Crane and his brother Niles. To me the key to the greatest practical jokes is spontaneity. And no one was ever more spontaneous than Moe Drabowsky.

Moe Drabowsky

When Moe Drabowsky's death was announced recently, you could scarcely blame his countless victims for being skeptical. These people had been taken in so many times by Moe that even a death certificate had to be notarized—he could be ready to strike again with a hotfoot or live snake gag.

Some people called Drabowsky "the Polish prince of pranks," others referred to him as the "king of comic relief." Some would simply call him a royal pain in the ass. He was a legend in the art of the prank. He was the Hornsby of the hotfoot. The Ruth of the rubber snake. Even the street-savvy and sophisticated Roy Firestone was sucked into the vortex of his practical jokes. In his mid-teens, Firestone spent two seasons in the Grapefruit League as a batboy for the Baltimore Orioles. The future sports interviewer and entertainer got a chance to rub elbows with the likes of Brooks Robinson, Frank Robinson, and Boog Powell, but it was Moe who made him an honorary stooge by sending him on an extended hunt for a left-handed bat. Drabowsky was adamant that he had to have it. "So I started looking for some left-handed bats," admitted Firestone. "He got me pretty good."

Firestone is hardly unique. Moe got many people "pretty good" throughout his pitching career. He put goldfish in the water cooler of the visitor's clubhouse. He coated their lockers with sneezing powder. On one infamous occasion, his Orioles were being shut out by Kansas City starter Jim Nash. Drabowsky called the Athletics' bullpen, disguising his voice as that of manager Alvin Dark. He ordered ace reliever Lew Krausse to start warming up. Nash saw the bullpen action and immediately came unglued, losing his shutout and the game. He left Limburger cheese or rotting fish in player's cars. Another time Drabowsky called a restaurant in Hong Kong from the bullpen and ordered Chinese food for 40.

The great thing about Moe was his spur-of-the-moment brilliance. He did things without a lot of forethought. During spring training one year, a bunch of the Orioles were relaxing by the hotel pool. Moe was on the balcony 12 stories above. One of his teammates spotted him and shouted, "Come on down, Moe. This is perfect. Warm water, beautiful women, cold drinks. The only thing we don't have is a TV." Two minutes later, a 26-inch TV landed in the pool, barely missing several Orioles notables. Now that's spontaneity!

Moe had a thing for snakes. He put them in teammates' shaving kits, lockers, and shoes. Even stars were fair game. He terrified Luis Aparicio by placing a live snake in his pocket. He put a small python into a bread basket at the head table during a sports dinner, giving the usually sure-handed Brooks Robinson the shakes. He placed wild mice in teammates' shoes, he lobbed firecrackers into occupied bathrooms. He even flirted with disaster by giving 6'5", 240-pound first baseman Boog Powell a hotfoot. If a player was relaxing at his locker reading the *Sporting News*, it was Drabowsky who lit them afire.

He was the class clown who helped keep the 1966 Baltimore Orioles loose enough to withstand the pressures of a pennant race. The Orioles went on to win the AL flag and the World Series. "As a starting pitcher, I had to work more than two hours to discover I

Moe Drabowsky, dubbed the "Polish Prince of Pranks," was the absolute master prankster of his—and probably any—era.

was horse manure that day," he explained to Bruce Shalin in his book *Oddballs*. "As a relief pitcher, I only had to work about two minutes to find out I was horse manure."

His mound work in '66 was impeccable, as he went 6–0 and won another game in relief in the World Series. In fact, he struck out 11 Dodgers in just 6 ²/₃ innings of work in Game 1 of that Series. His career marks were an 88–105 win-loss record, 55 saves, and a 3.71 ERA in 17 major league seasons.

He was as dedicated to comic relief as he was to pitching in relief. "If there were 20 guys sitting on the bench, Moe would crawl on his belly under 19 of them to give the last guy a hotfoot," Powell once said. Jim Elliott of the *Baltimore Sun* was so traumatized by Drabowsky's pyromania that he reportedly would not take his eyes off his shoes during pre- and postgame interviews. So Moe lit the distracted reporter's notebook ablaze.

On April 27, 1957, he was hit in the foot by a pitch. His teammate, Dick Drott, commandeered a wheelchair from a fan and pushed Moe to first base. Everyone laughed but umpire Stan Landes, who sent Drott, and not the supposed invalid, rolling to the showers.

Roger McDowell

Roger McDowell is immortalized as "the lone spitter" from the 1992 *Seinfeld* episode "The Boyfriend," which parodies the Zapruder film of President Kennedy's assassination. Mets first baseman Keith Hernandez reveals to Cosmo Kramer that the looger that glanced off him and hit his friend came from a grassy knoll above the exit ramp and was actually expectorated by McDowell and not by him.

McDowell may have been responsible for that one spitter, but the sinker was his big out pitch. McDowell was a competent major league relief pitcher from 1985 to 1996, throwing for the Mets, Phillies, Dodgers, Rangers, and Orioles. His lasting claim to fame was the fact that he was the winning pitcher in the Mets Game 7 victory over the Red Sox in the 1986 World Series. He was another of those relievers who had too much time on his hands in the bullpen. Aside from the usual firecracker and hotfoot routine, he also branched out into other acts of rebellion, often involving his wardrobe. He made his own quiet statement about Cincinnati Reds owner Marge Schott's ban on earrings by wearing them in the clubhouse for all to see. In the midst of a nationally televised game, he appeared with his uniform on upside down. He wore his shoes on his hands, his shirt on his legs, and his pants over his head. Away from the ballpark, he sometimes donned the McDowell tartan kilt.

Jay Johnstone

Although it is not my particular taste in eccentricity, the prank is a big part of baseball history. Jay Johnstone helped to elevate the practical joke to an art form. To Johnstone, a prank was a thing of beauty. It caused teammates and observers to stand back and appreciate the artistry. He was a practitioner of the Impressionist school. His style was reminiscent of Piersall, under whom he studied, with just a touch of Mo, Curly, and Larry thrown in for good measure. For Jay, each clubhouse was his canvas, waiting to be adorned with a master-piece of mischievous mayhem. The hotfoot was beneath Johnstone and his followers. They put time and energy and planning into their misdeeds, as any great artist must. They schemed, they planned, they connived, and they plotted. They are the creative side of eccentricity.

Every artist needs a subject, and Johnstone had numerous great ones during his career. Johnstone once hoisted teammate Steve Howe's underwear up the flagpole to see who would salute. When teammate Bill Russell committed four errors at shortstop in a spring training contest, Jay went to the trouble of roping off a section of seats behind first base, placing sandbags in front of the fence, and erecting a sign that warned: "Enter at your own risk. Bill Russell is playing shortstop today. All seats 25¢."

One of Johnstone's greatest works of art was a miniature, inspired by Ron Cey. While he was a member of the L.A. Dodgers, Johnstone was a teammate of Cey, the 5'9" third baseman whose stubby legs and jerky gait earned him the nickname "Penguin." In keeping with the artist's unsentimental code of ethics, Johnstone took it upon himself to ridicule Cey for all his shortcomings.

The artist arrived at the spring training site in Dodger Town early and went to work on his project. An hour and a half later, when Cey entered the clubhouse and went to his assigned locker, he almost fell over backward. His locker was now a three foot high enclosure complete with matching mini-stool and hooks for his clothes that were mere inches off the floor. Even the casual devotee of the art of the prank could have looked at the object and said with confidence: "Looks like a Johnstone to me!"

Another favorite target of Johnstone's was Steve Garvey. Garvey looked like a Ken doll in a baseball uniform. He was about as controversial as chicken salad. Sincerity oozed from every pore. Every hair on his head was neatly in place ("His hair isn't styled; it's carved," claimed Johnstone in *Temporary Insanity*), his posture was perfect, his jaw was square, and his smile was transcendent. His uniform was so starched and neat that it fairly glowed, and his glove received the kind of loving attention that some men give to religious relics. As you can imagine, all this was much too tempting for his somewhat less upstanding teammate.

On a steaming hot day in San Francisco, some fans had delivered a tray of baked brownies to the Dodgers dugout. The heat had made them soft and runny, and Johnstone stuck one to a baseball and ground it into the pocket of Garvey's mitt. Then, thinking several moves ahead as all artists must, he took the opportunity to secretly rub the excess chocolate onto the leg of Jerry Reuss's pants. He then alerted the Giants dugout to pay attention. Garvey put his glove on and attempted to take out the ball, which was now covered with chocolate mush. He dropped it like a hot potato, called time out, and went to the dugout for a towel. When the inning was over, he spotted the chocolate on Reuss's pants and drew some natural conclusions. The normally imperturbable Garvey then jumped on Reuss's lap and began to pummel the innocent pitcher.

Of all Johnstone's subjects, one stood out. Tommy Lasorda was his Mona Lisa. Lasorda, blessed with a girth as impressive as his temper, was a natural. "I thought I'd apologized for my sins," the Catholic manager once said, "but I guess the Lord is paying me back. He gave me Johnstone and Reuss." Johnstone once went for a hot dog while the game was still going on. At another time, he and Reuss disguised themselves as members of the Dodger Stadium grounds crew and dragged the infield. In fact, Reuss was often his partner in crime. The dynamic duo, with the help of Don Stanhouse, decided that all the media attention had gone to Lasorda's head and removed all the pictures of Frank Sinatra and his celebrity friends from his office — replacing them with pictures of themselves. They put a makeup mirror—the kind with bright white lights all around—in his office as a comment on his love of the spotlight. They locked Lasorda in his office after first disabling his phone so that he couldn't call for help (it's such attention to detail that makes a piece of art).

Not surprisingly, Johnstone is the author of two books, *Temporary Insanity* and *Over the Edge*, that record his zaniness in great detail.

Rick Dempsey

Rick Dempsey was a talented catcher whose best years were spent as a member of the Baltimore Orioles teams of the 1970s and '80s. The current first base coach of the O's was a more than competent fielding backstop and captured the World Series MVP Award for leading the Orioles to victory in the 1983 Fall Classic against the Philadelphia Phillies. But Dempsey's talents extended far beyond the usual baseball ones. He was also a frustrated thespian, and his performance of "swinging in the rain" would rival Gene Kelly in its choreography, if not its grace.

Dempsey is remembered fondly for turning one of baseball's most boring features—the dreaded rain delay—into an anticipated event. Not since "Spahn and Sain and pray for rain" had fans so looked forward to a downpour. After the grounds crew had covered the infield with a tarpaulin and the rain had made the surface slick, Dempsey would begin his act. Removing his cleats, he pantomimed a batter walking purposefully to the plate, hitting an imaginary pitch, and completing a frantic slip-and-slide, inside-the park homer scramble. The mad dash ended with a full belly flop across home plate like some crazed walrus. The fans went wild.

Dempsey had a knack for imitating the routines of various opposing batters, and he usually chose their home field to do so. He would hold his bat high in an exaggerated version of Carl Yastrzemski's stance in Boston, or mimic Robin Yount's distinctive hitting style in Milwaukee. Or George Brett's infamous pine-tar frenzy in Kansas City. But it wasn't only on the road that Dempsey

Baltimore's Rick Dempsey became famous for his one-man shows, which entertained the entire stadium during long rain delays.

was boffo at the box office. On at least one famous occasion he antagonized his teammate and battery mate, Hall of Fame pitcher Jim Palmer, by wearing underwear over his uniform pants. At the time, the handsome Palmer was as famous for his Jockey underwear ads as for his pitching.

In 1977 at Fenway Park in Boston, Dempsey stuffed his jersey with towels and imitated Babe Ruth hitting a home run into the right-field bleachers. If you can't imagine the splash that Babe would make sliding belly first across home plate, think tidal wave. The fans soaked it up (sorry!) and he responded to the applause by leading them in an impromptu version of "Raindrops Keep Falling On My Head."

You Can't Always Trust the Trainers

Sometimes the team trainers can be the worst pranksters because they have that dignified aura about them. Players generally trust the medical profession and you don't expect them to stoop to the players' level. Joe Garagiola, in his book *Baseball Is a Funny Game*, tells of an incident in the New York Giants clubhouse. Johnny Mize had just finished a brutal workout and entered the clubhouse drenched in sweat. He took his sweatshirt off and went for a drink. Trainer Frank Bowman quickly took the discarded sweatshirt and doused it with rubbing alcohol. When Mize returned, Bowman asked him how he was doing and Mize said that he was a bit tired, but otherwise felt good. Bowman looked at him with a clinical eye and told him that he would probably have more energy if he quit drinking the hard stuff. Mize was indignant. He assured Bowman that he didn't drink much and had only had a few beers the previous night. Bowman replied that it was his life to live, but he could see that Mize had been imbibing and furthermore he could prove it. He grabbed the shirt, threw it on the floor and tossed a lit match on the pile. The clothes burst into flames. "That's alcohol you sweated out, John!" said the trainer. Mize was mortified and after stamping out his shirt, he took him aside. "Please don't say anything about this to anyone," he begged.

Tug McGraw

If it's true that you are what you eat, Tug McGraw gave credence to the theory that you are what you throw. He not only threw a screwball, he was a screwball. He is best remembered for his phrase "Ya gotta believe," a rallying cry for the 1973 New York Mets and, poignantly, a rallying cry during the illness leading up to his death from brain cancer. Tug, father of country star Tim McGraw, was a happy-go-lucky personality off the field and an intense competitor when he got between the chalked lines.

When his name is mentioned, the image in everyone's mind is of Tug charging from the mound while slapping his glove against his thigh. He was exuberance personified. He carried his emotions on his sleeve, as evidenced by him patting his heart after a surefire home run curved foul. This human reaction endeared him to the fans who saw him as a player who really would play just for the love of the game.

Tug McGraw was a free spirit, though the classic story of the Astroturf is ascribed to him when actually it was Tom McCraw, who used to be with the Washington Senators and Cleveland. McCraw was asked if he preferred real grass or Astroturf, and thoughtfully replied, "I'm not sure, I never smoked Astroturf." I remember because Jethro Tull did a concert in Cleveland and the grass was all gone after the concert. I guess they smoked it all. They had to spray the outfield green to make it look like grass. It was all dirt—they hadn't re-sodded it or anything. We lost the ballgame on a roller that went up center field. Freddie Lynn charged it to scoop it up, but the ball took a bad hop over his glove and rolled to the fence. We lost. After the game, they asked him, "What happened, Freddie?" and he said, "I think it hit a roach clip."

As a member of the 1980 Phillies, McGraw was concerned that the city of Philadelphia was still fixated on the traumatic collapse of 1964: "The two worst things that ever happened to this city were W.C. Fields being born and the Phillies blowing the pennant in 1964. I think the fans can look at this team and forget about W.C. Fields and think about Benjamin Franklin or somebody."

When McGraw played for the Phillies in the mid-to-late '70s, he was a teammate of Jay Johnstone. After being swept in a doubleheader by the Pirates in Pittsburgh, several team members decided to drown their sorrows in alcohol. McGraw, who had lost both games, was leading the charge. Before long he was falling-down drunk but still astute enough to know it. He left the bar, hailed a cab, and asked to be taken to the nearest Pittsburgh police station as a kind of pre-emptive strike against himself. He introduced himself to the officer in charge and explained his situation: "I just lost both games of a doubleheader. On top of that, I've had too much to drink and I'm not sure that I can maintain control of myself. Please put me in jail." The desk sergeant was polite but suggested that McGraw would be much more comfortable sleeping it off back in his hotel room. An argument ensued in which Tug became increasingly insistent and belligerent. Soon, he was cursing the officer up and down and only then did he get his wish. He was bailed out at 6:00 the next morning, having saved himself from further trouble.

Milton Bradley

With a name like Milton Bradley, it would be surprising if you *didn't* have a few "toys in the attic," so to speak. The Los Angeles Dodgers outfielder and well-known malcontent has thrown balls at fans and was required by Dodgers management to take anger management classes. He recently expounded on his legacy, saying, "I want people to say Milton Bradley was a pretty good ballplayer and a pretty good person. Anybody who is going to stand between me getting there, then they need to be eliminated."

Clint Courtney

Clint Courtney was a near-sighted, bowlegged, follicularly challenged catcher for the Baltimore Orioles of the mid-to-late 1950s. A farm boy from Louisiana, this barnyard backstop used road trips to buy cattle and sometimes used his Cadillac to transport heifers. Teammate Dick Hall compared riding in his car to "being in a barn." Courtney, known as "Scrap Iron," was a pioneer of sorts, being the first catcher to wear glasses. The glasses were an inch thick, according to all reports, scarcely instilling confidence in his pitchers or the home plate umpire.

For some unimaginable reason, Clint was the victim of count-less practical jokes. One involved smearing large quantities of

Limburger cheese on the inside of his catcher's mitt. Whenever he opened the glove to catch the ball, the umpire looked suspiciously at the batter and the catcher, wondering who the flatulent one was.

Watching Courtney attempting to catch a Hoyt Wilhelm knuckleball was like watching a game of pin the tail on the donkey. He once bet outfielder Whitey Herzog a fifth of Scotch that Wilhelm wouldn't get a pitch past him. When a second-inning pitch hit him in the head and dropped in front of the plate, he quickly yelled to Herzog in the dugout, "See, it didn't get by me." Like Steve Sax and Chuck Knoblauch years later, Courtney developed a peculiar mental block about throwing the ball. He "forgot" how to throw the ball back to the pitcher on the mound. His solution was to throw to either first or third base and let them complete the relay, or walk to the mound and deliver the ball personally. He also went through a phase when he tried to throw out base stealers by throwing above-average sliders.

When Courtney was with the Washington Senators, he antagonized the home plate umpire by drawing a line in the dirt whenever he thought a bad call had been made. When he reached five and drew a line through the slashes, the umpire ejected him from the game.

Courtney died in 1975 while playing ping pong.

Leon Wagner

Another questionable fielder who was a bona fide character was Leon Wagner. Wagner was an original. He enjoyed the game of baseball so much that some people called him the "Good Humor Man," but he preferred the nickname "Daddy Wags." He was a piece of work. At the plate he was hunched over, like a vulture looking down at his prey from a lofty perch. His prey was fastballs, and he killed many of them. He was almost on top of the plate, as if defying the pitcher to hit him. Like Ty Cobb, he had his hands about five to six inches apart. But he could hit with power. When he broke in as an outfielder with the San Francisco Giants in 1958, he joined teammates like McCovey, Mays, and Cepeda, not to mention Matty, Jesus, and Felipe, the three Alous. (Anytime you try to replace a family that includes Jesus, it's difficult.) Even in this company and with limited playing time, he was able to make an impression. The hitting impression was positive, the fielding impression was not. In an early season game in 1959, he was taking a catnap in the dugout one day when his manager, Bill Rigney, startled him awake and told him to pinch hit. It was a real wake-up call. It was the bottom of the ninth and the Giants were losing to the hated L.A. Dodgers 4–2. Daddy Wags changed that with one swing, hitting a game-winning grand slam.

From San Francisco, Wagner was sent in 1960 to St. Louis where Stan Musial was in the twilight of his great career. Any hopes he had of replacing Stan the Man were quickly dashed. The following year he was then sent to the fledgling Los Angeles Angels, where he was installed as the regular outfielder. Hollywood proved the ideal spot for him to build his reputation. With the spotlight on him, he proceeded to hit 28 homers and bat a respectable .280. The offensive onslaught continued the next year, despite moving from a bandbox known as Wrigley Field to cavernous Dodger Stadium. Despite his reservations about playing in such a pitcher-friendly ballpark—he once complained, "This place is so big, Autry ought to use it for a ranch"—he raised his homer total to 37 with 107 RBIs and led the Angels to a shocking third place in the American League. When the MVP votes were tallied, he finished a strong fourth.

His fielding was laughable. I never saw him turn and run after a fly ball, he always backpedaled. I saw him three times catch a ball and then drop it over the fence. He would backpedal, hit the wall, catch the ball, and then come back empty-handed. Most people would go over the wall and bring it back. He never brought back anything. He's about as bad as I saw. He usually played with his back against the wall because he couldn't turn and catch it. He was ahead of his time in wanting to make all of his catches with one hand—in fact, he may have pioneered this trend. "I found out if you use two hands, the other hand just gets in the way," he reasoned. He earned the nickname "Butcher" and columnist

Jimmy Cannon described him as "an alien in the outfield." It was as if he were following fly balls with a broken compass. He assured Angels management that he had "all the tools" to be another Willie Mays, but, unfortunately, his tools were a shovel with a hole in it and a rusty hammer. He decided that he might need glasses, but they didn't make him Willie Mays either, although they did elicit one of the classic Wagner quotes. When looking at himself in the mirror with the new prescription eyewear, he cried out in shock, "Oh my God! I'm colored." (His may remind you of my reaction earlier in the book when I was informed that, unlike Satchel Paige, I was white.)

His throws from the outfield were more like shot puts. He once tried to retrieve a ball from under the bullpen bench and mistakenly threw a paper cup into the infield. He had two memorable collisions. In 1962 he collided in the outfield with teammate Billy Moran. Talk about a clash of two cultures! Moran was a southerner from Alabama and in 1962, the likelihood of this black man from Chattanooga, Tennessee, and this white man from Montgomery, Alabama, being friends was slim. But they were—which says a lot about both men. After the collision, Leon commented, "Hey, Billy, imagine me thinking I could knock down a white man from Alabama and get away with it."

Wagner made the most of his hip image, opening a men's clothing store in Los Angeles and promoting his wares using the slogan: "Get your rags at Daddy Wags." The business did not fare as well as he had hoped, prompting him to complain, "I've got a lot of friends in Los Angeles, but apparently they're all nudists." Considering the way he liked to "embroider the truth," as first baseman Bob Chance put it, the rag trade was ideally suited to Daddy Wags. His acting career also began to flourish while in California. He was a handsome man with high cheekbones, giving him an exotic look and inspiring the nickname "Cheeky."

When Wagner moved on to Cleveland in 1964, he was afraid that the spotlight would fade, but he continued to draw attention well out of proportion to his on-field talent. He retired after the

1969 season and his career statistics revealed a .272 batting average and 211 home runs.

My very favorite Leon Wagner quote was one about pitchers. He observed that "pitchers are white supremacists, even the black ones." I love it!

Bo Belinsky

Playboys have always been a part of major league baseball. You get a guy who's making a ton of money and is pretty good-looking, and "baseball Annies" are all over them. Some are able to resist. Others give in to the inevitable.

Bo Belinsky was the complete opposite of Mark Fidrych, but could have been Mickey McDermott's twin brother, or at least his soul mate. Where the Bird was oblivious to his success, Bo's good fortune led to destructive excess. Belinsky's world was a world of "broads," "Playmates of the Year," beaver-shooting, surfboards, "Go-Go's," booze, psychedelic drugs, and one-night stands. He hung out with people named "Mamie" and "Tina" and Ann-Margret—not to mention Walter Winchell and Hugh Hefner. He was, in short, not only a product of the '60s but the embodiment of the '60s. His baseball achievements, even his no-hitter in 1962, were just additional background stories in the soap opera that was his life. He lived out the fantasies of every teenage male of the decade. He was the ultimate hedonist. When my buddy Bernie Carbo came up as a naïve young rookie, he roomed with Belinsky. Carbo came into the room and there was Belinsky with a needle sticking out of his arm. Welcome to the big leagues, boy! He was freakin' firing up, and a rookie ballplayer was watching. Poor Bernie never had a chance.

Blessed with a ton of natural ability—a great arm and often unhittable stuff—it could never be enough to overcome the lifestyle that he chose for himself. "He had a million-dollar arm and ten-cent head," was the frank opinion of Buzzie Bavasi. For all the ink he generated in his eight major league seasons, you'd think he was the reincarnation of Cy Young. In actual fact, he won only 28 major league games, losing 51. "I got more publicity out of 28 victories than most guys do for winning 300 games," he once admitted.

Belinsky's apprenticeship was served in the pool halls of New Jersey. He was first and foremost a pool hustler. He and his cronies used to make forays into North and South Carolina and Georgia to swindle the locals out of their hard-earned money. They even dressed up in overalls and practiced their best vacant stares to look like easy pickings. So while most rookies arrive in major league camp just happy to be there, Bo arrived with street smarts and an over-abundance of confidence. In fact, he had the balls to hold out before he'd even thrown his first major league pitch. When the Angels drafted him from the Baltimore Orioles system in 1962, he balked at the paltry $6,500 they were offering him. He asked for an additional $2,000.

Bo quickly became a commodity, largely thanks to Angels publicity director Irv Kaze, who scheduled a press conference at a pool room. Bo proceeded to share his philosophy on tanning etiquette ("You can't be too dark," he once said), pool hustling, romancing beautiful women, and men's fashion. He arrived sporting diamond rings, a gold watch, sunglasses, and suede shoes. He informed the attentive press that all of his sartorial selections had a BB monogram.

Playing in the shadow of Hollywood didn't hurt. Blessed with swarthy good looks and an ample supply of confidence, he exploded on the scene with the fledgling Los Angeles Angels in 1962, winning his first five starts and pitching a no-hitter.

The no-hitter came on May 5, 1962. Bo allegedly crawled out of bed at noon after a night of passion with a woman he'd picked up in a club on Sunset Strip. He still had enough left to no-hit the Baltimore Orioles. "If I'd known I was going to throw a no-hitter today, I'd have gotten a haircut," he said after the gem. So much for that crap about sex ruining a ballplayer!

With ten wins and a no-hitter under his belt, he was the toast of Tinseltown and he played his celebrity to the hilt. He was not hard to spot driving around L.A. in a cherry-red Cadillac convertible. He dated beauties like Tina Louise, Ann-Margret, and Connie Stevens, not to mention Playboy centerfold Jo Collins (whom he subsequently

Bo Belinsky, shown here squiring actress Ann-Margret around town, saw his baseball career as a great vehicle to meet California's most eligible ladies. *Photo courtesy of Time Life Pictures/Getty Images.*

married), and most famously, Mamie Van Doren. Exhibiting the precociousness of youth and the cockiness that comes with early success, he even brought Van Doren to training camp one year and introduced her as his "physical therapist." Right, and Margo Adams was Wade Boggs's hitting instructor. Journalist Jeff Kallman claimed that, "A virgin in southern California came to mean any lovely who hadn't slept with Bo Belinsky."

Unfortunately, Bo's saga does not end happily. He was involved in an early hours hotel room brawl with an elderly *L.A. Times* sports reporter named Braven Dyer and was exiled to the Angels' minor league affiliate in Hawaii. He subsequently played for the Phillies, Astros, Pirates, and Reds before major league baseball gave up on him entirely. Writing in *Sports Illustrated*, Pat Jordan said that his name was "synonymous with dissipated talent." After his playing days were over, he abused alcohol and drugs and became alienated from his twin daughters (from his failed marriage to paper heiress

Janie Weyerhaeuser) and younger sister. He managed to overcome his demons and remained clean and sober for the last twenty years of his life.

Bo settled in Nevada, became a born-again Christian ("Can you imagine finding Jesus Christ in Las Vegas?" he said), and died of a heart attack on November 23, 2001, after a long battle with bladder cancer. Eleven months after his death, the Angels won their first World Series. He once admitted to Pat Jordan: "You can't beat the piper, Babe. I never thought I could. But I'll tell you who I do feel sorry for. I feel sorry for all those poor bastards who never heard the music."

On Opening Day, 1954, Don Larsen was the starting pitcher for the Baltimore Orioles. He was not yet the pitcher who would make history by pitching a perfect game for the Yankees in the 1956 World Series against the Brooklyn Dodgers. The young Larsen was nicknamed "Goony Bird," and was to finish the '54 season with a 3-21 record. One day he was being bombed by opposing hitters. Eventually the manager strode to the mound and ended the misery. Back in the O's clubhouse, Larsen lost it, throwing equipment across the room and kicking lockers. The team's PR man, Richard Armstrong, tried to calm the sophomore player. "Don, tomorrow's another day," he said. "You don't understand," replied a distraught Larsen, "Somebody stole my Flash Gordon comic book."

Even when he pitched his perfect game in the '56 Series, he still showed decided signs of goofiness. In the seventh inning of the game, he broke a cardinal rule of baseball: not talking about a no-hitter for fear of jinxing it. Puffing on a between-innings cigarette, he turned to Mickey Mantle and said, "Look at the scoreboard, Mick. Wouldn't it be something? Two more innings to go." This may not seem like such odd behavior, but in the baseball world it is the equivalent of walking under a ladder outside 1313 Thirteenth Street while a black cat is passing by. Perhaps the bad luck was just delayed for awhile. Larsen ended his career with an 81-91 record.

Dean Chance

Bo's close friend and former teammate Dean Chance was an original member of the Los Angeles Angels (later to become the California Angels, the Anaheim Angels, and the Los Angeles Angels of Anaheim, and soon to be known as the "Angels from the Land of Fruits and Nuts") when the expansion franchise took the field in 1961. Owner Gene Autry stocked his team with players made available from the rest of the American League. Most were dogs. Dean Chance was the pick of the litter. Chance won the Cy Young Award in 1964—there was only one award for all of Major League Baseball at that point—with a 20–9 record and an ERA of 1.65. He tossed 15 complete games that year, including 11 shutouts in 278 innings. Before his career was over, he had added a second 20-win campaign for a total of 128 victories and 115 losses in 11 seasons. His ERA was 2.92.

Chance was a playboy. He was good-looking, talented, and played in Hollywood. I always tell the story about the Beatles being at Fenway Park. They came into the clubhouse to meet us, and later John Lennon came out and sat in the bullpen with me. Sparky Lyle was out there with me and he was shootin' the breeze with Dean Chance, who was with the Indians at the time. Chance was trying to convince this little usherette to go home with him, and the Cleveland bullpen all breaks out in song: "All we are saying is give Chance a piece..." And John Lennon looks over at me and says, "Oh, I think I could use that..." That story isn't true, but it does show that baseball is "an arena for the imagination."

Schaefer, Germany

What do you call German hotdogs? Frankfurters? Whatever they call them, Germany Schaefer was definitely one. They say Germany has no sense of humor, but this Germany was a regular Sergeant Shultz, and just about as competent. In fact, it's ironic that this fun Hun (I wonder if his wife called him "Hun") actually brought about a major league rule change. In 1908 Schaefer's Detroit Tigers were playing Cleveland. Schaefer was on first base, and a speedster by the name of Davy Jones was on third. The manager called for a delayed double steal, hoping to steal a run. The pitch came in high and hard, but the Cleveland catcher didn't take the bait and did not make a throw as Schaefer reached second unchallenged.

To everyone's surprise, on the next pitch Schaefer scrambled back to first and slid in safely in a cloud of dust. He may have been the first and only German to willingly retreat after capturing enemy ground. He then announced loudly that he was going to steal second again. The catcher was understandably disconcerted and somewhat confused and, when the next pitch was delivered, he rifled a throw to second, allowing Jones to score from third. The league quickly created a rule preventing such a move from happening again. It makes one wonder if Schaefer could have stolen home from first and gone to bat again, like a baby returning to the womb, or the swallows to Capistrano.

Schaefer was a utility player who could fill in at any position, although his hitting was erratic at best. Unlike his namesake country, Germany was never power-crazy. Fans in an enemy ballpark once got on him for his shortcomings as a hitter, and Schaefer responded by hitting a home run. He proceeded to slide into first, second, third, and home. He then bowed elaborately, tipped his hat to the crowd, and declared, "Ladies and gentlemen, this concludes today's performance."

Schaefer was once involved in a game in which it began to rain heavily and steadily. It was obvious to everyone from the fans to the players to the bat boy that the game should be called, or at least that there should be a rain delay. But the umpire allowed them to play on, oblivious to the deluge and the dangers it posed for potential injury. The ump finally got the message when Germany came to the plate dressed in hip rubber boots and raincoat, carrying a bat in one hand and an umbrella in the other.

Mickey Mantle invited teammate Billy Martin to join him on a hunting trip on a friend's ranch in Texas. When they arrived, Mantle went in alone to let his friend know they had arrived, while Billy remained in the car. Unbeknownst to Martin, Mickey's friend had asked him to do him a favor. He had an ancient mule that was sick and going blind. The kind thing was to put him out of his misery, but the mule had been with him for years, and he couldn't bring himself to do the deed himself. He asked Mantle if he would do it for him. Mantle quickly agreed, though maybe a bit too quickly. When he got back to the car, he pretended to be agitated, cursing the ranch owner and vowing to get revenge on him. Billy asked what the problem was, and Mantle explained that his so-called friend wouldn't let them hunt after all.

Mantle's anger seemed to escalate with every passing moment. "I am so mad at that guy that I am going out to that barn and shoot one of his mules," he said. As they approached the barn, Martin tried to calm his teammate down. "We can't do that!" he pleaded. Mickey pushed him aside, entered the barn, and shot and killed the mule. When he exited the barn, Martin was standing there with his gun, and smoke was coming from the barrel. Mantle panicked, fearing the worst. "What did you do, Billy?" he asked nervously.

"We'll show that son-of-a-bitch," said Martin. "I killed two of his cows, too!"

Mickey McDermott

Mickey McDermott became a dear friend of mine, but our relationship had a rocky start. Mickey was invited by my former USC coach Rod Dedeaux to take part in the annual USC versus Ancient Warriors game. The game features the current USC team against former major leaguers. I was the ace of the Trojans staff at that point, and I guess I thought I was pretty hot stuff. This old guy came to the plate, and he looked like he should have been in rehab — which, as it turned out, he should have been. He looked familiar to

Like Belinsky, Mickey McDermott is viewed by many as a baseball tragedy who wasted his talent, but I prefer to remember the Mickey whose life was full of so many other things besides just baseball. *Photo courtesy of Bettmann/CORBIS.*

me. I threw him my best fastball and he got hold of it and knocked it over the wall. I couldn't believe it! I guess I acted like a spoiled kid throwing a tantrum. I recognized the guy from seeing him at the Santa Anita race track, where he had been taking tickets. After the game, I was rambling on about the shame of having some decrepit old ticket-taker hitting a home run off me. Well, Mickey heard of my tirade and sent me a note saying, "I hit home runs off better pitchers than you'll ever be." End of story—or almost.

I soon did some research and found out he wasn't kidding. For example, I discovered that Mickey's father Maurice had been replaced by Lou Gehrig as the first baseman for the Hartford Senators of the Eastern League. I discovered that by the time he was 13, Mickey was averaging 20 strikeouts a game and that he was playing against adults. In fact, he went for a tryout with the Dodgers when he was still 13, and the Brooklyn scout, Mule Haas, wanted to sign him—and almost certainly would have if it hadn't been illegal. He was then pursued and signed by the Red Sox when he was 15 years old. His father had doctored his birth certificate to indicate he was 16. His bonus consisted of two flatbeds of beer and $5,000 for his proud father. He was a member of the Boston Red Sox organization.

Years later, Mickey still recalled his first major league experience. "I was 15 years old when I signed and I'm with Scranton, right after the war. We've got about 150 guys on our roster. I'm sitting on the bench and next to Mel Parnell, who later became my roommate in the major leagues. A ball rolled nearby and Mel turned to me and said, 'Hey batboy, get the ball.' I said 'Go f*ck yourself! You get the ball.' He said, 'Oh my God, what a fresh kid you are.' Then they read the roster off for pitchers to pitch batting practice, and my name came up and I started throwing, and he said, 'Geez, I guess you're not the batboy.' That was cute."

McDermott pitched three no-hitters in the Red Sox minor league system; the first came when he was 17 years old. He played his first Red Sox game in 1948, but his lack of control forced him back to the minors. With the Louisville Colonels, he struck out 20, 19, 18, 17, and 19 opponents over the span of five games! He was called up to the Red Sox, who were going nowhere fast. His first major league victory came when Ellis Kinder had to leave the game in the first inning because he was too drunk to pitch. McDermott continued to struggle with his control, but in 1953 compiled a fine 18–10 record. In 1954 he was sent to Washington in exchange for Jackie Jensen.

Anyway, fast-forward to the 1980s. I hadn't set eyes on McDermott since the USC game. I was doing one of the Red Sox fantasy camps, and McDermott was on my team. By now I knew a lot more about him. I went over to him, introduced myself, and offered my apologies and an explanation. "I knew I'd seen you at Santa Anita, what was I supposed to think?" I told him. Mickey just laughed. We had a big party after the fantasy camp was over, and I got to know him. We soon discovered we were kindred spirits and remained friends until his death a few years back. I mean, here was a guy who was on field in Cuba during the 26th of July Movement when Fidel Castro overthrew Batista. Gunfire was happening all around him. He was also playing in Venezuela when Dominican Republic leader Trujillo attempted to assassinate the Venezuelan president, Romulo Betancourt. He was hardly fazed by all that because he had pitched in Yankee Stadium.

There are two ways to consider Mickey McDermott. You can think of him as a tragic figure, a talented southpaw with unlimited potential who wasted his potential and squandered a chance to pitch his way into the Hall of Fame. Fellow Red Sox pitcher Mel Parnell, among many others, admits, "He could have been one of the best pitchers in baseball, but he just didn't take it seriously."

Ted Williams agreed. "Ted once signed a picture for me," McDermott said. " 'To the one and only Maurice.' One time Ted took me aside and said, 'Listen, Bush, I've seen a lot of kids come into the big leagues, but you've got more talent than anyone I've ever looked at. But there's one word in the dictionary that you do not know how to spell, you do not know what it means, and you never will.' I said, 'What's that?' He said, 'It's called discipline, Bush.' " Birdie Tebbetts said that Mickey had a chance to be "the greatest left-hander of his generation. SPORT magazine's Al Hirshberg expressed the popular opinion of baseball experts when he wrote: "McDermott has the most conservative observers comparing him with Grove, Gomez, and Feller."

The other way you can look at Mickey McDermott's career and life is as a success. You can think of him as a guy who enjoyed every minute of his career and came out of it with enough memories and friendships to last a lifetime. I prefer the latter view of McDermott. He was a genuine original, a one-of-a-kind baseball nut. He had a defibrillator, a pacemaker, and god knows what else. The only original part he had left was his mind—and that was one of a kind. At the age of 63, he won $7 million in the Arizona State Lottery. It didn't slow him down. He was involved in a car accident and thrown in the drunk tank for 60 days, charged with DWI. That finally did the trick and from 1993 on he was sober.

The razor-thin McDermott played for the Boston Red Sox of the 1950s, where his teammates included Ted Williams, Johnny Pesky, and Walt Dropo. In fact when McDermott was a rookie, the 6'5", 240-pound Dropo was his roommate when he first arrived in Boston. He and the 138-pound pitcher became best friends for life. "He was the biggest son of a bitch I ever saw in my life," McDermott claimed. "I thought the Ringling Brothers Circus truck must have broken down and Gargantua was rooming with me. I asked him if he had any bananas. I called him 'Moose' and asked if he could leave his head to the Elks Club to be mounted."

"I was sort of like a son to Joe McCarthy," recalled McDermott. "He took a shine to me. Mel Parnell went to Joe, and McCarthy said, 'Oh, you're rooming with McDermott, aren't you?' Mel said, 'We've been on road trips for a year and I haven't seen him yet. I'm rooming with his suitcases.'

He called me in his office once and, of course, with a McDermott and a McCarthy, the Irish flag immediately went up. He said, 'Maurice, have you got a girlfriend?' I said, 'Yes, sir.' He said, 'Did you ever hear of a pitcher named Lefty Gomez?' I said, 'Yes sir.' He said, 'Well, don't become Lefty Gomez. He left his fastball in the sheets.' I didn't know what the f*ck he was talking about. I was only 18 years old. I thought, What the hell would he leave his fastball in my sheets for? I was looking for it for three days."

McDermott related this great story about a man who is definitely not an eccentric, the man who Ted Williams said should be in the Hall of Fame with his brother Joe, Dom DiMaggio. "Joe McCarthy was a very marse man—they called him 'Marse Joe.' I almost never seen him laugh. When he laughed, it was like a big New Year's Eve party. One time Dom DiMaggio struck out on a terrible call. Usually, players were yelling and screaming obscenities at this point. Dominic never turned around or hollered at an umpire. He was known as the Little Professor because that's what he looked like. He wore spectacles and was very scholarly looking. He got into the dugout and he put one knee on the top step of the dugout and he rested there for a minute. He took his glasses off and started wiping them off, and finally he looked out to the umpire and said, 'I have never witnessed such incompetence in all my life.' McCarthy fell off the bench laughing. What in the Christ kind of ballplayer says that?"

McDermott was a talented lounge singer and often performed at The Cave and other Boston venues. On one famous occasion, Dropo brought his date to the Boston nightclub where Mickey was performing. In order to impress the pretty young thing, he had arranged to have a table near the stage. McDermott spotted him in the crowd and said, "Ladies and gentlemen, we have a celebrity with us tonight. Sitting in the front row is the great first baseman of the Boston Red Sox, Mr. Walter Dropo." Dropo waved and took a bow, acknowledging the warm round of applause from the audience. He smiled modestly at his beautiful companion, pleased that she was now aware of his stature in this city. "In fact," McDermott went on when the applause had died down, "he's so good that they named a town here in Massachusetts after him. It's called Marblehead."

McDermott's singing career didn't impress his baseball foes. He told me, "Once in a game against Cleveland, I pitched 16 innings and then loaded the bases. Birdie Tebbetts, who we'd traded to Cleveland, was standing on the steps of the dugout and hollering at me: 'Sing your f*cking way out of this, McDermott.' "

Pitcher Mel Parnell once drew the short straw and ended up rooming with the young fireballer. "McCarthy said, 'Be a father to this kid.' I said, 'Father, hell, I can't keep up with him.' He would go out to a men's clothing shop, take the shirt off his back, buy a new one, and leave the other shirt there. When the Red Sox left a city, he'd depart the hotel with whatever was in his suitcase. He left shoes and articles of clothing all over the place. I picked up after him for awhile, but finally gave up."

Even "Mr. Red Sox," Johnny Pesky, ran afoul of McDermott's wild lifestyle. Bosox management decided that the youngster needed a role model. They felt that if he moved in with a dedicated family man like Pesky, he might settle down and focus on baseball. It was a miserable failure, as Mickey recalled years later: "They gave Johnny a car one time as a tribute on Pesky Day at Fenway. I borrowed it that night and picked up some broad—and I kicked the window out trying to get laid in the back seat. Pesky was going to kill me. I just told him, 'Why didn't you leave the windows open? You knew I was 6'3"; you're only 5'11".' "

McDermott was traded to the Yankees, where he played under Casey Stengel, a strange pairing by any standard. One classic episode says it all about their relationship. There are several versions, but here it is, straight from McDermott's mouth:

> When I was with the Yankees, we were on a road trip in Boston. Since I'd played with the Red Sox, I knew all the hotels and I knew how to sneak in late at night. I was staying at the Kenmore Hotel, and there is a service elevator there. About 4:00 one morning, I had a big stack of White Castle hamburgers under my arm, and I was bombed out of my gourd. I figured I'd sneak in the basement to avoid breaking curfew. So I came in the alley entrance and pushed the button for the service elevator, way down in the bowels of the hotel. The elevator gave a jerk and started moving up, traveling at the speed of a glacier. Finally it ground to a halt at my floor. Now the problem was, I'd forgotten that goddamned Stengel also played and managed in Boston, and he knew all the secret entrances, too. The elevator door opened, and he was standing there. He looked at me with disgust, shook

111

his head, and said, 'Drunk again!' I hiccupped and said, 'Me too, Skip!' He couldn't fine me. He thought it was too funny."

Mickey remained a close friend of Ted Williams and used to visit Ted during the annual induction ceremonies at the Ted Williams Hall of Fame in Florida. Ted, of course, was a close friend of George H.W. Bush. He used to campaign for him when he ran for President. McDermott remembered one occasion when Bush was an honored guest at the ceremonies:

They were both pilots during the war. So Bush and his wife Barbara and Jack Kemp were there, and I was walking by the rostrum. Ted hollered out to me, "Maurice, come on over here."

"Have you met the President?" he asked.

I said, "No, Ted, I have never met him."

"Oh," he said, "Maurice McDermott, this is President Bush."

I said, 'Well, for chrissakes, George, how the hell are you?'

Williams almost fainted. "Jesus Christ," he said, "he's calling the President of the United States George!"

I said, "Wait a minute, Theodore, he played against Walt Dropo when he was at Yale and Dropo was at Connecticut. Right, George?" Bush gave me the high five and laughed his ass off.

Williams was dying. The marine corps came to the rescue. "Jesus Christ, bush," he said to me. "You'll never change."

Steve "Psycho" Lyons

When Steve "Psycho" Lyons was traded in 1986 from the Red Sox to the White Sox for Tom Seaver, one wag suggested it was like swapping Psy-cho for Cy Young. It was a great line, one Lyons would almost certainly have used himself if he'd thought of it first. Lyons played the game of baseball like a little kid, and every major ballpark was his own playground. When he played the infield, he used to leave messages scrawled in the dirt for his counterpart on the opposing team. Stuff like, "What's up?" or, "Wow, you must have great range to get to this ball." Sometimes he conducted games of tic-tac-toe or hangman with his counterpart that went on for several innings. It gives hope to all those who think baseball is too businesslike, to know that other players almost always played along. "Only two guys wouldn't play with me," he claims. "Fred McGriff and a guy from Baltimore."

The "Psycho" label was inspired by his intensity and his occasional tantrums, and not because of any fear that teammates may have had in the shower.

Casey Stengel and fellow baseball icon Jackie Robinson did not see eye to eye. When Robinson got a lucrative endorsement contract, Casey saw an opportunity to needle the pioneer of baseball integration. "He was a great ballplayer once," he said. "But everyone knows that now he's Chock Full o' Nuts."

Psycho's biggest claim to fame was dropping his drawers in front of 35,000 fans and a national TV audience during a 1990 game. It happened after he had slid into first base and was focused on shaking the dirt from his pants. He blamed it on a "brain cramp," but hey, mooning an entire country could happen to anyone, right?

His fan club is called the Psycho Ward.

Gene Conley and Pumpsie Green

You rarely hear Gene Conley's name without hearing Pumpsie Green's in the next breath. In July of 1962 in New York, Red Sox 6'9" pitcher Gene Conley and infielder Pumpsie Green, the first black player to play for the Sox, went AWOL. Conley had been the losing pitcher that day in a game against the Yankees and was feeling down. When the team bus got stuck in rush hour traffic, the two men jumped ship and headed for a bar. They then checked into a hotel and had a few more drinks. At some point, Conley decided that it would be an excellent idea to make a pilgrimage to Israel. Why Israel? Who knows? With names like Conley and Pumpsie, it was hardly "the land of their people." Eventually Green chickened out, but Conley proceeded to the airport, where only the lack of a passport prevented his departure. Red Sox owner Tom Yawkey fined them both. Oy vey!

Conley was a member of a very elite fraternity, a two-sport athlete at the very highest level. He played major league baseball and he played basketball for the world champion Boston Celtic teams of the early 1960s. Of course, it all had to end someday, and when that day came in 1964, it hit him hard, as recorded in Donald Honig's book *Baseball Between the Lines*:

> I wandered around for awhile, a lost soul on the streets of this town in North Carolina. Then I walked into a church and sat down in the back, all by myself. There was a service going on. After the singing this Baptist minister started preaching. All of a sudden it hit me real hard and I caved in and started crying. I just sat there in that last row and cried and cried, trying to keep my head down so as not to upset anybody. Then I felt a hand on my shoulder and I looked up. An elderly Southern gentleman was standing there gazing down at me.
>
> "What's the matter, son?" he asked. "Did you lose your mother?"
>
> I shook my head, the tears still running. "No, sir," I said. "I lost my fastball."

| Misanthropes,
Malaprops, and Magicians

Some ballplayers are as adept at word play as they are at playing baseball. They can turn a slick double play and then go to the clubhouse and deliver a snappy double entendre without breaking a sweat. Some even turn the occasional triple entendre, although there's a lot of luck involved in that particular feat and most people have never witnessed one.

Other ballplayers commit jaw-dropping errors in syntax with the ease and flair that Dick Stuart used to commit jaw-dropping errors at first base.

Joe Schultz

Joe Schultz was brought to national attention in Jim Bouton's book *Ball Four*. Schultz was the manager of the Seattle Pilots when Bouton was writing the diary that turned into the book. Not only did the book give us insights into the day-by-day lives of players, but it also afforded the general public a look into the managerial brain trust that ran the team. I wish I'd done that with Zimmer. I could have had an encyclopedia. Any idea that managers spend sleepless hours devising strategy pretty much went out the door when Bouton's book hit the stands. Schultz's favorite advice to his players after a loss was, "We'll get 'em tomorrow. Now go out and pound that Budweiser." (He might as well have suggested having sex in a canoe because in Canada—where they brew the beer a tad stronger—they used to tell me that Budweiser was like sex in a canoe: both are f*cking near water.) On other occasions, Schultz would make a trip to the mound to give the pitcher a pep talk. According to Bouton, those talks went something like this: "What the shit. Give 'em some low smoke and we'll catch an early plane the hell out of here." Sage advice—and much in keeping with some managers I have had in the past.

I remember those meetings. We'd go through the lineup player by player, and after every name, I'd yell, "High and tight, then down and away." If a real good hitter's name came up, I'd say, "Walk him." They'd say, "Don't give 'em anything good to hit but throw strikes." Garbage like that.

Schultz' favorite expression was "shitf*ck." Bouton quoted him saying it 211 times in his book. In fact, when the manager moved on to Detroit, he was known as "Ol' Shitf*ck." It doesn't have quite the impact as "Ol' Ironsides."

Bouton, a pretty bright guy, was dumbfounded by the strategic game plans that were mapped out by Schultzie. "What a great guy Joe was," he said. "I remember we were playing a doubleheader one day and he gathered us together and said, 'Men, between games we have a choice of ham, roast beef, or tuna salad.' Could Knute Rockne think of inspiring words like that? Could Vince Lombardi?"

Once pitcher John Gelnar, scheduled to start the next day, was at the far corner of the dugout keeping a chart on Orioles hitters. Suddenly Schultz yelled at him and motioned urgently for him to come to his end of the dugout. At the time, Seattle was a run behind late in the game, and Bouton and the rest of the Seattle Pilots strained to listen, assuming that Schultz was seeking some statistical information about the Orioles hitters that would give the Pilots an edge. Instead, Schultz pointed across the infield and said, "Gelnar. Gelnar, look over there by that section 23 sign. Check the rack on that broad."

Jerry Coleman

Jerry Coleman, the man I call Mr. Malaprop, is a professional talker, which is really scary. I mean, he gets paid for his skill with words. If Lowell Thomas had reported from the battle front with the accuracy Jerry Coleman brings to baseball announcing for the San Diego Padres, we might well have lost the war. Radio announcers are supposed to paint a word picture for the listener. What Coleman achieved was finger-painting at best. He once reported to his horrified radio audience: "A fly ball to deep center! Winfield is back, back....He's hit his head against the wall. It's rolling toward second base." On another occasion he intoned definitively, "They throw Winfield out at second base, and he's safe." And imagine the mental images that were conjured up when this thought balloon was sent floating across the airwaves: "There's a hard-hit ball to LeMaster...and he throws Madlock into the dugout."

Coleman is the greatest source of misinformation this side of Fox News. He might be fair, but is he balanced? "[Larry] Lintz stole the base standing up. He slid, but he didn't have to." And what must Folkers's wife have thought about the meatloaf she served for supper when she heard, "Rich Folkers is now throwing up in the bullpen."? Think perhaps he was better at the out-of-town scores? Think again. "Kansas City is at Chicago tonight, or is Chicago at KC? Well, whatever the case, Kansas City leads in the eighth 4–4."

Einstein proved that space is curved and time is relative, so time travel is possible, but could he explain this? "Gaylord Perry and [Willie] McCovey know each other like a book. After all, they've been ex-teammates for many years." And they call *me* the Spaceman.

Ralph Kiner

There was nothing funny about Ralph Kiner when he was playing baseball. Certainly pitchers saw nothing humorous when he stepped to the plate. No less an authority than Ted Williams ranked him in the top 20 hitters of all time. He hit 369 homers in just 10 seasons and his 14.11 at-bats-per-home-run ratio is Ruthian.

It was when he replaced his bat with a mic that we saw the other side of Ralph Kiner. He was a funny, funny man, and the fact that most of his humor was unintentional made it even funnier. As an announcer for the New York Mets, he has imparted the following information to fans: "This one is hit deep to right and it is way back,

Ralph Kiner was an absolute killer in the batter's box during his Hall of Fame career, but he was also something of a butcher behind the microphone.

going, going, it is gone, no, off of the top of the wall." He has also told listeners that Bruce Sutter was "going to be out of action for the rest of his major league career." Admittedly it's tough to describe the physics of a knuckleball, but saying that watching Phil Niekro's knuckler is "like watching Mario Andretti park a car" surely does not paint the correct mental picture. Often Mets fans had whiplash from shaking their heads in bewilderment at statements such as "Solo homers usually come with no one on base," or "Strawberry has been voted to the Hall of Fame five years in a row now."

It gets better. He said of a ballplayer whose father had once played in the majors: "There's a lot of heredity in that family." Occasionally his commentary was positively Berra-esque, as in "Two-thirds of the earth is covered by water. The other third is covered by Garry Maddox." Or Stengel-esque, as in "All of his saves have come in relief appearances." Or just plain ridicul-esque as in: "If Branch Rickey were alive today, he'd be spinning in his grave," or "The Mets have played so well at Shea this year because they have the best home record in baseball."

Lefty "Goofy" Gomez

As a rule, the New York Yankees are about as eccentric as corn flakes. Their image is as conservative as the *Wall Street Journal*. Their pinstripe uniforms might as well be three-piece pinstripe suits. That's what makes any island of zaniness in that ocean of blandness stand out like an intellectual in Bush's cabinet. Lefty "Goofy" Gomez was a pitcher for the New York Yankees from to 1930 to 1942. Despite his nickname, there was nothing goofy about Gomez when he was pitching. Funny, yes; goofy, no. He was an astute and intelligent man who once said that he "talked batters out of hits." His forte was wit, and he took on the role of court jester on the Yankees teams of the 1930s and early '40s and used his self-deprecating humor to keep the team loose.

Gomez won 20 games on four different occasions. In 1934 he was 26–5. That same season he topped the league in complete games, shutouts, innings pitched, ERA, strikeouts, wins, and winning percentage.

He once said, "When Neil Armstrong first walked on the moon, he and all the space scientists were puzzled by an unidentifiable white object. I knew immediately what it was. That was a home run ball hit off me in 1933 by Jimmie Foxx." Actually, Gomez had something of a Foxx fetish. He claimed that Foxx "has muscles in his hair." He was once on the mound when the Beast of Boston strode to the plate. Gomez just stood there as the crowd and his teammates got restive. Finally, his catcher Bill Dickey walked to the plate and said, "Okay, Lefty. How do you want to pitch to Foxx?" Gomez just gazed straight ahead and replied, "I don't want to pitch to him at all. Maybe if we wait long enough, he'll give up and go home." He claimed the best way to pitch to Foxx was to "make your best pitch and back up third base. That relay might get away and you've got another shot at him."

Gomez was a skinny 6'2" southpaw who as a rookie weighed about 160 pounds soaking wet. Gomez was advised by Yankees owner Ed Barrow to put on some weight before his sophomore year of 1931. "Put on 20 pounds, young man," said Barrow, " and you'll make 'em forget Lefty Grove." It was less than successful, according to Gomez. "I put on the 20 pounds," said Gomez, "and I damn near made 'em forget Lefty Gomez."

In one game, El Goofy was unusually wild and proceeded to load the bases. Manager Joe McCarthy made a trip to the mound to calm his pitcher down and discuss how to pitch to the next batter. "Okay, Lefty," he said. "The bases are loaded." Lefty was just a little testy. "I know they're loaded! I didn't think they gave me a second infield." It was this sense of humor that got him through many a tough jam. He once said, "A lot of things run through your head when you're going in to relieve in a tight spot. One of them was, 'Should I spike myself?'" Gomez was engaged to a vivacious brunette actress named June O'Dea. One day after Lefty had lost a game 1–0 in extra innings, his future wife felt that he needed some consoling. "You just had bad luck today, Lefty," she said soothingly. "Don't let it worry you. You'll beat 'em tomorrow."

"Tomorrow!" shouted the tired and frustrated pitcher. "Who the hell do you think you're marrying—Iron Man Joe McGinnity?"

One time a promising rookie pitcher named Charley Devens arrived in spring training. Devens was a Harvard graduate with impeccable lineage. His father was a prominent Boston banker, and his family had traveled extensively in all parts of the globe. His parents weren't particularly crazy about the heir to the family fortune becoming a mere baseball player. The father was particularly adamant that young Charley not spend any time at the Yankees farm team in Newark, New Jersey, and exacted a guarantee from Yankees management that he would stay with the parent club. Gomez did not know this. When the team had assembled and were awaiting their assignments, Gomez noticed Devens's luggage. There were labels that indicated that he had traveled to Cairo, Paris, Rome, and other centers of culture and beauty. "You've traveled a lot, haven't you, Charley?" Gomez ventured. "Why, yes, I suppose I have, Mr. Gomez," said the well-mannered Devens. "Tell me," said Gomez, "have you ever been to Newark?"

Another youngster who was the target of his wit was future Red Sox first baseman Walt Dropo, who went on to win the Rookie of the Year award. When the 6'5", 140-pound prospect Dropo was playing in the high minors, he faced the Yankees farm club in Binghamton, managed by Gomez. When Dropo was emerging from the clubhouse to take batting practice, Gomez shouted at him, "Hey, kid, your breakfast's waiting for you in the batting cage. And so is your teething ring." Dropo ignored him until he reached the cage and found a tire suspended from a rope, a bale of hay, and two bushels of apples.

Gomez loved to talk baseball, and one evening he got into a heated argument with Jimmie Dykes. The subject was the proper way to pitch to a hitter with two men on base. They fought to a draw and decided to ask Mike Kelly to cast the deciding vote. They went to his room and woke him from a sound sleep. Kelly was not interested in responding. "Get lost. Wait until tomorrow," he said. Gomez was shocked. "What? You want us to leave those two men on base?"

Gomez finally left the Yankees in 1943 to join the Boston Braves of the National League, but it was fairly obvious where his loyalties lay. "The trouble with the National League," he complained to Braves manager Casey Stengel, "is that McGraw's been dead for years and you fellows don't know it."

Even in retirement, Gomez continued to entertain. "I was the worst hitter ever. I never even broke a bat until last year when I ran over one while I was backing out of the garage."

When Mark Fidrych was making headlines by talking to the ball, Gomez chimed in with, "I talked to the ball a lot of times in my career. I yelled, 'Go foul. Go foul.'"

My former teammate George "Boomer" Scott, former first baseman for the Boston Red Sox and Milwaukee Brewers, wasn't infected with a particularly active sense of humor. He was more of a carrier. It wasn't that Boomer was really that funny or eccentric; it was just that he came from Greenville, Mississippi. It's like anyone that comes from down there—you know they're going to rank number 49 or 50 in any category. Boomer was the same. People from Mississippi just thank god that Alabama is down there, too. People from the South may read this book—or have it read to them—and rise up against me, but they did that about a hundred years ago and got their asses kicked. It's true, they can't fight that. I married a girl from Mississippi and had three children by her and raised the IQ of the state by three points, so I did my part.

Boomer was of those guys who could have made the Hall of Fame but, because he ceased playing a position, he got out of shape faster and his career ended prematurely. There were lots of those guys. Just another case of specialization breeding extinction. He was the greatest defensive player I ever played with. He was a fabulous fielder, a great hitter, and a wonderful ballplayer, but when he started to get big, they put him at first, which made him get bigger and hastened his demise. Thank God for interleague play which now forces teams to play their designated hitters as position players so they stay in some sort of shape.

Scott and Luis Tiant had some classic verbal sparring sessions. Unfortunately, no one knew what the hell they were saying most of the time. George was hilarious, but people couldn't understand him. You'd be driving home from the ballpark three hours later and all of a sudden you'd get what he said and you'd have to pull over because you were laughing so hard. You have to speak Ebonics and fluent Spanish to understand George and Tiant. The Tower of Babel was a piece of cake compared to our clubhouse when those two got going. I told Boomer one time, "Boomer, we've got a store up here in Boston called Toys 'R' Us, but down where you live it's called We Be Toys." We were back and forth at each other all the time.

He also had a chip on his shoulder and felt that he was under-appreciated. He almost won the Triple Crown in 1975 in Milwaukee.

Gomez brought a lot of smiles to a lot of people during his career and after. He used to introduce himself as "the guy that made Joe DiMaggio famous," and claimed that "the secret of my success was clean living and a fast outfield."

He might have added "a quick wit" to his list. Gomez attended the 1965 World Series with Tommy Henrich. Sandy Koufax was slated to pitch the first game but because it fell on a Jewish holiday, the Dodgers juggled the rotation to accommodate Sandy's religious beliefs. Don Drysdale took the mound instead. Unfortunately, Drysdale got shelled in the third inning, with the Minnesota Twins scoring six runs. Dodgers manager Walter Alston proceeded to the mound to remove the big righty. Gomez turned to Henrich and told him that he knew exactly what Alston was saying to Drysdale: "He's saying, 'Why couldn't you have been Jewish instead of Koufax?'"

Here are a few more of his classics:

- "Hell, Lou [Gehrig], it took 15 years to get you out of a game. Sometimes I'm out in 15 minutes."
- "I'd rather be lucky than good."
- "I'm throwing as hard as I ever did, but the ball is just not getting there as fast."
- "I've got a new invention. It's a revolving bowl for tired goldfish."
- "I want to thank all my teammates, who scored so many runs, and Joe DiMaggio, who ran down so many of my mistakes."

- "No one hit home runs the way Babe [Ruth] did. They were something special. They were like homing pigeons. The ball would leave the bat, pause briefly, suddenly gain its bearings, then take off for the stands."

Mickey Rivers

There is no polite way of saying this without offending someone. When Mickey Rivers walked onto a baseball field, he looked like he just crapped his pants. Whew, glad that's over.

But it's true, Mick the Quick had that mincing little gait that belied the lightning speed he showed when he got on base. He was the master of the outrageous put-down. When Reggie Jackson boasted loudly that he had an IQ of 160, Rivers's derisive rejoinder was: "Out of what, a thousand?" He said of New York Met Danny Napoleon, "He's so ugly, when you walk by him, your pants would wrinkle."

Rivers marched to his own drummer and every once in a while he seemed to be channeling one. Here's one example: "There ain't no sense worryin' about things you got control over, 'cause if you got control over 'em, ain't no sense in worryin'. And there ain't no sense worryin' about things you got no control over, 'cause if you got no control over 'em, ain't no sense worryin.'"

He once said that, "My goals this season are to hit .300, score 100 runs, and stay injury-prone." After a lengthy losing streak while betting on the ponies, he finally won and cashed in with a big smile on his face. He later disclosed that he had placed a wager on every horse in the race. He explained to teammate Lou Piniella that he "had to break my luck." He may have been quick, but he wasn't that swift.

George "Boomer" Scott, the supersized first baseman for the Milwaukee Brewers and Boston Red Sox, used to wear a necklace made out of pieces of white seashells. When asked what they were, he used to glare menacingly and answer: "They're the teeth of American League pitchers."

Phenomenal Smith

When you have a name like Phenomenal Smith, you'd better be pretty damn good. Unfortunately, this 20-year-old pitcher for the Brooklyns of 1885 was not quite the phenom he thought he was. Maybe if he'd called himself "So-So" Smith, he might have had a longer, albeit mediocre, career. Smith made one fatal mistake before his first big-league start against the St. Louis Cardinals. He announced to anyone who would listen that he was so phenomenal that he didn't need his teammates to win. This kind of crap from an unproven rookie goes over like a pregnant high jumper. Hell hath no fury like a fielder scorned. The game proved to be one of the biggest travesties in baseball history.

The Brooklyn nine treated any ball hit to them as if it were coated with dog crap. Shortstop Germany Smith (no relation) committed seven errors, and catcher Jack Hayes made two—not to mention the five passed balls that sailed past unmolested. Infielders and outfielders didn't even get close enough to some balls to have them ruled errors. In all, there were 14 errors on the Brooklyn side. Brooklyn ownership subsequently fined the players $500 each, but they had gotten the result they wanted. Phenomenal Smith was released with phenomenal speed.

George Brett

One of the most bizarre, headline-grabbing events in baseball history took place in 1983 during a game between the New York Yankees and the Kansas City Royals at Yankee Stadium. Of course, it was initiated by my arch-nemesis, Graig Nettles, also known as Mr. Nice Guy. Like most hitters, George Brett used pine tar on his bat to get a better grip. Nettles had noticed in the previous series in Kansas City that the tar extended further up the bat handle than the rules allowed. Like the little tattletale he is, he ran to tell manager Billy Martin, and the two conspired to use this information against Brett at some future date.

Brett's bat remained quiet during the Kansas City series, and there was no reason to blow the whistle on Brett. But back in New

York on July 24, batting against Goose Gossage in the top of the ninth, Brett homered with two out and a man on to give the Royals a 5–4 lead. Billy Martin charged from the dugout like a ravenous rat after a piece of cheese. He demanded that home plate umpire Tim McClelland check the bat for pine tar. The batboy was carrying the bat back to the dugout, but the umpire retrieved it and examined it as Martin egged him on. "The tar is too high," Martin said. "It shouldn't be more than 18 inches above the handle. This is more than that. It's an illegal bat. The homer shouldn't count!" The fans weren't sure what was going on, but they knew something was up. The umpires convened and decided to measure the pine tar, but they didn't have a ruler so they laid it across home plate, which is 17 inches across. The pine tar clearly went several inches beyond. The umpire signaled that Brett was out and the homer didn't count. Then all hell broke loose.

Brett charged from the dugout like a man possessed. Royals manager Dick Howser loudly protested. One of the umpires intercepted him en route to confront McClelland. He tried to restrain him and calm him down, but he was furious. While Howser protested loudly, wily veteran Gaylord Perry took the bat from the umpire and headed to the dugout. The Royals started playing hot potato with it, trying to fool the umps with the old hidden bat trick. It was to no avail. The umpire tracked it down and recovered the evidence. The game ended, and the Yankees celebrated the 4–3 win. "It turned out to be a lovely Sunday afternoon," said Martin.

Several days later, American League president Lee MacPhail overturned the ump's decision and reinstated Brett's homer. Even though the bat was technically illegal, the "spirit of the rule" dictated that the game should be re-commenced on August 18 from the point at which Brett had homered. Martin was now apoplectic.

When the game resumed on August 18, Martin immediately claimed that Brett had failed to touch all the bases when he hit the home run a month earlier. He argued that the current umpiring crew—which was a different crew from the "pine tar" game—could not possibly know if Brett had touched all the bases. But crew chief

Davey Phillips had done his homework. He quickly produced an affidavit that had been signed by the previous umpiring crew. The document confirmed that Brett and the runner who scored ahead of him had both touched them all. Martin argued and was ejected from the game. The remainder of the game was played out in just over 12 minutes, and the score stood at 5–4 Royals. Yankees pitching ace Ron Guidry played center field for the Yanks, and left-handed throwing outfielder Don Mattingly played second.

More than 20 years later, Brett remembers the incident fondly. Since 1980, the same year that he made a legitimate run at hitting .400, Brett led the Royals to a World Series appearance against the National League champion Phillies. Brett was hampered during the Series by a painful case of hemorrhoids, and the Royals lost in six games ("If a tie is like kissing your sister," said Brett, "losing is like kissing your grandmother with her teeth out.") Ever since that, fans in every ballpark showered him with catcalls about his embarrassing ailment. Finally, thanks to the July 24, 1983, game, George Brett's name was now associated with pine tar and not Preparation H. "Now, I'm the pine tar guy," said a grateful Brett. "It was the greatest thing that ever happened in my career."

The pine tar bat and Brett are both in the Hall of Fame.

Mark Fidrych

Mark Fidrych was called Bird because his drooping-shoulder posture resembled that of Big Bird, the big yellow bird on Sesame Street. It was an apt nickname. He was a bird of a different feather, a rare species that may be on the endangered species list. He was a right-handed pitcher with the sensibilities of a lefty.

Fidrych captured the imagination of not only Detroit Tigers fans but baseball fans around the world. For one thing, the story quickly spread that he talked to baseballs. There is no evidence to suggest that he actually did—and less to suggest they talked back. The fact that he was actually talking to himself and not the ball doesn't take away from his legend in the least. He certainly did seem to treat them as if they were human. He once insisted that the umpire deposit a well-hit ball back into the ball bag. His reason? "It could goof around with the other balls and let the other balls beat the heck out of him and smarten him up," he said, "so the next time he comes out he'll be a pop-up."

Fidrych fluttered into the majors in 1976, after being selected by Detroit in the 10th round of the 1974 draft. When manager Ralph Houk gave him the great news that he was heading north with the team, his first question was, "Mister Houk, how do you gotta dress in the big leagues?" The first thing that impressed Fidrych when he walked into a big league clubhouse was not rubbing elbows with Ron LeFlore or Rusty Staub.

"The first time I walked into a big league clubhouse I went, 'Wow! Free orange juice! Free chewing gum! Free chewing tobacco! I don't even chew tobacco, but I think I'm gonna start!'" he told Steve Rushin of *Sports Illustrated*. The Bird's home perch soon became the mound at Tiger Stadium.

Watching Fidrych pitch was like watching a kid at play in the sandbox, a big innocent kid who was having the time of his life. He was totally consumed with what he was doing, not the least distracted by the adults around him and intent on building the best darn sandcastle ever. One minute Fidrych was on his hands and knees smoothing out the pitching mound. The next minute he was cleaning the rubber. Most endearing of all were his apparent instructions to the ball, which were actually instructions to himself. Fidrych was 19–9 in his rookie year with the fifth place Tigers, with an ERA of 2.34. He also pitched 24 complete games. The Tigers attracted an average of 18,268 additional fans in games that Fidrych started that year, and he won the American League Rookie of the Year Award.

The Bird's formal introduction to America came on June 28, his first national TV appearance. His timing couldn't have been better. This was America's bicentennial summer—suddenly the eagle was to have some competition as a symbol of America's can-do character. Going into the game, only the state of Michigan and serious baseball fans around the country knew about the rookie rook. They knew from the box scores that he was 7–1 and boasted an impressive 2.19

Mark "The Bird" Fidrych injected so much fun and passion into the game in 1976 with his eccentricities and his childlike love for the game. When asked one night, after beating the Yankees, about his reaction to Yankees captain Thurman Munson's charges of showboating, he innocently asked, "Who's Thurman Munson?" *Photo courtesy of MLB Photos via Getty Images.*

ERA. But they hadn't seen him in all his full-fledged glory. With the ABC *Monday Night Baseball* team introducing him "up close and personal," Fidrych didn't disappoint. Featuring a hard and heavy slider and mixing it with a 90 mph fastball, Bird allowed the Yankees only seven hits en route to a 5–1 victory. It was the way he did it that caught the imagination and affection of the country, however. He groomed the mound like an attentive mother hen. He looked at the ball and talked in its direction like it was Yorick's skull and he was Prince Hamlet delivering a soliloquy.

When the last pitch had been delivered, the Tiger Stadium crowd of 50,000 stood as one and chanted his name—well, not his name. They chanted "Bird, Bird, Bird!" over and over again. He responded with several curtain calls—his teammates actually had to push him from the dugout each time.

After the game, Thurman Munson, the no-nonsense, ever-so-tough, ever-so-talented Yankees catcher, concluded that the Yankees had been disrespected by this fresh rookie and his antics. He called Fidrych "fly-by-night" (which is pretty funny when you think about it), and "a showboat." Naturally the press flocked (sorry!) to Bird's locker to get his reaction to the Munson slight. His response left the media scrum momentarily stunned: "Who's Thurman Munson?" said Fidrych. "They didn't ask me another question," he recalled years later. "They just went running out of the clubhouse." But he wasn't trying to be funny, mean-spirited, or disrespectful—Mark Fidrych *did not know who Thurman Munson was!* His Tigers teammates quickly informed him that Munson just might be one of the best catchers in the game.

Casey Stengel also had a close encounter of the bird kind. In 1918, when he was playing for the Pittsburgh Pirates in a game against his former team, the Brooklyn Dodgers, Stengel was greeted with boos when he stepped onto the Ebbets Field diamond. Stengel responded by doffing his baseball cap. To the delight of the fans, a tiny sparrow flew out.

Ironically, and fittingly, Munson would be catching Fidrych when he started the All-Star Game for the American League. By then, Munson, who could subdue a perceived enemy with a glare, knew that his new battery-mate was the genuine article, and the unlikely duo struck up a friendship.

Fidrych proved equally refreshing and lacking in pretense away from the ballpark. In a meeting with then-President Gerald Ford, he asked the President if his son Jack—a soap opera actor—could score him a date. Nothing—not being photographed by Annie Leibovitz and appearing on the cover of *Rolling Stone*, being selected to star in an Aqua Velva TV commercial, meeting Frank Sinatra or being given a spanking-new Thunderbird—changed him. The 1976 season proved to be his first and last complete campaign. In spring training the next year he tore cartilage in his left knee and a month later tore the rotator cuff in his right shoulder. For all intents and purposes, his career was over.

Fidrych was what baseball should be all about—a kind of wide-eyed innocence coupled with the sheer joy of playing a game that he loved. He still wears his double-knit pants and drinks his 12 Buds a day. We will not see his like again. The Bird has flown the coop.

Luis Tiant

Luis Tiant is another former teammate of mine. He was the funniest guy I met in baseball. In fact, he may just be my favorite player of all time. When he came to Boston, it was as a reliever and possible spot starter. There's a pecking order in baseball and at that time the relief pitcher was at the bottom. No one was ever sent to the bullpen as a reward. Finally they saw the light and made him a starter.

He was the center of attention in any game he pitched. Luis was not only the heart and soul of the Red Sox, he was also the funny bone. He kept the team looser than Perry Como on Valium. He used rubber snakes to terrify Luis Aparicio, questioned Yaz's fashion sense, and generally transformed the Red Sox clubhouse into an amiable Animal House. One day he was pitching and a hitter drove the ball to dead center field, and Luis yelled, "Go foul! Go foul!"

His main target was Tommy Harper. When Tommy came to the Red Sox, he was reunited with his old friend from their days together in Cleveland. When Tommy came over to the Indians, he had the reputation of being moody. Basically he wanted to remain anonymous. With the Indians, Luis single-handedly brought him out of his shell and made him a part of the team. He did it by making him the target for various forms of good-natured physical and verbal abuse. Harper loved it, and it was the start of a beautiful friendship.

Before Luis intervened, Tommy used to enter the clubhouse and go about his business with as little fanfare as possible. He didn't want attention drawn to him. So of course, Tiant did just that. It began innocently enough with Luis accusing Tommy of having "alligator breath." He would stagger around the dressing room and pretend to be passing out from the bad breath. The rest of the team cracked up, and eventually so did Harper. The next time he entered the clubhouse, he heard a scream like that of a fire truck. "Eeeeeaaaaaaaaaiii!" Startled, he looked around and there, under a bright red fireman's hat, was Tiant. Luis was carrying a fire extinguisher, which he proceeded to aim at Harper and slip its nozzle into his mouth. "No more alligator breath," he shouted with glee as he completed his task and sped away with his siren sounding, "Eeeeeeeaaaaaiii." The whole clubhouse was in stitches, Tommy included, and he was now Luis's permanent foil. Turns out he really liked being included. Luis did wonders for Tommy.

When Tommy came to the Red Sox in 1972, he arrived at spring training in Winter Haven. As he tells it, he got lost on the way from Tampa and arrived very late at night. The next day he was apprehensive all the way to the ballpark, knowing that Luis would be ready for his arrival. "There was no doubt in my mind that he was going to get there early just to put something in my locker or set up some kind of joke on me," he said in *El Tiant*. Previous to meeting Luis, such things would have been outside of Tommy's focused little world, but no more. "Just thinking about him doing something like that made me laugh. And sure enough, the moment I walked through the door, I could hear that high, squeaky voice, yelling and screaming, telling everyone in the room that 'the ugliest man in the world just joined our team.' I looked at him and he looked at me and we laughed so hard we cried."

Every time—and I mean *every* time—Luis would go to the toilet, just before you heard the flush, you'd hear Luis say, "Goo-bye, Tommy!"

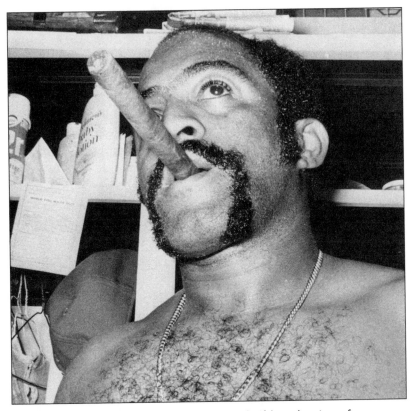

His wacky delivery wasn't the only eccentric thing about my former teammate Luis Tiant; he was one of the funniest men I ever met in baseball and always kept our clubhouse in stitches.

One day in spring training, Yaz came into the clubhouse carrying a huge fish he'd caught. Luis started going on about how this ugly fish looked just like Tommy. "It's even got teeth like Tommy," he chirped. Later that afternoon, when Tommy came in the clubhouse, there was the fish draped in Harper's Red Sox uniform—its mouth propped open with tongue depressors and a Red Sox hat on its head.

After being hit heavily in an old-timer's game in 1988, Luis returned to the dugout, where fellow Red Sox players rubbed his sore arm. "My arm's fine," he said, turning his ass to the players. "Here, massage this."

Of course, Tiant's delivery alone makes him an eccentric. The mother of the Dionne quintuplets didn't go through as many contractions before her delivery as Tiant did before his. I used to say that a Tiant start was like a symphony orchestra that he was conducting. The maestro takes the mound with his baton and everyone waits for the concert to begin. He starts to conduct. The banging and clanging starts and it shakes the ballpark. Then comes the middle part of the symphony and things become very calm and sweet and it almost lulls you to sleep. And then all of a sudden you sense that the end is approaching and the crowd starts getting noisy again. The whole gang is letting loose with the instruments, then— BOOM—the concert is over. That was Louie: hard at the start, sweet in the middle, and then the big finish with a flourish.

His own description was even better. He had a million different deliveries, but one was called the "jaw breaker." "My head stopped exactly seven times," he said. "First I looked up, then I looked down; then my jaw pointed toward second base, then toward third. Then it pointed toward center field, then behind my back—and then, just before I throw the ball, I pointed it upstairs to where Mrs. Yawkey was sitting."

Luis would smoke his cigars in the shower, which takes a lot of talent—and practice. "[After] so many years, the water would hit [my] face and hair but not hit my cigar," he said.

Danny Ozark

Another manager who communicated in his own language was the Philadelphia Phillies' Danny Ozark. When the Phillies lost 10 consecutive games and were in danger of dropping out of first place, he comforted his players and Phillies fans with the observation that "even Napoleon had his Watergate." He provided this inspirational assessment of outfielder Mike Anderson: "His limitations are limitless." Little wonder that, as he put it, he "had a wonderful repertoire with my players."

He convened a meeting prior to a 1975 game against the Cincinnati Reds, the vaunted Big Red Machine that would go on to win the World Series against the Boston Red Sox. He carefully went through the Reds lineup and offered advice about how to pitch to them. His strategy was as follows:

He suggested that because lead-off man Pete Rose was a good fastball hitter, they shouldn't "give him anything good to hit." Of number two hitter Ken Griffey, he said he was also a good fastball hitter and should be pitched away. Joe Morgan was also a great fastball hitter, he cautioned, and should be made to swing at bad pitches. "Pitch him high and tight and then low and away." The cleanup hitter, Johnny Bench, was a good fastball hitter and can hit it deep, so he should get a diet of curve balls down and away.

It was at this point that Larry Bowa interrupted to point out the obvious. "So far, skip, we've got the bases loaded and one run in. What do we do now?"

But on other occasions he was much less pessimistic. When the Phillies were seven games behind in the 1975 National League pennant race, he declared, "We're not out of the pennant race." Unfortunately his math skills didn't match his optimism, since the Phillies had only six games left to play.

But despite it all, he was convinced that there was no morale problem on his team. "This team's morality is not a factor," he assured the press.

He admitted to reporters that he didn't always give direct answers to their questions: "Don't you know I'm a fascist? You know, a guy who says one thing and means another."

Babe Herman

Babe Herman is often referred to as a "baseball buffoon." A label like that doesn't just happen, it has to be earned. What evidence is there of such buffoonery? Well there is Exhibit A, of course. Like "Bonehead" Fred Merkle, Herman was defined by a single bizarre incident that occurred in 1926, his rookie year with the Brooklyn Dodgers. The 6'4", 190-pound Herman was a very good-hit, virtually-no-field first baseman whose best year was 1930, when he batted .393 and accumulated 241 hits. His career average was .324. Despite being one of the worst fielders in the annals of the game, he was one of its best batsmen. So why the guffaws whenever his name is spoken? On August 15, 1926, during a game with the Boston Braves at Ebbets Field, Herman put a charge into a ball and drove it against the outfield wall. With his head down and running at full bore to leg out a triple (author Tom Meany likened him to "the Headless Horseman of Sleepy Hollow"), he arrived at third only to find that three's company. Herman was so intent on making it to third that he hadn't noticed that:

1. teammate Chick Fewster had stopped at third
2. teammate Dazzy Vance had retreated to third to avoid being caught in a rundown

Unsure of the ruling, the third baseman tagged all three and let the umpire sort it out. The funniest scene was the pursuit of Fewster into right field by Braves second baseman Doc Gautreau. Gautreau finally applied the tag. The ump ruled that the lead runner has the right to the base; therefore both Herman and Fewster were called out. He had doubled into a double play, and came very close to tripling into a triple play. Dodgers manager Wilbert Robinson was asked about the play after the game. "That's the first time those guys ever got together on anything all season," he said. Strangely, instead of faulting Herman, he picked on Fewster. "Tagging was too good for him," he said. "They should have hung him."

The incident did spawn one of the funnier zingers of the era, however.

> First Fan: "The Dodgers have three men on base!
> Second Fan: "Oh yeah? Which base?"

Was this just an isolated event? It would be nice to say yes, but the answer is no. Babe was part of a group that came to be known as the "Daffiness Boys." He did his part to make the label accurate. On at least two infamous occasions, he negated teammates' home runs by stopping on the bases to admire the arc of the ball while the home-run hitter absentmindedly passed him. This turned the homers into singles and presumably friends into enemies.

When he was told by a teammate that a mutual friend had lost everything during the war, Babe turned to him and said, "What did he do, bet on the Germans?" He told the Brooklyn writers that he was smarter than they thought. He liked to read books in his spare time, especially biographies of great generals. The reporters were skeptical. "What did you think of the Napoleonic era?" asked one. "I thought it should have been scored a hit," he replied.

Soon, stories of Babe Herman's goofiness were circulating throughout the baseball world, and Herman was starting to resent it. He felt that the stories damaged his reputation and therefore, potentially, his very livelihood as a ballplayer. He once cornered respected writer Frank Graham and conveyed these reasonable concerns. Graham was sympathetic and promised that any future stories originating from his pen would pay greater homage to Babe's undoubted intellect. "Thanks," said the relieved Babe. He then reached into his pocket and drew out a half-smoked cigar, which he stuck in his mouth. Graham, still trying to soothe the player's hurt feelings, struck a match and offered to light his stogie. Much to his surprise, he saw that the cigar was already lit and Babe was already blowing impressive smoke rings into the air. "Never mind," he said between puffs, "it's already lit."

Graham was flabbergasted. "Forget what I just said!" he told Herman. "The deal's off! Anyone who carries lit cigars around in his pocket deserves whatever he gets."

Herman's fielding was so bad that reporters started to wonder if Babe was gun-shy due to having been hit in the head by a fly ball. One brave scribe, Tom Meany, even ventured to ask him that very question. "That's a joke," said an angry Herman, "but it ain't funny. I'll promise you this: if I ever get hit in the head by a fly ball, I'll walk off the field and never come back." Meany probed deeper. "How about getting hit on the shoulder, Babe?" Herman flicked the ash off his cigar and replied, "Oh, no. On the shoulder don't count."

Rube Waddell

Rube Waddell is confirmation of Yogi's assertion that "baseball is half mental" and that so are some of its players.

Anyone who turned cartwheels on his way to the mound and still pitched well enough to make the Hall of Fame is a flake in my book. Waddell, a Philadelphia A's southpaw, did just that and more. He was cocky enough to wave his outfielders from the field in a spring training game and then strike out the side. He wanted to do the same in a regular-season game, but the rules specify that nine men must be on the field. He overcame that obstacle by having his outfielders move in to the fringes of the infield and sit down. He then proceeded to mow down the next three batters on strikes. He once doused his arm with cold water before a game and told puzzled teammates, "The fact is, my fastball is so good today I might burn the catcher's mitt if I don't cool it down." Was he full of bravado? Sure. Was he playing with a full deck? Debatable.

While pitching in the minors, he had the unnerving habit of changing from street clothes to uniform as he ran across the field before the game. The fact that he didn't believe in wearing underwear made this practice particularly offensive, especially at the turn of the century.

Waddell wasn't the brightest bulb in the scoreboard. When he was fined $100 for what his manager claimed was "a disgraceful hotel episode in Detroit," Rube jumped on his accuser with righteous indignation. "You're a damn liar," he said. "There ain't even a Hotel Episode in Detroit."

Waddell was one of the best left-handed pitchers in baseball history. His fastball was explosive and his curveball backbreaking. He also had precise control—at least while pitching. He was often out of control in his private life. Connie Mack had to hire a private dick to keep him from repeatedly disappearing. "He's got a million-dollar arm and a two-cent head," said the frustrated Mack.

Rube may not have been street-smart, but on the mound he was a genius, or at least an idiot savant. From 1902 to 1907, he topped the league in strikeouts. His only real competitor for the title of best pitcher was Cy Young himself. Ironically, Cy had also been considered something of a rube when he came up to the majors. In 1904 Rube set a brand-new, seemingly unassailable strikeout record with 349 Ks. The record stood intact for six decades.

Waddell worked his rivalry with Young for all it was worth. When the two faced each other in a 1905 showdown, it was the Rubester who came out on top in a 20-inning classic. Decades later, taverns and bars from California to Maine boasted that they had the game ball from the Waddell-Young game—it seems that Waddell exchanged countless "game balls" in exchange for some highballs.

Nevertheless, where others had tried and failed miserably, Mack managed to tap into Waddell's limitless potential. He became almost like a father figure—or perhaps a warden—to the country boy. Because he knew that Rube had no money sense, he used to dole out his $2,500 salary in $10 allowances. Mack also knew how to get the most out of his pitcher on the mound. After he'd gone out and pitched a grueling 17-inning victory, Mack enticed him to start the second game of the doubleheader. He threw a shutout. His reward? A fishing trip.

In the midst of this success, Waddell took a brief sabbatical with the Pittsburgh Pirates. However, unaccustomed to his "ways," they soon returned him at the request of manager Fred Clarke, who expressed his reservations to the ownership in subtle terms, as follows: "Sell him, release him, drop him off the Monongahela Bridge; do anything with him you like, so long as you get him off my ball team!"

A roommate usually gets to know a ballplayer well, and Waddell's longtime roomie was Ossee "Schreck" Schreckengost, a catcher who did not like Rube's habit of late-night snacking on Limburger cheese sandwiches and crackers. The smell of the cheese was as overpowering as a Waddell fastball. Fed up with the nocturnal noshes of his nibbling neighbor, Schreckengost actually went so far as to hold out in signing his 1903 player contract until Connie Mack and the team added a clause that specifically forbade Rube from eating cheese and crackers in bed.

Some people have hinted that Waddell might have been mentally challenged. It's true he wrestled alligators, was married to two women at the same time, left the mound and ran after fire trucks, and twirled batons at the front of parades. It's true that he was an actor and rugby player and a fisherman prone to taking over bartending at every watering joint he visited. It's also true that he arrived at the ballpark drunk many times and pitched well, although his fielding was understandably erratic.

The parade incident took place in 1903 in Jacksonville, Florida, where the Athletics were training. Waddell disappeared from camp and no one knew where he had gone. Teammates Socks Seybold and Danny Murphy knew there was a minstrel show in town and decided to go. Seybold jokingly said, "Let's take a look at the parade. Maybe we'll find Waddell in it." To their shock and amusement, when they got there, Waddell was not only in the parade, but was leading it. But then Rube had a habit of showing up where he wasn't expected. In Washington, the A's were enjoying a rare day off. Manager Connie Mack was visiting friends when he heard a fire engine approach a burning building. Soon, a courageous fireman was risking his life at the second-floor window, pouring water on the flames. Mack was admiring the heroic lad when suddenly he realized that he looked familiar. It was Rube Waddell.

The last half of Waddell's career was played under a cloud of scandal. He had led the A's to the 1905 World Series with a league- and career-best record of 27–10. That's why his failure to play in the series was so devastating and suspicious. He claimed that he injured his pitching arm in a fight after making fun of a teammate's new straw boater. Naturally, there was talk of betting, syndicates, and illegal bribes. The A's lost the Series four games to one, and Waddell's reputation has been forever tarnished. In 1908 he was shipped off to the St. Louis Browns, where he played for three more seasons before retiring.

Lee Allen in his book, *The American League Story*, summarized Waddell's 1903 adventures:

He began that year sleeping in a firehouse at Camden, New Jersey, and ended it tending bar in a saloon in Wheeling, West Virginia. In between those events, he won 21 games for the Philadelphia Athletics (even though he didn't bother to hang around for the final month of the season); played left end for the Business Men's Rugby Football Club of Grand Rapids, Michigan; toured the nation in a melodrama called "The Stain of Guilt"; courted, married, and became separated from May Wynne Skinner of Lynn, Massachusetts; saved a woman from drowning, accidentally shot a friend through the hand; and was bitten by a lion.

Waddell salvaged his reputation in 1912 when he heroically assisted residents of Hickman, Kentucky, during a flood. But just to ensure that his reputation as an eccentric was ensured, he also used his spare time teaching three wild geese to jump rope.

Perhaps fittingly, Waddell died on April Fools Day, 1914. He was penniless at the time of his death. The inscription on his headstone—written by his former roommate Schreckengost—said it all: "Rube Waddell had only one priority, to have a good time." Waddell was elected to the Hall of Fame in 1946.

Bob Uecker

Bob Uecker is a pure baseball entertainer. Unlike Dizzy Dean, he did not possess a lot of baseball talent, and whereas Dean's humor came from self-aggrandizing and braggadocio, Uecker made mediocrity an asset. He was once told by a minor league manager, "There's no place in baseball for a clown." That man couldn't have been more wrong.

Known to one and all as Mr. Baseball, Uke knows irony when he spews it. To borrow from one of his most memorable lines, Bob Uecker must surely be "in the front row" of baseball characters. Uecker may well be the funniest man in baseball. He has made

The hilarious Bob Uecker turned self-deprecating humor into an art form, but you know he had to be able to play a little to have the career he did in the big leagues.

more mileage from a truly mediocre major league career than anyone this side of Joe Garagiola. How mediocre was it? The 6'1", 190-pound catcher played six seasons, from 1962 to 1967, and batted .200 with 14 homers and 74 RBIs. From the very beginning, he got no respect, no respect at all. "I really wanted a glove, but we were poor so my father went out and shot a cow," he once quipped.

"I remember I signed with the Milwaukee Braves for a $3,000 bonus," he recalls. "That bothered my dad at the time. We were a poor family and he didn't know where he was going to come up with that kind of money."

It got worse. "They said that I was such a great prospect they were sending me to a winter league to sharpen up," he recalls. "When I stepped off the plane, I was in Greenland." And worse. He recalled his first major league game in Milwaukee as one of his proudest moments. Things were going well and the fans seemed to be watching his every move with great interest. The more they stared, the prouder he was. Then, in the third inning, his manager called him back to the dugout and told him he was wearing his athletic supporter outside his pants. And still worse. "In 1963 I was named Minor League Player of the Year," he once boasted. "It was my second season in the bigs."

Uecker's highest hit total was 43 in 1966. "I had slumps that lasted into the winter," he claims. In those six major league seasons, he played for five different teams: the Milwaukee Braves (1962–1963), the St. Louis Cardinals (1964–1965), the Philadelphia Phillies (1966–1967), and the Atlanta Braves (1967). He was brought to the Braves specifically to catch knuckleball pitcher Phil Niekro. When Braves trainer Harvey Stone was rubbing down Niekro's arm after a 2–1 win over the Pirates, he mentioned that the pitcher could probably start a game again the next day. Atlanta vice-president Paul Richards was skeptical. "No, he couldn't either," he said.

"Why not?" he was asked. "Does he need more rest?"

"No," said Richards, "but Uecker does. Every time Phil pitches, it's Uecker who needs four days off."

He once explained his two top career highlights: "I got an intentional walk from Sandy Koufax and I got out of a rundown against the Mets." On another occasion he added a third: "In 1967 with St. Louis I walked with the bases loaded to drive in the winning run in an intrasquad game in spring training." He also was quick to point out his contribution to the World Series–winning St. Louis Cardinals in 1964. "I came down with hepatitis," he explains. "The trainer injected me with it."

Even after he had retired, he got no respect. He was invited to an old-timers game in Philadelphia and told to report to Shibe Park, which had been torn down years earlier.

By now you have probably accepted the fact that Uecker was not a great ballplayer. "I didn't receive a lot of awards as a player," he once admitted. "But they did have a Bob Uecker Day Off for me once in Philly." He got very little respect from his own teams. "When I looked at the third-base coach, he turned his back on me," he says. Opposing teams were no more impressed with his abilities. "I remember I'm batting against the Dodgers in Milwaukee. They led, 2–1 in the bottom of the ninth, bases loaded, two out, and the pitcher has a full count on me. I look over at the Dodgers dugout and they're all in street clothes."

My coauthor, Jim Prime, once interviewed Uecker for a book he was writing on Ted Williams. He repeated Ted's youthful commitment to be the very best: "When I walk down the street after my career is over, I want people to point to me and say, 'There goes Ted Williams, the greatest hitter who ever lived.'" Jim asked Uecker if he had similar goals, and whether he thought he had reached them. "After my career, I didn't walk down streets. I walked down alleys." Perfect.

He probed deeper, asking him to compare his hitting style with that of the Splendid Splinter. "Our hitting styles were similar in that we both used a bat. I was more of a choke hitter...I choked every time I was up there." He explained the huge discrepancy in their career statistics thusly: "He [Ted] took time off for the wars to rest. I didn't have that opportunity. I had to stay and play. I got tired."

Lest you think that Uecker is little more than Rodney Dangerfield in cleats, think again. The reference to Uecker as "Mr. Baseball" is intended to be ironic, but he actually does represent baseball's Everyman. Here is a ballplayer whom we can identify with. Few of us can imagine being Ted Williams or Alex Rodriguez or Manny Ramirez, but we can all imagine being Bob Uecker. The saddest fact is that Uecker, despite all his self-deprecating talk, was good enough to be a major leaguer, something 99.99 percent of us will never be.

You might think that it would be consistent for Uecker to end his life by being hit by a beer truck. Well, not quite. Actually, it was beer that jump-started his new career. Uecker came back to the national spotlight in the early 1990s as a pitchman for Miller Lite in a hilarious commercial. The commercial begins with Uke striding down the aisle to his seat at Dodger Stadium. He is the cock of the walk, confident that his role as a former major leaguer gives him preferred status. "You know," he says. "One of the best things about being an ex–big leaguer is getting freebies to the game. Call the front office and—*Bingo!*" He seats himself in a VIP seat near the field. An usher instantly approaches and informs him that he is seated in the wrong section. Ever the cockeyed optimist, Uecker's parting comment is, "Oh, I must be in the *front rooow!*" The next time we see poor Bob he is so far up in nosebleed territory that even a St. Bernard would get woozy. When the commercial was running, Uecker couldn't walk down a street without someone yelling "Bingo!" It was a classic casting job and represented every thing we love about Bob Uecker: optimism in the face of abject failure, a kind of undeserved pride in a job not very well done, and a healthy—if inaccurate—self-image.

Let's give the last word to Mr. Baseball. "Baseball hasn't forgotten me," says Uecker. "I go to a lot of old-timers games and I haven't lost a thing. I sit in the bullpen and let people throw things at me, just like old times." Not only that, but Mr. Baseball's genes are strong. "The biggest thrill a ballplayer can have is when your son takes after you. That happened when Bobby was in his championship Little League game. He really showed me something. Struck out three times. Made an error that lost the game. Parents were throwing things at our car and swearing at us as we drove off. Gosh, I was proud."

It was reported recently that Uecker was being stalked by a fan. This has to be a put-on. I mean, come on, who's going to stalk a .200 hitting ex-catcher? Maybe an ex-pitcher with a 6.15 ERA.

Graig Nettles

Graig Nettles wasn't everyone's cup of Gatorade. When I was asked how I liked Nettles's book *Balls*, I pointed out that he missed it by an inch or so. It should have been called *Asshole*. Of course, I had reason to dislike the Yankees third baseman. A brawl at Yankee Stadium on May 20, 1976, almost ended my career. I was blind-sided by Nettles and fell awkwardly on my pitching shoulder. I was out of action until mid-July and was never the same pitcher after the incident.

He had the reputation of provoking fights and then disappear-ing before the fisticuffs started. His nickname was "Puff," but announcer Joe Garagiola pronounced it "Poof." He said, "They call him Puff because he's always provoking fights and then, when they start—Poof—he's gone." I recently met Nettles at a baseball func-tion and was pleased to see that he hadn't aged well. He didn't get up, just sat there. He looks like a duvet cover. So I won that war.

Nettles was the Yankees' version of Don Rickles. Some of the best comedians have come from poor ghetto backgrounds and have used humor as a way of escaping their harsh conditions. There are baseball ghettos, too—like the early Mets and the Washington Senators of the '40s and '50s. Both teams seemed to have a higher than average number of flakes and kooks. So how do you explain Graig Nettles? In a baseball sense, he was born into privilege as a member of the New York Yankees and yet he was a funny guy—cruel and boorish but funny. Of course the Bronx Zoo of George Steinbrenner and Billy Martin, et al, breeds the kind of acerbic, cynical humor that is necessary to survive in such an atmosphere.

Nevertheless, Nettles provided some perspective and outspoken commentary on a team dominated by the Boss, George Stein-brenner, and run—off and on—by the erratic, volatile Martin.

"Every year is like being traded—a new manager and a whole new team," said Nettles.

And, "Some people dream of being in a circus, others of being a major league baseball player. As a member of the New York Yankees, I'm getting to do both."

And, "It's a good thing Babe Ruth isn't here. If he was, George Steinbrenner would have him bat seventh and say he's overweight."

He did have some great lines about fellow players. Of Luis Tiant, the Cuban-born twirler who had come to the Yankees from

Boston, he said, "We've got a problem here. Luis Tiant wants to use the bathroom, and it says no foreign objects in the toilet." When Sparky Lyle lost his closer role to Goose Gossage in 1978, Nettles told him he had gone "from Cy Young to sayonara." So he had his moments.

Dick Stuart

Dick Stuart was like Michael Jackson. He wore a glove for no apparent reason. What a beaut! Before a game between the Chicago Cubs and the Pittsburgh Pirates, the public address announcer issued the usual pregame statement to the Forbes Field crowd: "Anyone who interferes with a ball while it is in play shall immediately be ejected from the ballpark." Pirates manager Danny Murtaugh turned to his pitching coach and said, "I hope Stuart doesn't think that includes him."

While he was a member of the Boston Red Sox, Stuart once received a standing ovation for scooping up a gum wrapper that had blown onto the field. Funny? Sure. But the thing is, the crowd was genuinely surprised that this human sieve was able to stop it.

Get the picture? Dick Stuart wasn't exactly Hal Chase. He was sometimes referred to as Old Stonefingers. Other times he was called Dr. Strangeglove or Cement Hands because it was rumored that his first baseman's glove was manufactured, not by Rawlings or Spalding, but by the Portland Cement Company. When he was taking infield practice with the California Angels, shortstop Jim Fregosi threw a ball low into the dirt. Stuart dug it out with his bare hand, as the crowd applauded. "C'mon Fregosi, hit my glove," complained Stuart. "Why?" Fregosi shot back. "There's no way I could hurt your hands. They're pure U.S. Steel!"

In both Pittsburgh and Boston, Stuart was concerned with one thing and one thing only: hitting. Trying to prevent opposing players from getting hits was not a priority for him. Nor was baserunning. He continually missed or misread his coach's signs. When the Pirates coaches had finally had enough and confronted Stuart about the situation, he offered a solution to the problem.

"Why don't you just point to where you want me to go?" he suggested.

Not only was Stuart an atrocious fielder, he was no day at the beach for management either. He was once a guest speaker at a postseason banquet in Boston, where prominent members of the baseball community were gathered. Red Sox manager Billy Herman was also at the head table. Stuart turned to him and said, "Hope you have a great winter, Billy." Herman nodded his thanks, as Stuart added, "Because you sure had a horseshit summer."

Steve Dalkowski

Steve Dalkowski, also known as "White Lightning," was a very mortal 5'11", 170 pounds. He also wore Coke-bottle glasses that shouted "Nerd!"

He may be the fastest pitcher in the history of the sport. Stories of him shattering umpires' masks with pitches abound. He also threw baseballs through backstops. He once unleashed a pitch that tore off a section of a batter's ear. Today that pitch would be called "the Tyson trimmer."

Dalkowski's resume is one that would earn him a job with any major league team in any era, *if* certain facts were omitted. For example:

> **Steve Dalkowski Resume (first draft)**
> Include: Struck out 18 in a high school contest. Allowed no hits and no runs.
> Omit: I walked 18 in the same game.
> Include: In 1957, I pitched 62 innings and struck out 121, which is an average of 18 Ks per game.
> Omit: I won only one game that year. I walked 129, including 39 wild pitches.
> Include: On August 31 of 1957, as a player for Kingsport, I struck out 24 Bluefield batters.
> Omit: I walked 18 and lost the game 8–4. I also recorded 6 wild pitches and 4 HBPs.
> Include: I struck out $104,000 bonus baby Rick

Monday four times in one game.
Omit: He made it to the majors. I did not.

How fast was Dalkowski? Some say 110 mph.

Oh yeah, he never made it to the major leagues. In fact, even his minor league record was unimpressive. He boasted a nine-year, 46–80 bush league record and an ERA of 5.59. He struck out an impressive 1,396 hitters. But perhaps the statistic that best explains his languishing in the minors is that he also walked 1,354 in 995 innings.

He reportedly assisted the dry-cleaning industry in Knoxville, where one player confessed to having soiled his pants when an errant pitch whizzed past his head. Bob Lemon, a former Yankees manager, claims that he once saw Dalkowski hit a guy in the back with a pitch—and the guy was standing in line to buy popcorn. "The guy came up to me afterward and asked if I'd autograph the ball," Dalkowski claims. Some cynics suspected that at times Dalkowski was intentionally wild just to unsettle hitters and perhaps gain more media attention.

While pitching for Earl Weaver in South Dakota, he once struck out 20 batters—and walked 18. Oh yeah, he also pitched a no-hitter. This may well have been when Weaver learned to swear.

Dalkowski was almost always "wild high," and low-flying aircraft had to be on alert.

Despite being the perennial "hopeful" at Baltimore Orioles camps each spring, Dalkowski never pitched an inning of major league ball. The closest he came was an exhibition appearance against the Cincinnati Reds on 1959 in which he struck the side out in order. His hygiene—or lack thereof—was noted by pitcher Steve Barber, who had the misfortune of having his locker next to Dalkowski's. "He had his sweatshirts and stuff in the locker…and they smelled so bad, I told him, 'If you don't wash those things by tomorrow, I'm going to cut them up.'"

The Sporting News of June 30, 1979, quoted Cal Ripken Sr. on other negatives.

"Dalkowski could do some drinking," Ripken said. "He couldn't stop. He liked to stay out, drink, and have some fun. He'd always be borrowing money to buy booze and was broke from payday to payday."

Steve Barber described a night in which he and Dalkowski's roommate, Bo Belinsky, accompanied Steve to a bar the night before he was to pitch. According to Barber, the fireballer was just as prone to drinking highballs as he was to pitching them. "Hey, guys, come over and look at this beautiful sight," Dalkowski reportedly said to his friends. Two dozen scotch and waters were lined up on the bar in front of him. He consumed them all and then insisted on stopping to buy a gallon of wine on the way home. He downed that as well. "The next night they just carried him off the mound in the fourth inning," Barber told.

More than once, his drinking and carousing got him in trouble. He once rammed a police car with a teammate's brand new Cadillac. When the police called manager Earl Weaver to see if he wanted to post bail, Weaver replied, "Goddamnit, let him stay there tonight."

Nevertheless, Weaver showed surprising restraint and was something akin to a father figure to the troubled young man in his charge. As manager at the Baltimore Orioles Double-A farm club in Elmira, New York, the future hall of fame skipper administered IQ tests to his players. Dalkowski reportedly scored a 60, and Weaver decided that the kid had to be handled with kid gloves. He revised his tactics and made any instructions simple and straightforward: throw fastballs in the strike zone. The strategy worked, if only for a while.

In 160 innings of work, Dalkowski posted a 7–10 record with a ERA of 3.04. He walked 114 and struck out 192, by far his best show of control. During one amazing stretch, Dalkowski fanned 104 batters while walking only 11 and allowed a single earned run. But just as it seemed he'd turned a corner, disaster struck. During the next year's Orioles spring training opener against the Yankees, he entered the game in relief and struck out Roger Maris, Elston

Howard, and Hector Lopez. The next inning he faced Phil Linz, and when Dalkowski delivered the first pitch to him, he heard a pop in his elbow. He was never the same after his rehab—with his fastball topping out at about 90 mph.

The Orioles bid their one-time wunderkind a regretful farewell in 1965, and he became a baseball gypsy, moving from team to team and minor league city to minor league city. By 1966, he was out of baseball.

We have something in common. Dalkowski and I were the inspiration for "Nuke" LaLoosh of *Bull Durham* fame. Nuke is actually an amalgam of both of us.

Don Stanhouse and Mike Hargrove

Pitcher Don Stanhouse had two nicknames. He was called "Stan the Man Unusual" because of his unorthodox behavior on the mound and off. His Baltimore manager Earl Weaver, who couldn't stand him, called him "Full Pack," because that's how many cigarettes he could smoke during a Stanhouse outing. Only reluctantly would he bring him into a game. Stanhouse spent so much time between pitches, it sometimes seemed as if he didn't want to throw the ball at all. Stanhouse explained the logic behind his delaying tactics: "My stuff is so bad, the longer I hold onto the ball, the better my chances."

When Stanhouse pitched against Cleveland's Mike "the Human Rain Delay" Hargrove, it was like watching paint dry—only slower. Someone once timed one of their excruciating encounters. Countless fidgets, fouls, and filibusters later, 12 minutes had expired and it looked as if both the procrastinating pitcher and the hesitating hitter might be arrested for loitering. Hargrove was actually the inspiration for an American League directive which instructed umpires to keep wandering hitters confined to the batter's box.

Legendary columnist Dick Young—whom I couldn't stand—writing in *The Sporting News*, described Hargrove's resultant slump in meteorological terms: "One theory opposing players have is that umpires won't let him [Hargrove] out of the batter's box to go through his lengthy between-pitches routine, thus turning the Human Rain Delay into a spot shower."

I got Billy Martin fired from Texas, and Hargrove inadvertently helped because of that rule. If you didn't throw the ball in 20 seconds, it was an automatic ball. So Hargrove got in the batter's box and got ready to hit. He stepped out and adjusted his cup, his pants, his helmet, and won't put his freakin' right foot in the batter's box. I was in the dugout and I started timing him. It got to 20 seconds, and I took a bat and pounded it on the wooden steps at Arlington, yelling, "Strike one!" as loud as possible. The umpire stepped out, and Hargrove stepped out, and it went another 20 seconds, and I yelled, "Strike two," as loud as I could. It was unbelievable. I was just disrupting the game like hell, and Billy Martin went nuts in the Rangers dugout and started swinging on the bat racks and scratching under his arms like he was a monkey—and the next night, owner Brad Corbett fired him. So if you wonder why we fought tooth and nail all those years, that's where it started. We had a running feud all the way down the line. That's why when the Yankees–Red Sox brawl broke out years later, he still had a grudge, and when I was on the mound he was hoping something would break out. He and his Yankees henchmen charged from the dugout lickety-split like banshees and tried to take me out, and they succeeded.

Hargrove later became a manager of the Cleveland Indians. When it looked as if the Indians would make it to the 1998 ALCS, he said, "I have a good feeling about the club, but that could be gas."

Six | The Superstitious and the Bizarre

As I've said, baseball is the perfect theater for the bizarre. It's sort of like the Eagles' "Hotel California" without the harmony: "You can check out anytime you want, but you can never leave."

Kevin Rhomberg

It's safe to say that in his three-year major league career, Kevin Rhomberg touched many people, but only if they touched him first. As a member of the Cleveland Indians from 1982 to 1984, Rhomberg played in all of 41 games. He had one home run, three RBIs, no doubles, no triples, and four walks. So, why do ballplayers and fans still speak of him in reverential tones?

Well, Rhomberg was a tad superstitious. In fact, his superstition was very singular and distinctive. Whenever he was touched by another human being, he had to touch that person back. Sounds harmless, doesn't it? But think about it. Think about the people you encounter in the run of a day, week, month, or year. Then think about the game of baseball and the various situations that put you in direct contact with other ballplayers on your own and opposing teams. And think about the less than sympathetic mentality of fellow ballplayers.

Bill Mazeroski, the Hall of Fame second baseman of the Pittsburgh Pirates, was known as "No Touch" for his ability to turn the double play. Cleveland manager Mike Hargrove christened Rhomberg "Touch Me." You see, Rhomberg's need to touch was not just some innocent quirk, it was an obsession. Failure to repay a touch resulted in lost sleep, agitation, and outright panic.

Naturally, ballplayers went out of their way to prevent him from carrying out his plans. One player tagged him with a ball and then threw it out of the ballpark, sending "Touch Me" on a two-hour scavenger hunt. Pitcher Rick Sutcliffe even intruded on the sanctity of the clubhouse bathroom to reach under the stall and make contact with Rhomberg's toe. Not knowing who the toe molester was, Rhomberg was forced to touch every player in the clubhouse. (There are no reports that he was ever touched by an Angel, but in a game against New York, the home plate umpire was forced to order the Yankees to stop touching Rhomberg.)

If he was unable to touch a person, according to Larry Stone in the *Seattle Times*, he sometimes sent that person a letter in lieu of the contact. "This constitutes a touch," the letter announced.

There are numerous stories of players who touched him and then used elaborate tricks to escape and hide. But like some kind of Sherlock Holmes, he tracked them down and touched them. In one particular case, teammate Dan Rohn thought he had eluded him, until a 3:00 AM knock on his hotel room door proved otherwise.

This unending game of tag reached its apex one day when pitcher Bert Blyleven was driving with Rhomberg to the ballpark. Blyleven touched Rhomberg and then jumped out of the car and disappeared. The Associated Press reported that only the intervention of Rhomberg's wife, Denise, resolved the very touchy situation. "Let him touch you," she pleaded with Blyleven, "or he won't sleep all night."

A relief pitcher who was definitely touched was Jim Kern, who toiled for the Texas Rangers of the late 1970s and early '80s. Kern was known by his teammates as "the Amazing Emu" due to his skinny 6'5" frame and bird-like gait. Kern embraced the moniker, often responding to calls of "Emu! Emu!" with otherworldly screeches of an indeterminate avian variety.

Kern became a certified eccentric before he even reached the major leagues. In one minor league game, his team held an insurmountable lead in the late innings. Relief pitchers with too much time on their hands are unpredictable at best. An idle mind is the devil's workshop and all that. Kern and his fellow bullpen inmates thought the game was over and had turned their attention to the fans in the adjacent bleachers. They were swapping balls for peanuts, popcorn, hotdogs, and pop. Eventually they had given away all the warm-up balls and had stuffed themselves with food and drink to a point where they could hardly move. When they looked up from their "game within a game" things had changed considerably. In the space of a half inning, the opposing team had scored five runs and were still threatening. The swollen savers were in a fix. They could barely move—and they had no balls left to warm up. Necessity is the mother of invention, and Kern and company devised a scheme. The bullpen catcher squatted in his usual spot and pretended to catch Kern's nonexistent offerings. The scheme worked, for awhile. Several days later team management fined the phantom throwers $250.

Babe Ruth claimed he had only one superstition. "Whenever I hit a home run, I make sure I touch all the bases," he said.

While with the Cleveland Indians, where he fell under the questionable influence of John Lowenstein, Gaylord Perry, and Fritz Peterson, Kern was also known to cultivate spiders in the dugout. They captured moths and fed them to their pet arachnids. "We each had a spider, and it was a contest to see who could grow the biggest one," he told writers Bruce Nash and Allan Zullo. "We wanted to get one big enough so it could answer the phone and warm up five guys at once."

Sparky Lyle

Kern's bullpen partner in Texas was my old Red Sox teammate Sparky Lyle. Together, Kern and Lyle earned the Rangers bullpen the name "the Cuckoo's Nest." The Boston Red Sox made one of the all-time dumb deals in baseball history when they dispatched him to the Yankees for Danny Cater, and it was all because of the infamous birthday cake incident. You see, Sparky had a little tradition that some people might consider a tad eccentric: he liked to sit on birthday cakes. That's all well and good. Everybody has to have a hobby. And at least he was smart enough to do it before the candles were lit. Sparky's mistake was in not being selective. He dropped his trousers and sat his bare ass on Red Sox owner Tom Yawkey's birthday cake. Unfortunately, Yawkey's wife found out about the incident and the next day it was "good-bye Sparky, hello Danny Cater." Sparky went on to become famous for his relieving and for his book on the dysfunctional Yankees called *The Bronx Zoo*.

Maybe it was the Texas heat, but in July of 1980, Sparky began to throw baseballs to a group of Little Leaguers who had arrived en masse. Soon the supply of balls was depleted but the demands of the young ballplayers were not. Soon, a young lady requested Sparky's hat, and Lyle obliged. Another fan asked for his glove, and soon it was hurled in his direction. His uniform shirt was next, followed by his pants, sweatshirt, and cleats. He was into it like Gypsy Rose Lee at the Ziegfeld Follies. Finally, when only a cheap pair of shorts were between him and the raucous crowd, he ceased the striptease and left the field in his underwear, receiving a standing ovation that would have made a porn star proud.

While with the Yankees, Sparky sometimes arrived at spring training wearing fake casts. He was perfectly okay, of course, but afterwards Billy Martin and George Steinbrenner complained of minor coronary infarctions. In 1977 Sparky saved 26 games for the Yankees and had a 13–5 record to lead them to the World Series, which they won. The Boss gave all the Yankees diamond-studded championship rings, but Lyle was skeptical. He was lounging around at home and tried to cut the glass top on his coffee table. "It was then that I discovered that the table was worth more than the ring," he said.

Lyle was a piece of work. His Yankees teammate Fred Stanley once decided that it would be kind of cool to make a bar from a

The Yankees have one of Sparky Lyle's more out-
landish hobbies to thank for his one-way ticket from
Boston and subsequent Cy Young Award.

casket. He somehow got hold of one and had it shipped to him at
Shea Stadium, where the team was playing while Yankee Stadium
was being renovated. Lyle couldn't resist temptation. He put on
some ghoulish make-up and donned a shroud and lay down in the
casket, closing it after him. The Yankees manager at the time was
Bill Virdon and it was his custom to have strategy sessions before
every game. The Yankees were listening intently as Virdon ana-
lyzed the strengths and weakness of the entire Baltimore Orioles

lineup. Suddenly the coffin lid creaked open very slowly. All conversation ceased as Lyle sat up and said in his best Bela Lugosi voice: "That's all well and good, but how do yoouu pitch to Brooks Robbb-innn-sonnn?"

Turk Wendell

What is it about relievers, anyway? Maybe the pressure gets to them. Maybe they are nuts to take the job in the first place. Maybe their gallows humor is just to relieve the tension. Maybe that's why they're called relievers. Whatever the reason, there are a hell of a lot of relievers in this book: Moe Drabowsky, Tug McGraw, Roger McDowell, Sparky Lyle.

You can add Turk Wendell to this group. He possessed a tough slider and had a durable arm, which made him an effective pitcher. His particular quirk was superstitions. Wendell was a walking, talking, chewing, leaping, squatting bundle of quirks. He had more superstitions than the offspring of a leprechaun and a troll. He wore number 99 as a tribute to Charlie Sheen's character in the movie *Major League*. He insists that no matter the size of his contracts, the figure must end in .99 ¢.

Wendell not only used to step over the baselines on his way to and from the diamond, he leaped them like a somewhat less graceful Rudolf Nureyev. In another *Swan Lake* move, he used to squat when his catcher was standing up and stand when his catcher was squatting. The Nureyev comparison went out the window when he took the mound and started to chew four (not three, not five) plugs of black licorice, spit them out after each inning, and then retire to the dugout to brush his teeth. He would draw three crosses in the mound and wave to the center fielder, slamming the rosin bag with a flourish before his initial pitch.

A dedicated outdoorsman and hunter, Turk eats a raw bit of the heart of each new species he kills, endearing him to Ted Nugent and revolting animal lovers everywhere. He sports a necklace of animal teeth taken from his kills, but fortunately does not wear fur jerseys.

That one looks a little high as Eddie Gaedel draws a walk in his first—and only—major league at-bat, courtesy of eccentric owner Bill Veeck.

Bill Veeck

Bill Veeck was the Phineas T. Barnum of baseball. He is well deserving of his reputation as the most outrageous promoter in the history of the game. He would stop at nothing to bring fans to the ballpark. He employed exploding scoreboards, horse races, on-the-field weddings, clowns, disco record burnings, and jazz ensembles, to name just a few events. In 1948 he brought Satchel Paige—then 42 years of age—to his Cleveland Indians to pitch. Paige proved that Veeck wasn't interested in all sizzle and no steak by winning six games and losing only one for the pennant-bound Indians.

One of his most bizarre acts was to send Eddie Gaedel, a 3'7" midget, to the plate for his St. Louis Browns in 1951. He borrowed the idea from a James Thurber story titled "You Could Look It Up," in which this very thing happens. In the real-life version of the story, Gaedel drew a walk, but his baseball career proved to be as short as he was. He was subsequently barred from baseball by American League president Will Harridge.

In his book *Veeck—As in Wreck*, he expressed outrage at the decision. "Naturally I was bewildered and alarmed and shocked. I was a few other things, too: 'I'm puzzled, baffled, and grieved by Mr. Harridge's ruling,' I announced. 'Why, we're paying a lot of guys on the Browns' roster good money to get on base and, even though they don't do it, nobody sympathizes with us. But when this little guy goes up to the plate and draws a walk in his only time at bat, they call it "conduct detrimental to baseball.".…Now that midgets had been so arbitrarily barred,' I asked, 'were we to assume that giants were also barred?' I made dark references to the stature of Phil Rizzuto, who is not much over 5' tall, and I implied very strongly that I was going to demand an official ruling on whether he was a short ballplayer or a tall midget." Veeck stated that he would, reluctantly, accept the League's decision. "I thought that was rather big of me," he said in his book.

Veeck's manner of introducing Gaedel to his manager of the day, Zack Taylor, was to insert him into a birthday cake and have a mascot for Falstaff beer, Sir John Falstaff, release him. I like it.

Jim Piersall

Jim Piersall was the poster boy for eccentricity. (It takes one to know one.) He once got in a fight with Billy Martin, so he couldn't have been that crazy, but Mickey McDermott confirmed that he was. "They finally found out he was whackier than shit, some part of the brain wasn't working without this functional liquid or something, but the pill they finally gave him worked. They sent him down to Birmingham and I got in a fight with him and then he started telling stories about Vern Stephens. I went to Boudreau and said, 'Hey, there's something wrong with this kid. I knew him from Scranton and I think he's sick or something.' Well, he was sick alright and it wasn't his fault. They sent him to Birmingham, and in the first game he got up to home plate and the umpire called him out on a bad pitch. He didn't holler, he didn't say nothin'. He just reached in his back pocket and pulled out a water pistol and shot the umpire with it, and the f*ckin' umpire fainted dead away.

A virtual poster boy for baseball eccentrics, Jimmy Piersall rounded the bases backwards after his 100th home run.

After all the stories he'd read about Piersall, he said, 'I thought he sonofabitch was going to kill me.'"

Mel Parnell remembers his former teammate, too. "I remember pitching a game in Chicago," he said, "and I could hear a roar from right field. I turned to look and all I could see was the number on Jimmy's back. He was facing the stand, leading a locomotive cheer of P-I-E-R-S-A-L-L. If the ball had been hit to right field, he would never have been able to make a play on it. That was Jimmy. A great fielder but…"

When Piersall hit his 100th homer, he ran around the bases backwards.

Ichiro Suzuki

Some ballplayers don't treat their wives with the same loving tenderness that Ichiro Suzuki lavishes on his bats. Ichiro stores his bats in a humidor worthy of the finest Cuban cigars. When not in the humidor, the bats are standing upright in the Seattle Mariners dugout, ready for use.

Other players have had love affairs with their bats. Shoeless Joe Jackson named his bat Black Beauty. Ted Williams occasionally used to visit the Louisville Slugger factory to ensure that he got only the finest wood with the tightest grain. He then used to spend hours grooming the bats by rubbing them with a bone to toughen them. But Ichiro carries it a few steps further. He once forgot himself and threw his bat aside. He felt such guilt and shame for the action that he let it stay with him in his hotel room that night. Separate beds, of course.

In the summer of 1982, John Montefusco was pitching a game for the San Diego Padres against the Cincinnati Reds when suddenly he stepped off the mound and motioned for home plate umpire John Kibler to come and inspect the baseball. This alone was unusual—it's usually hitters who want the balls to be examined for imperfections. "It looks alright to me," said Kibler, after giving it the once-over. Montefusco pointed out that the ball had the word *Spalding* clearly printed on it. Spalding had lost the contract to supply balls to Major League Baseball six years earlier, and all balls were now supposed to be made by Rawlings. To top it off, Montefusco claimed that he had been the last pitcher to throw a no-hitter using a Spalding ball. It was a 9–0 win for the Count's Giants over the Braves on September 29, 1976. Believe it or not...

According to Jim Caple at ESPN.com, he gives equal attention to his gloves, which are handcrafted by a 70-year-old Mizuno craftsman named Yoshii Tsubota. Caple suggests that "Ichiro regards them so reverently it's as if he knew the cows personally, oiling the leather as religiously as George Hamilton preparing for an afternoon at St. Tropez."

Ichiro also has a special Japanese pillow made out of buckwheat (I assume it's the organic kind and not that kid from *The Little Rascals*). He uses a special hand-held massager to massage the bottoms of his feet before and after games. "The bottoms of your feet are very important," he told Janie McCauley of the Associated Press. "There's a saying in Japan that the bottoms of your feet are like your heart." Geez, Nettles must have a ton of calluses!

John Lowenstein

John Lowenstein was a .255 hitting outfielder and designated hitter for Cleveland, Texas, and Baltimore from 1970 to 1985. I roomed with him once in Venezuela. Who cares, you might well ask? Who cares, indeed. While with the Indians, the man they called "Steiner" was so uninspiring that he inspired a fan club known as the Lowenstein Apathy Club, LAC for short. Membership was automatic…if you couldn't care less. Naturally, the movement really caught on and soon attained the momentum of molasses. During games, fans held up huge banners that read, "Hey Steiner:" surrounded by yards and yards of blank white cloth. Such heartfelt sentiments were widespread. He was like Jean Paul Sartre, the existentialist. His answering machine message said, "I'm not here. You're not here. There is no message. There is no beep."

Indian fans lobbied—lethargically, of course—to have a day for Lowenstein while the team was on a road trip. He received countless fan letters expressing extreme passivity about their hero. One can only imagine how many additional fans just didn't have the motivation to mail them at all. Some of the letters were written in invisible ink. Lowenstein refused to give his autograph to his faint-hearted fans, sometimes explaining that he'd "left it in the clubhouse." He was the kind of guy who would tell a kid that the game couldn't start until he found the key to the batter's box.

When he moved on to Baltimore years later, the enthusiastic ennui had died down. In a 1980 game between the Orioles and the Oakland A's, he made an effort to regain his public's more active form of apathy. While running to second base, he was struck in the neck by a ball thrown by the first baseman. He fell as if he'd been pole-axed and remained motionless. As concerned players from both teams, managers, umpires, and coaches gathered around,

Steiner remained apparently comatose. Finally, a stretcher arrived and he was carefully loaded aboard and carried toward the dugout. The capacity Baltimore crowd looked on in stunned silence. "Just as they brought me near the dugout," he said, "I suddenly rose up with both fists clenched and let out a bloodcurdling yell. And the whole place just exploded." And the cry of "Apathy forever!" was reborn.

Lowenstein hung out with pitchers. We let Carbo do that with our Buffalo Heads club in Boston. The Buffalo Heads were a counter-culture group of players—mostly intellectual pitchers like myself—who gathered for scholarly conversation and occasional recreational refreshments. Somewhat akin to the Algonquin Round Table.

Lowenstein and Sparky Lyle actually had something in common. They both had birthday cake fixations. But while Sparky sat on them, Lowenstein used to give them the "finger-plunge" test, ramming his digit into the cake to test the taste. If it passed, all was well. If not, the cake was used as batting practice, with pieces flying in all directions.

George Theodore

I was trying to find a way to describe George Theodore to readers who haven't seen him. Comparisons eluded me until I happened to catch the movie *Napoleon Dynamite*. George Theodore is the original Napoleon Dynamite. He just decided to tackle baseball instead of tetherball. Theodore was a nerd's nerd. His middle name was Basil, for pete's sake! He had style-proof aviator glasses that just served to accentuate the 6'4", 190-pound frame that earned him the nickname "Stork." Some pronounced it "dork." One writer commented that he "looks like he swallowed a coat hanger." They had to add additional police presence at Shea Stadium to keep bullies from running out on the field to give him wedgies.

The most exciting thing they could think to say about him on his baseball card was: "He likes marshmallow milkshakes." I mean, he must have led a pretty boring existence. They might as well have said: "He wears shirts." Well, not always. When he (almost) made his major league debut, he entered the game in the sixth inning as a pinch runner. He jogged to first with his warm-up jacket on, a rookie move, but not that bad. When the umpire told him to remove it, he had no shirt on—he hadn't been issued one yet. On another occasion, he lost a shoe trying to steal second. In 1973, he was involved in a 1-3-6-3-4-3-9-2 rundown play.

Theodore was awkward, which is a drawback for athletes at any level, let alone in the major leagues. He once ran into teammate Don Hahn in the outfield—a collision that is legendary for its brutality—and laid them both out. They had to be carted off the field on stretchers.

Theodore was actually much cooler than Napoleon. He was left over from the 1960s, like me. He liked to philosophize, like me. He courted writers, like me. He loved the game of baseball and it showed, like me.

Theodore probably inspired more kids than Mickey Mantle, and I'll tell you why. Mickey Mantle was "the Mick." No one could hope to be Mickey Mantle, but one look at Theodore and everyone thought they could be a major leaguer. Even dorks. The Stork played for just two years, during which he hit two home runs, one each year. I also hit two major league homers—in 14 years—and I only walked once. I never met a pitch I didn't like. He batted .259 the first year before dipping below the Mendoza line with .158 in his farewell tour.

Fritz Peterson and Mike Kekich

Fritz Peterson and Mike Kekich have to be enshrined in this book as a duo due to a bizarre event that took place in March of 1973. The two Yankees pitchers held a press conference to announce a rather unusual trade. Peterson traded his wife, youngest child, and family pet (a dog) to Kekich for his wife, youngest child, and family pet (a dog). According to Jim Bouton, "The latest word was that Peterson's wife, child, and dog refused to report, and Kekich was demanding the return of his players." There was no word of any unborn children to be named later.

Ed Delahanty

Big Ed Delahanty was one of baseball's greatest stars at the turn of the century. He is as famous for his death as he was for his impressive baseball credentials. Some people leave baseball with a pop-up, others with a homer; Delahanty made his exit by plunging over Niagara Falls. In 1902 Delahanty, as a member of the Washington Senators, had led the American League in hitting with an average of .376 and doubles with 43. In 1903, his sixteenth big league season, he was batting at a .333 clip when he failed to show up for a game in his hometown of Cleveland. He was suspended by the team and reportedly went on a bender. On July 2 he got aboard a train in Detroit and headed for New York, where he was scheduled to rejoin the team. He was drinking heavily on the train and became obnoxious to other passengers. Finally, some of these passengers decided to take matters into their own hands. They asked the conductor to protect them. By this time, Big Ed was much too drunk to listen to reason. The conductor threw him off the train on International Bridge, but on the Canadian side of the falls. What happened after that is uncertain, but Big Ed ending up plummeting over the Falls to his death. Whether he jumped, fell, or was pushed has been the subject of endless conjecture ever since.

The writers of the time covered up the details of his death, not wanting to sully the reputation of a genuine baseball hero with a lifetime average of .346. In actual fact, Big Ed was not a very nice man. Baseball writer Robert Smith gave this frank assessment: "Men who met him had to admit he was a handsome fellow, although there was an air about him that indicated he was a roughneck at heart and no man to tamper with. He had that wide-eyed, half-smiling, ready-for-anything look that is characteristic of a certain type of Irishman. He had a towering impatience, too, and a taste for liquor and excitement." Wow, that description fits half the population of Boston. Smith went on to say, "He created plenty of excitement for opponents and spectators when he laid his tremendous bat against a pitch."

Delahanty was self-destructive, one of the first—but certainly not the last—American heroes to succumb to his own celebrity. He drank too much, became despondent, and took his own life. Or at least that's the theory.

Len Koenecke

And speaking of bizarre deaths, Brooklyn Dodgers outfielder Len Koenecke died one of the strangest in 1935. His is a cautionary tale for baseball managers, general managers, and owners. Koenicke's Dodgers had lost to St. Louis 1–0 the previous day, and he had been released by manager Casey Stengel. Death was a result of him being hit over the head by a small fire extinguisher during a desperate mid-air brawl over Toronto. He was killed by the two-man crew of an airplane that he had chartered in Detroit. Koenecke had flown from St. Louis on an American Airlines commercial flight but had been extremely disruptive, striking a stewardess and attacking passengers. He was put off the plane in Detroit and chartered the small plane to fly to Buffalo.

During the charter flight, Koenecke was sitting up front with pilot Williams Joseph Mulqueeney. Mulqueeney's friend and assistant Irwin Davis occupied the back seat in the small craft. The ballplayer had been drinking heavily and seemed disoriented and "under great stress." He began to poke the pilot in the shoulder and refused to stop, despite repeated warnings. He then flew into a rage and tried to wrestle the controls from the pilot. With the plane careening out of control, Davis intervened, and all hell broke loose. Koenecke bit Davis in the shoulder, and the two battled on the floor as the pilot struggled to stabilize the plane. The despondent former Dodger then tried to throttle the pilot from behind before Davis was able to stop him. The three-way battle went on for 10 or 15 minutes, during which the pilot lost his bearings. By now, the aircraft was so far off course that they were in Canadian airspace and approaching Toronto. In real danger of crashing, the pilot decided to take action. He waited for an opportunity and then struck the ballplayer over the head with the extinguisher three times. Koenecke died instantly. With the combat at an end, he was able to spot an open area of pastureland that was part of the Long Branch Racetrack and bring the plane down safely. It was later found that Koenecke had been severely depressed and was probably trying to commit suicide.

Later there were unsubstantiated rumors that Koenecke might have been making sexual advances to the pilot or his friend. Whatever the case, he was dead.

Koenecke was once a highly rated prospect. He was a good hitter and, when focused, a great fielder. Unfortunately, he was often not focused. As a rookie in 1932 with the New York Giants, he showed early indications of just how erratic he could be. In a game against the St. Louis Cardinals, Dizzy Dean came to the plate in a bunting situation. Instead of laying one down, Diz swung away and blooped the ball over the head of the charging third baseman and into left field. Koenecke was caught unawares and he compounded his inattention by loafing on the play. Dean took full advantage of the mental lapse and rounded second, drawing a desperate and wild throw from Koenecke. The ball went over everything, allowing Dean to score—all on a bloop hit by a pitcher who should have bunted. Giants manager John McGraw retired less than a month later, and Dean always suggested there was a connection. "When [McGraw] sees a rookie pitcher get a home run on a bunt," he said. "That's too much for any man."

Two years later, Koenecke, now with Brooklyn under rookie manager Casey Stengel, led the National League with a stellar .994 fielding average and only two errors. He batted .320 with 14 home runs and 73 RBIs in 1934 before slumping to .283, four homers, and 27 RBIs in 1935. The moral of this story is: don't have a bad year, it could kill you.

There are no experiences from my career that I can draw on to explain this bizarre episode. Sure, I was pissed off when I was traded to Montreal for Stan ("Don't ever mistake me for 'Big'") Papi, but I didn't take it out on the Air Canada pilots. And I would never have even *sprayed* Zimmer with a fire extinguisher, even if he were on fire—*especially* if he were on fire. In fact, I wouldn't piss on him if he were on fire. As far as wrestling around in a plane, the only thing I can recall that comes anywhere near was during a trip to Oakland when an announcement was made "to return the flight attendant to her full and upright position."

Bo Diaz

Bo Diaz came to the Red Sox for one season at the end of my time in Boston. He was my catcher for a while. He was a good guy and had a good little arm. He was killed when he was hit on the head by a satellite dish on his house in Caracas, Venezuela. If only he'd been born a few years later, the dishes would have gotten smaller and he might have survived.

Turk Farrell was a fire-balling right-handed pitcher for the Phillies, Dodgers, and Astros. He once won a 14-inning game that ended after 1:00 in the morning. He then proclaimed, "Nobody beats Farrell after midnight."

Bill Faul

My friend Bernie Carbo once claimed that a flake is just someone who isn't boring, someone who has fun in the game. He used right-handed pitcher Bill Faul as an example. Bernie played with Faul in the minor leagues and saw his exploits up close and personal. Faul's idea of a postgame meal was to bite off the head of a live parakeet and swallow it. Bernie was quite shocked the first time he saw it and mentioned it to his teammates. They just yawned and said that he should have been there the previous day when Faul had chewed up a live frog and gulped it down.

In the major leagues, as a member of the Detroit Tigers, Faul used to hypnotize himself before every start. When he was snapped out of his trance-like state, he was ready to take on the world. Teammates shied away from him because he seemed to be possessed. The Chicago Cubs acquired Faul before the 1965 season and, before his first start as a Cub, his new teammates got a taste of his unorthodox routines. He brought a record player to the clubhouse and spun a record that will never make the top 10 on any hit parade. The lyrics were as follows: "You're going to keep the baaalll dowwwn, you're going to keep the baaalll dowwwn. You're going to pitch loooowww and awaaay, loooowww and awaaaay!" I sang that tune myself for years.

Speaking of eccentricities, that year Faul was a part of three triple plays: one on July 14, one on July 25, and one on October 1.

Chuck Knoblauch

There is a whole group of ballplayers who suffer from a kind of anal-retentive inability to give up the ball. This condition causes them to hold onto the ball too long and then make errant throws. Steve Sax had it. In his case they called it Sax disease, but there are various forms. Rick Ankiel, Mackey Sasser, Chuck Knoblauch, and Mike Ivie couldn't throw the ball back to the mound properly. It's all part of Ernest Becker's denial of death philosophy.

In 1999 Chuck Knoblauch's infield play suddenly became erratic. He had trouble throwing the ball to first base, even on the simplest play. On the golf course, they call this condition the "yips." They started to use him as a DH to remove the pressure, but when he returned to the field, so did his problem. He consulted psychiatrists and psychologists to no avail. The errors continued to pile up, and soon fans beyond first base in opposing cities added to the pressures by wearing protective helmets. The precaution wasn't entirely in jest. He would often make errant throws that went 20 feet over the first baseman's head. He even hit announcer Keith Olbermann's mother in the head with one attempt. He was moved to left field by manager Joe Torre. His throwing woes spread like a cancer to his at-bats, and he batted an embarrassing .056 in the 2001 World Series. He finished up with the Kansas City Royals and then retired. How does a guy who played in four All-Star Games end up not being able to throw a baseball to first base?

I swear this is true. I was visiting Cooperstown for a charity event in June of 2006 and I struck up a conversation with the room maid while I was watching the College World Series on TV. It looked like North Carolina was going to win over Oregon. They had two pitchers—one was a first-round draft choice for the Red Sox, the other was a first-rounder for someone else. The first guy was throwing 96 mph and the other 98 mph. There were runners on, but the batter hit a little bleeder to the second baseman and he fielded it, but then he gagged on it! Held it too long and threw it away. Oregon won. I asked the maid her name and she told me it was Debbie Knoblauch. You can't make this stuff up! I started to watch her and, sure enough, every time she threw dirty towels into the hamper, they missed wide left. I booed her out of the room.

Jackie Brandt

It's difficult, if not impossible, to write a book on flakes and not include a guy whose nickname was "Flakey." Jackie Brandt, who played for five different teams between 1956 and 1967, could well be ground zero for the term. A teammate said that "things seem to flake off his mind and disappear." While trying to question his own degree of flakiness, Jay Johnstone once invoked the name of the godfather of flakes: "Flake? Who's a flake? Jackie [Brandt] once played 27 holes of golf in 101-degree heat before a doubleheader." Well, assuming it takes one to know one, he's got to be one (and, by the way, Brandt claims it was 36 holes, not 27). He went 7-for-8 in the two games. "Two doubles, two homers, and three singles," he recalls, before adding, "I was loose." Brandt was indeed a flake's flake.

Some players have questioned the Baltimore outfielder's intensity, and little wonder. Blessed with an abundance of skill, he once said, "This year I'm going to play with harder nonchalance." Even his excuses were strange and wondrous. He reasoned that the harder he ran, the more his "eyeballs jumped up and down." A 1962 issue of *The Evening Sun* quoted him thusly: "I'm trying to make myself think I'm trying harder. When you bust a gut and make things look easy, it's hard to do the same things and make them look hard." He also claimed to have lost the ball "in the jet stream." Hello, Yogi, are you in there?

He was not much more aggressive at the plate. After he struck out on a full count with the bases loaded, his manager asked, reasonably, what pitch he was guessing, fastball or curveball. His reply? "Neither. I was guessing ball."

He was beaned six times, a stat in which he seemed to take a lot of pride. If he hit a home run, he was known to slide into first, second, third, and home. He once did a back-flip in an unsuccessful effort to avoid the tag in a rundown between third and home. The crowd loved it, and everyone but the French judge gave him a "10."

But perhaps his greatest legacy was that he was the inspiration for the term "flake." Before that, eccentric players had to endure a variety of descriptors. They now have Jackie Brandt to thank—or blame—for uniting them under a single banner.

The late Broadway Charlie Wagner was best known as Ted Williams's former roommate. The nattily attired Wagner was not particularly superstitious, but in 1938, when the Red Sox went on a winning streak, he was forced to be. During the eight-game victory streak, the players were coerced into eating whatever foods they had been eating on the day the streak began. Unfortunately, Wagner had consumed a large glass of prune juice that day. "I was on prune juice for eight straight days," he recalled. "I'm glad we finally lost."

Charles "Victory" Faust

At last, a chance to give this book a classic touch, add some class, culture, and sophistication. With a name like Charles "Victory" Faust, this guy has to have all three coming out his wazoo, right? Well, not quite. Unfortunately, our flakey Faust bears little resemblance to the fictional version. Unlike the protagonist of Johann Wolfgang von Goethe's tragedy, he did not yearn for experience and knowledge. He yearned only to win a pennant for the New York Giants. This hardly makes him unique, you may rightly say. Most of today's major leaguers surely had similar dreams. True, but they at least had played some baseball at some level. Faust hadn't, and that's what makes him more like Forrest Gump than a Faustian hero.

Charles Faust was what, in a less enlightened time, they used to call "feeble-minded." But no, he wasn't an owner. A farm boy from Marion, Kansas, some writers have even characterized him as the "village idiot." But like I said, he wasn't an owner. Medically speaking, he suffered from a condition known as hebephrenia. Among other symptoms, he would have been delusional and would have experienced hallucinations. According to the *Encyclopedia and Dictionary of Medicine and Nursing*, he would have had "absurd delusions, senseless laughter, and silly mannerisms." Sounds like a ballplayer to me.

Legend has it that he went to a fortune-teller in Kansas, and she foresaw that he would leave his home state and win a pennant for the Giants. Unlike the literary Dr. Faustus, he made no deal with the devil in order to reach the majors, unless, as some of his players did, you consider John McGraw to be Mephistopheles incarnate. He made his way to St. Louis where, during batting practice, he left the grandstand and approached the Giants' bench. He said that he wanted an audience with the Giants' fiery, tempestuous manager. He announced that he was there to lead the Giants to the World Series. "Mr. McGraw," he said, "my name is Charles Victory and I cam here from Kansas because a fortune-teller told me that if I joined the New York Giants I could pitch them to a pennant." The usually intense, no-nonsense McGraw must have been amused by this brash interloper because instead of sending him packing, he offered him a job as the Giants' mascot, a kind of San Diego Chicken, sans the feathers. He was a frenetic sight on the field before games, exhibiting his unique pitching and fielding style. He immediately became the team's good-luck charm as they went on an impressive winning streak.

The players began to actually believe that Faust was making a difference. So did the manager. When a game was on the line, McGraw would send him to the bullpen to warm up. As crazy as it seems, it worked. Faust the benchwarmer led them to a record of 37–2. After the Giants had clinched the National League flag, Faust was rewarded by actually being brought into a game in relief. He pitched the ninth against the Boston Braves and allowed only a single run, arguably a better performance than George Plimpton mustered in any of the sports he took on. He was given another shot on the last day of the 1911 regular season and came to the plate. He was hit by a pitch and allowed to run the bases, stealing second and third.

Faust's magic was not enough to carry the team to victory in the World Series, but then the psychic had only guaranteed a pennant, not a world championship. Nevertheless, his grateful "teammates" voted him a $1,000 World Series share. He returned in 1912, and the Giants once again responded to his presence with a record of 54–11. Unfortunately, McGraw was losing patience with Faust, who was making demands and distracting the manager from more important matters.

If you look him up in your *Total Baseball* encyclopedia, you will find one line devoted to him in the pitching register section. He appeared in two games for the 1911 New York Giants of the National League, pitched a total of 2 innings, and gave up 2 hits and 1 run (earned). His ERA was 4.50.

Perhaps fittingly, the story of Faust has a tragic ending. He was committed to an "insane asylum," prompting the *New York Herald* to cruelly headline: 'Charlie Faust Sent to Bughouse League.' He died on June 18, 1915, at the age of 35. E.L. Doctorow once called Faust "a pathetic pantomime of his own solitude." Whatever you may say about the man, you have to say this. He lived out the dream of every red-blooded American male. He played in the major leagues and he has a line in *Total Baseball* to prove it. Not a bad epitaph for anyone.

Al Hrabosky

Al Hrabosky, the "Mad Hungarian," had an act. It consisted of the mustachioed relief pitcher coming to the mound in a key situation. His face was set in a combination glare and trancelike state. Before key pitches, he would walk behind the mound and rub up the ball, finishing by slamming the ball hard into his glove. The act worked. Batters were intimidated by the Mad Hungarian and more often than not, Al strode from the mound with a save.

"The Mad Hungarian," Al Hrabosky, used to get a little fired up out there in the late innings of games. *Photo courtesy of Getty Images.*

Off the mound, Hrabosky was somewhat less intimidating. He once appeared in the bullpen wearing his protective cup and jockstrap on the outside of his uniform.

It turns out that Hrabosky was also a great—if unorthodox—motivator. Jay Johnstone reported that in 1978 Hrabosky brought a hand grenade into the clubhouse of his slumping Kansas City Royals. In his best Patton voice, he reportedly said, "Look, you sons of bitches, if we don't get our act together and start winning, they're going to blame this on me, and I ain't taking it alone." Brandishing the grenade for all to see, he continued, "I'm taking some of you suckers with me." He then threatened that if the team didn't start to win he was "pulling the pin and blowing all of you to hell and back." He finished by placing the grenade in his locker and exiting the clubhouse. Now *that* is a motivational speech!

The Royals went on to win the AL West title and, as Johnstone tells the story, the players were in the midst of the division-clinching celebration when suddenly the mad moundsman took the grenade from his locker and pulled the pin. As players took cover behind whatever furniture was near, he assured them that he had the pin and there was no reason to worry…and then he started to panic. The pin was bent, he said, and couldn't be re-inserted. Finally, after much help from his teammates/detonation-prevention crew, the situation was defused. Although Hrabosky's strategy worked on this occasion, fooling people into thinking that you have such WMDs is not condoned by Major League Baseball or responsible world leaders. Mr. Bush and Mr. Blair, take note.

Jack McKeon

Another motivational genius is Jack McKeon. At 76, McKeon may be old chronologically, but he is still young at heart. He is one of the few managers today who roams a bit off the well-beaten managerial path. In his autobiography, McKeon talks about a minor league player he coached in the mid-1950s named Juan Vistuer. Vistuer was an aggressive base runner—a bit too aggressive for McKeon's liking. On more than one occasion he ran his team out of potential scoring situations by charging through the coach's stop sign at third.

McKeon resorted to extreme measures to rid the young player of his habit. In short, he threatened to shoot him if he ran through another sign. Vistuer smiled at his manager, acknowledging the joke. The only problem was, McKeon went out and purchased a pistol and loaded it with blank cartridges. Sure enough, the very next time Vistuer ignored the stop sign and barreled for home, McKeon pulled out the weapon and fired in his direction. "He was halfway home," recalled McKeon, "and hit the ground so fast.

Never ran through another stop sign. Taught him a lesson." It's called the Dick Cheney school of baseball, and if it catches on there could be a barrage of gunfire across Major League Baseball.

Ted Williams

Yes, fans, even Ted Williams was a flake. In fact, his antics—on the field and off—would have made him famous even if he'd been a .220 hitter with acne and not the greatest hitter who ever lived. Many people think of Ted as a brooding, ill-tempered, media-baiting superstar who was so obsessed with hitting a baseball that he was one-dimensional, even boring. Well, I'm here to tell you that the Kid was a kid at heart. When he first arrived in the major leagues, Ted was open, carefree, and full of enthusiasm. Jack Kerouac loved Ted Williams. He admired the way he did everything in a continuous stream of consciousness. He didn't edit himself or revise himself. He was the living embodiment of Kerouac's writing.

Even later in his career, he loved the give-and-take of the locker room. He engaged in classic verbal exchanges with Red Sox trainer Jack Fadden. It was always Ted who got things going.

> Ted: Am I the greatest ballplayer you ever saw, Jack?
>
> Fadden: Theodore, I could name 50 guys I'd rather have.
>
> Ted: Fifty? Name one!
>
> Fadden: How about Joe DiMag? Can you field like him? Can you run like him?
>
> Ted: No.
>
> Fadden: And when it comes to throwing, you're the world's highest-paid shot putter.
>
> Ted: Well, I'm still the greatest hitter and the greatest fisherman.
>
> Fadden: Greatest fisherman? Listen, there was a guy who produced more fish in one minute than you could in a year.
>
> Ted: Who the hell was that?

Fadden: Didn't you ever hear about the Sermon on the Mount? About the loaves and fishes?

Ted: My God, you had to go back far enough to top me, didn't you?

Does this exchange confirm Williams as the egotistical monster that Boston dailies made him out to be, or as someone who could laugh at himself? How about this one?

When Pedro Ramos was a rookie pitcher for the Washington Senators, he struck out Ted. After the game Ramos, who idolized Williams, went to the Red Sox clubhouse and asked Ted to sign the ball. Ted reacted as only Ted can. "Get the hell outta here. I'm not signing any ball I struck out on." Ramos was crushed and slowly turned to leave. Seeing the effect his words had on the young pitcher, Ted quickly softened. "Give me the damn ball, I'll sign it." Ramos left the clubhouse on cloud nine. The next time the two faced each other, Ted hit a gigantic home run into the right field bleachers at Fenway. As he was rounding the bases, he looked over at Ramos and said, "Go find that son-of-a-bitch and I'll sign it for you, too."

It was Ted's intensity and focus that makes this funny. Same as when Tigers catcher Birdie Tebbetts tried to destroy Ted's legendary concentration by telling him a long, drawn-out joke. As Birdie told the story, strike one exploded in his mitt. He continued to talk as strike two zoomed past Williams. All that was left was the punch line, but Ted laid into the third pitch and hit it out of the ballpark. As he crossed home plate, he stopped and, with exaggerated interest, asked Tebbetts, "And then what happened, Birdie?"

When did it all change? When did Ted change from carefree to embittered? Actor and former Red Sox farmhand Paul Gleason had a theory: "When Ted was young, he was an exuberant, ebullient, enthusiastic fellow who loved baseball and loved life, and when he saw how fickle the fans could be he was sensitive enough, he said, 'Okay, I'm not giving them that part of myself. I'm not going to share my enthusiasm with them anymore. F*ck 'em. I'm not tipping my hat.'"

It was his quest for perfection that caused many of his eccentric actions. He was once so disgusted with his performance on the golf course that he threw his golf clubs into a lake adjacent to the 18th hole. In a tantrum that only Ted could throw, he walked to his car only to discover that the keys were in the golf bag. He returned to the lake, rolled up his pants, and waded in. He picked up the golf bag, rummaged through it until he found the keys, and chucked it back in. The point is, he didn't calm down in all that time. He didn't think better of his initial rash reaction. That was Ted Williams.

Remember that Ted is the same guy who claimed that he could smell smoke when he hit a foul tip off a good fastball pitcher. Sometimes a player is just superhuman, not eccentric.

Most of his commentary on the writers was X-rated. Here is one of the milder examples: "Pour hot water over a sportswriter and you'll get instant shit." It was endearing comments like this that made Ted Williams the nemesis of every scribe in Boston.

Ted was as passionate about politics as he was about hitting, and the lefty swinger was definitely a right-winger. He once flew with John Glenn when both were serving in Korea. Years later, a dinner honoring Ted was held in Boston. Glenn, who by now had won fame as an astronaut and a respected U.S. senator, was one of the speakers. When it was Ted's turn to reply to all the nice things that had been said about him that evening, he turned to Glenn and said, "I just wish I could have voted for you. But you had to be a f*cking Democrat."

Bernie Carbo

Without my buddy Bernie Carbo, there could never have been a Carlton Fisk. Without his game-tying three-run homer in the bottom of the eighth, there would have been no foul pole homer in the bottom of the twelfth. "That home run is my present to the citizens of Boston," he once said.

When he first came up with the Red Sox, he was in the clubhouse, and Red Sox owner Tom Yawkey approached him wearing a brown shirt, brown pants, and brown shoes. He welcomed Bernie to the ballclub and asked if he needed anything. Bernie thought he was the clubhouse guy and asked him to go and get him a couple of Fenway Franks.

Bernie is famous for traveling with a stuffed gorilla named Mighty Joe Young. When he was unhappy about not getting enough playing time, he dressed Mighty Joe in a baseball uniform and sat him in the dugout, often under scrawled graffiti that announced: "Bernie Carbo still lives!" The gorilla also accompanied Carbo on flights, at restaurants, during interviews with the media, and on Boston radio talk shows. He was the unofficial predecessor of Fenway's now ubiquitous Wally, the Green Monster. In some ways, Carbo was as much a mascot as Mighty Joe. He described his relationship with baseball to writer Edward Kiersh: "Baseball owners in my day were Nixon, and I was Woodstock."

In 1977 Carbo slugged a bases-loaded homer against Seattle Mariner's left-hander Mike Kekich. After the game, reporters gathered around his locker to ask him about the grand slam. "Grand slam?" said a startled Carbo, who had failed to notice that the bases were loaded while he was at bat. Another reporter asked when he had last homered off a southpaw pitcher. Carbo laughed. "Now I know you're pulling my leg, because he was a right-handed pitcher," he said confidently. "[Red Sox manager Don] Zimmer would never let me hit against a left-hander with the bases loaded."

Today, Bernie is a hairdresser and owns a unisex beauty salon in Detroit.

Seven

Come Back to the Diamond, Dizzy Dean, Dizzy Dean

It's no coincidence that this is the shortest chapter in this book. Let's look at one character from days not long ago and ask yourself if it could happen today:

Sammy White

Talk about players with unusual glove work. Sammy "Catch That Ball or Bust" White was a catcher for the Boston Red Sox. Whereas Dick Stuart made a boob of himself with the glove, White made a glove by himself with a boob. You see, White used to use women's falsies as padding in his catcher's mitt. Mel Parnell told a particularly fitting story:

> Sammy White was a great catcher, probably the best I ever threw to. There wasn't much room behind home plate at Fenway. He always said, "Just throw it, if I can't catch it, I'll block it." What more confidence could you give a pitcher than that? You aren't afraid to throw the ball down low because you knew darn well he would block it, if not catch it. Sammy used to use a woman's falsie as his sponge in his glove. When you think about it, it's the ideal thing because it fits the hand perfectly and creates that air vacuum between the rubberized sponge and the glove, which would soften the impact of the ball hitting in his glove.

181

One day he goes over to the wall after a foul ball and hits the wall and the glove flies off and darned if the falsie doesn't land in a girl's lap. She was so embarrassed, her face was as red as can be. Everyone wanted to laugh but they couldn't. It took Sam to think of that.

Today that would be called a "wardrobe malfunction" and all parties would end up on *Larry King Live*, discussing their childhood.

Mickey McDermott, another of Sammy's batterymates, agrees that the catcher liked to keep abreast of new techniques. He described one story: "Sammy goes into a department store and he sees these falsies in a barrel. He says to the lady clerk: 'What size do you have there?' She said: 'You mean for your girlfriend?' he said: 'No, for me.' She said: 'Oh, my god!' He buys two of the falsies and painted the nipples red, and they fit between his two fingers perfectly and when they were doubled up, they made a great sponge for the catcher's mitt—because when you set down and catch fastballs all day long, your hand gets killed." Makes sense.

So is there any downside to this practice? McDermott thinks so, "There was a close play at home one day where the lead runner from third was coming home and the anchor runner was coming around third and almost caught the lead runner. It should have been a sure bang-bang double-play at home plate for Sammy. But as he tagged one, the other runner hit him, and his glove flew off, and there were the two big shiny tits with bright red nipples lying in the middle of the field. The place went nuts. They thought he was a cross-dresser and they'd knocked his bra off or something."

White was involved in another infamous incident while catching for the Red Sox. In a game at Fenway Park, the Detroit Tigers were leading the home team 3–0 in the top of the sixth inning. Bill Tuttle was on second base for the Tigers, and Red Wilson came up and beat out an infield hit. Tuttle advanced to third on the play and kept on going. Red Sox shortstop Milt Bolling threw home, but umpire Frank Umont called the runner safe.

In a 1986 game between the Milwaukee Brewers and the Toronto Blue Jays, Buck Martinez was catching for the Jays. When Brewers slugger Gorman Thomas ambled to the plate, he casually asked Martinez what the pitcher was planning to throw to him. The catcher looked him in the eye and replied that it would be a fastball. Sure enough, he signaled for the heater and the pitcher obliged. Gorman swung mightily and missed. He turned to Martinez with a hurt expression on his face and said, "What did you do that for?" Further proof that the truth sometimes hurts.

Sammy went ballistic, tearing off his mask and verbally assaulting the umpire. Finally, after he had vented his anger on the man in blue to no avail, he picked up the ball and heaved it with all his might into center field. Unfortunately, the ball was still in play, and Red Wilson took the free double-pass through second and on to third. White was now the last line of defense. Ted Williams finally retrieved the ball and threw it back to the infield. Again, unfortunately, White and Red Sox manager Pinky Higgins were still arguing the play with umpire Umont. Seeing this, the Tigers third-base coach waved Wilson home. He scored easily as the three-man conference was still in session. It wouldn't have mattered. White had been ejected the moment he threw the ball away and would not have been eligible to make the play anyway. Higgins protested the game on grounds that time was called automatically when White was ejected. Not so. The umpire explained it his way: "White was not thrown out of the game until he threw the ball. When he threw the ball, he put it in play, and we couldn't call time until the play was finished. And it didn't finish until Wilson crossed the plate."

Sammy is one of the few catchers to be removed from a game because his pitcher couldn't find the strike zone. I say again, people, you can't make stuff like this up!

No one like Sammy White exists in today's game. If CNN spends two months debating the infamous wardrobe malfunction by Janet Jackson at the Super Bowl, today's politically correct sporting establishment is definitely not going to tolerate a flagrant display of falsies.

Barry Zito

Barry Zito is living proof that there are still non-conformists in baseball. He may be the only surfer dude in our list of eccentrics. The winner of the 2002 Cy Young Award in the American League is an ace of the Oakland A's talented staff. He is the stereotypical incense-burning Californian and, like me, he's a southpaw who attended USC. He helped the Trojans to the 1998 NCAA championship. Where I am known as the Spaceman, he is often referred to as Planet Zito.

He combines the philosophic principles of yoga and the baseball principles of Yogi. I like his attitude. He recently said, "I'm okay being the veteran, but I'm still just a kid." That's the way I've always felt. He also was quoted as saying, "Some people pray to a totem pole, some people pray to a sun, some people pray to a god. It all works for them. It all comes back to what you think." Once again, I agree. But this is what really sold me on the guy: "I refuse to be molded into some stereotypical ballplayer that has no interests, really, no life, no depth, no intelligence." And this: "There's a part of me that wants to go streak and run outside and jump around and go swim in the ocean and do everything. The other part of me wants to bear down and repeat this kind of performance next year and in the years to come." And especially this: "I can relate to anyone. I can hang out with stoners, skaters, surfers, stockbrokers, lawyers, athletes, rappers. I feel I can hang out with any group of people and find common ground to talk with them."

Zito confesses that he's "big into having routines. I'm almost a little anal about it, but you have to be, especially at this level."

He's a perfectionist who sets high personal standards. "I'm not happy when I pitch seven innings and give up two runs and get a win."

Zito's fastball is in the 90 mph range. He has to get by on his smarts, not a bully pitch. He has a fantastic 12–6, knee-buckling curveball that has earned him nicknames such as 12–6, Rip-Curl,

Barry Zito, playing hacky sack with a baseball before the start of the 2006 ALCS, is a flaky, California-born left-hander from USC. Sound familiar?

Captain Hook and—eccentrically—Bert. He also has a very respectable change of pace.

Need proof that he dances to a different tune? "When I'm doing well, it's like I'm in a nice little ballet," he said, and as a former prima donna myself (see Chapter 1), I know what he's saying. "Everything is going slow all around me," he added. "It's very peaceful." Twice, Zito has been cast as a toy soldier in the Oakland Ballet's production of *The Nutcracker*. I'd love to get together with him and discuss our pas de deux.

He also packs his own satin Tempur-Pedic pillow on road trips. It is reportedly fuchsia in color. He also takes a foam roller, which he uses to massage his hips, not to mention bath salts and candles to use while soaking his aching muscles after pitching. But he is an eclectic eccentric with tastes that also run to mountain bikes, rock guitar, and stuffed animals in addition to surfboards.

Zito once bought his own autographed baseball cards on eBay. Why, you may well ask, did he bid high prices for cards when he could just get some new ones and sign them? "Because they're authenticated," he explained.

Perhaps it is the fact that he's the son of show-business parents, but his timing and sense of the dramatic are impressive. His uncle is Patrick Duffy and he once did a cameo in an episode of *JAG*. In that particular show, he played a pitcher who stands trial for assault with a deadly weapon for hitting a batter in the head with murderous intent. I know the feeling.

Ozzie Guillen

Chicago White Sox manager Ozzie Guillen recently got himself into a ton of trouble for swearing at a reporter. He used a word that is politically incorrect but is used all the time in baseball. He called him a cocksucker. Really that's not bad. It's used so often in baseball that it's the rough equivalent of "rascal" or "scalawag." Nevertheless, to quell such insurrections, I suggest that he be sent to work with the guys from *Queer Eye for the Straight Guy*, where he can get sensitivity training and learn macramé.

The White Sox should be ashamed of themselves. They did not support their manager. He may not be politically correct, but he is a refreshing change from the robotic accountants who presently serve as managers in the major leagues. You know who we're talking about. Without a chart, a computer, and a file folder crammed full of statistics, they would be forced to make decisions on their own.

Ozzie actually admits to having fun managing his White Sox. Some people think that's a bad thing. Ozzie Guillen is a throwback to the days when managers were totally involved in what's happening on the field. He manages with emotion and instinct. No computer printouts, no complex charts or statistical analyses for him. All you had to do was watch Ozzie in the 2005 postseason to know that he is passionate about the game of baseball. Even when his Chicago White Sox were leading the American League Central by 15 games, he was hardly nonchalant. In fact, it was not unusual for him to throw up before games.

Ozzie tells it like it is. Chicago writers feel that he leaves no thought—however trivial—unexpressed. He expects the maximum from his players and doesn't spout the usual political correctness when they screw up. Before the White Sox won the World Series, ending an 88-year drought, he told *Sports Illustrated*, "Chicago is a city of f*cking losers. We've got to come up with another sport for Chicago, just to win something."

Ozzie is not laid back and he does not let the fact that English is his second language—profanity being his third—prevent him from using it to great effect. When Buck Showalter made postgame comments questioning Guillen's baseball knowledge, Ozzie let go with a barrage that indicates he knows the use of irony and sarcasm in any language. Because of his subtlety, I have italicized the sarcastic parts so that the less intuitive reader will be able to identify them.

> When the *best manager in the history of baseball* talks about you, that means you're on somebody's mind. And when you're beating the crap out of the *best manager in baseball*, and we beat the shit out of them, it makes me feel a lot better....To me, I think [Atlanta manager] Bobby Cox was the best. To compete against the guy [Showalter] that *invented baseball*, and beat him, that's something you should feel good about as a rookie manager.
>
> I could have made a big deal about it, but I was professional enough because I respect the guy that was coaching first base....John Wetteland did something in the big leagues. [Showalter] never

even smelled a jock in the big leagues. He didn't even know how the clubhouse in the big leagues was when he got his first job...."*Mr. Baseball*" never even got a hit in Triple-A. He was a backup catcher or a first baseman all his career. Now all of the sudden he's the *best ever in baseball*....There are so many different things he might be jealous [of]...I was a better player than him, I've got more money than him, and I'm better looking than him.

Ozzie is a follower of an Afro-Caribbean religion called Santeria that combines elements of African religion and Christianity. The rituals associated with it seem bizarre by North American standards. Each person is born under a specified guardian saint that they must worship. The rituals sometimes require the sacrifice of animals and birds, and each saint has his or her favorite. Significantly, the blood of the goat is a very common offering. Just imagine, if only Ozzie had been managing the Cubbies, that billy-goat curse would have been history!

During the 2005 championship season, Guillen dismissed questions about pitch counts and pitch selection. "First of all, I'm not that smart," he said proving that he *is* a smart manager, "and second, I'm not that good," proving that he *is* that good. "I trust my catchers." (In my next life I want to come back as a member of Ozzie's rotation!) He allowed that the White Sox were sometimes lucky but promised that if the team could hold together until October, "it will be my turn to make witchcraft." Which he then proceeded to do.

During the 2005 World Series, Guillen used basic but effective sign language to call his relievers in from the pen. When he wanted the jumbo-sized closer Bobby Jenks, he stretched his hands wide as if he were gripping a refrigerator. If he wanted the services of a more modestly proportioned model, he held his hands closer together. It was a great visual for the TV audience and an indication of how this manager doesn't take himself or the game too seriously.

But it would be a shame if the politically correct police stifled Ozzie. *The Onion*, my source for all information, described a scenario that I could certainly see happening:

Ozzie Guillen Fined $10,000
For What He Just Thought

August 10, 2006

CHICAGO—MLB disciplinary officials announced that Ozzie Guillen would be fined $10,000 and ordered to undergo sensitivity psychoanalysis for the "irresponsible, offensive, and completely unacceptable" thoughts that passed through the White Sox manager's mind during Wednesday night's game.

"During the fourth inning of yesterday's White Sox–Yankees contest, Mr. Guillen's mind conjured a series of insensitive, wildly inappropriate—I would even go so far as to say depraved—thoughts and images," said Bob Watson, MLB vice president of on-field discipline. "Baseball is a social institution with a responsibility to espouse proper values, and there is absolutely no excuse for anyone to entertain thoughts which portray people in a negative or demeaning light, regardless of their race, color, creed, culture, sexual orientation, gender, weight, or personal beliefs."

"Major League Baseball would like to offer its most profound, heartfelt apologies to those portrayed inappropriately in Mr. Guillen's mind, including African Americans, Cuban Americans, Caucasian Americans, Dominican Americans, 'immigrants,' the sportswriting community, the gay community, the White Sox fan community, the communities of Schaumburg, Illinois, and New York City, the umpiring crew, Yankee right fielder Bobby Abreu and his female relatives, members of the Peace Corps, and women—

particularly the female fan seated in Section 32, Row B, Seat 7," Watson added.

Watson's report alleges that Guillen carelessly composed his thoughts without considering the fact that millions of fans would know exactly what he was thinking in the event that television cameras inevitably cut to a shot of his sour expression. And according to commissioner Bud Selig, the idea of remorse never crossed Guillen's mind.

"Ozzie's thoughts were in poor taste, and the sheer volume and scope of them—all of which occurred over a 17-second span of time—seem to indicate that they were premeditated," Selig said. "I also must strongly emphasize that our organization neither shares nor condones Mr. Guillen's views on statutory rape, regardless of whether or not they are ever vocalized."

Guillen's thoughts upon learning of his punishment earned him an additional $5,000 fine and a three-game suspension.

"I'm not going to change the way I think," Guillen said during an apology late Wednesday. "Anyone who knows me will tell you I can't control my thoughts."

"I acknowledge that the things that entered my mind today might have offended certain groups of people, but you have to realize I didn't mean anything by it," Guillen continued. "After all, my mother is dead, too, and I would never want anyone digging up her corpse and paying drunken, uh, Arabs to do those things to her. And as for people of Middle Eastern origin, I was only imagining those terms being used to refer to just one specific 'filthy raghead,' not a whole region of them."

"Also, I would never, ever do that kind of thing to a person in real life, even if I had a worn-down radial-saw blade and 100 milligrams of hydrogen cyanide at my disposal," Guillen added.

A recent poll indicates that 97 percent of baseball fans were offended by Guillen's thoughts, with an astounding 12 percent of those polled actually having been personally attacked, insulted, or killed within Guillen's inner tirade.

"Ozzie needs to remember that people have families...My nine-year-old daughter was watching at home, and even though she isn't old enough to understand what a 'tire-iron abortion' is, I'm sure she understood that what he was thinking was not nice," said Chicago resident and White Sox fan Brian McVeigh. "And this isn't the last time he'll be on TV. What will I have to explain to my daughter next time she sees Ozzie thinking? Bestiality? Knife rape? Auschwitz?"

Guillen, however, claims that if he truly meant what he thought, he would have just come out and said it.

"Am I going to have to explain everything I think from now on?" Guillen asked reporters. "Do I really need to tell you people that I don't actually want fuel truck after fuel truck to plow into an orphanage? That I don't really want to feed baby rats to [White Sox pitcher] Jon Garland so they chew their way through his intestinal system and expel themselves out his rectum in unison? That I actually love and respect my wife? Can't you people figure this out on your own? I'm not that bad a guy."

"F*cking faggot assholes," Guillen added.

Jim Bouton
More than any other person, Jim Bouton showed us that ballplayers are human beings. Up to that point, most fans had their doubts.

They thought that ballplayers played the games and then went home, maybe stopping for a milkshake and visiting a children's hospital on the way home. They arrived early the next day in order to practice the old hit and run. That was until *Ball Four* hit the bookshelves. Bouton's actual career was almost little more than a prop, a chance to observe and soak up all that makes up a major league team. In a sport where few players even read books that didn't have superheroes on the cover, Bouton was actually writing a book—a book about them! (Reliever Jim Kern once spotted a sportswriter reading *Blind Ambition*, John Dean's book about Watergate. Kern grabbed the book, tore out the last few pages, and ate them as if they were so many M&Ms. "Now figure out how it ends," he said.)

It was his book *Ball Four* that made Bouton, if not a flake, certainly a rebel. Some players had different names for him, names like "Judas" and "Benedict Arnold" and "backstabber." He was ostracized by players, but he did a great service to fans. Bouton showed us that ballplayers were not all heroic. Some were flawed, some were mean-spirited, and some were downright nasty. Strangely, though Bouton was vilified by many of his colleagues and shunned by the fortress known as Major League Baseball, fans liked what they read. For the first time they knew that Mickey Mantle liked to look up women's skirts. In short, they knew that the players they idolized were just average people with one special talent—and not a life-and-death talent either—just a talent to throw, catch, or hit a baseball.

Miguel Batista

Bouton was about as close as baseball gets to an intellectual. Happily, there is another intellectual in today's game—and he actually reads books without pictures in them! His name is Miguel Batista. Naturally, he's a pitcher. Batista, a native of the Dominican Republic, is a renaissance man. He's bright, articulate, and funny. How weird is that!? He writes poetry and fiction and has priorities well beyond the baseball diamond. In fact, he didn't begin to play competitive baseball until the age of 15 and even now he isn't consumed by it. Although he loves the "beauty of the game," he hopes to become a criminal lawyer someday. He has written a novel about the search for a teenage serial killer in Arizona. He writes completely in longhand because he feels disconnected from the word when using a keyboard. "Typing is like taking the stars out of the sky," he told John Lott in a December 19, 2003, article in Canada's *National Post*.

Baseball clichés do not issue from his lips. His commentary is invariably thoughtful and thought-provoking. "I have become everything my mom always feared I would become: a man of my own mind that is not afraid to go against the crowd," he told Lott.

When he joined the Toronto Blue Jays from the National League Arizona Diamondbacks, he fielded reporters' questions about whether he would miss taking his turn at bat. "My hits are just like comets," he quipped. "They come every four years."

Batista is my kind of pitcher. Despite his surname, he is far from being a dictator on the mound. He is a democrat. He believes in getting the infielders involved. Recently, his ERA had ballooned to 5.21 and he was being criticized for not throwing more fastballs. "I had been leading the league in weak ground balls and bloopers," he explained. He refused to change his philosophy and eventually the cheap hits turned into outs. "I was approaching it from the standpoint that I was doing my job, making those people hit the ball soft," he said.

The man they call Miggy is also like me in that he doesn't believe in specialization. He wants to start and finish the game. "I believe that baseball has evolved to a point to where a lot of starters don't go out there with the mentality of throwing a complete game, and that's totally bad for the game," Batista said recently.

It was Hall of Fame hurler and fellow countryman Juan Marichal who convinced Batista that finishing games made him the master of his own fate. Marichal certainly practiced what he preached—he finished 244 games in his career and he won 243 games in his career.

For me, the most impressive thing about Batista is that he is a good world citizen. He cares about the earth and works to make it a better, fairer place. He is a philanthropist who donated money to build the first baseball field on Native American land in Arizona. Despite his numerous good works in the community, he doesn't want attention drawn to him. "I don't really like my name to be mentioned," he said, "because I'm the type of man who believes that real charity doesn't care if it's tax-deductible or not." Wow! What a concept!

He knows that baseball clubhouses bear little resemblance to the Algonquin Round Table, as he related to Lott in the *National Post*. "In 1998 I walked into the Montreal Expos clubhouse with a book in my hand, a biography of Mahatma Gandhi. Here comes the head trainer, going, 'Is that what I think it is?' I said, 'What?' He says, 'You might be the first player I've ever seen in 35 years that brought a book in here without any pictures in it.' For me that was shocking. He acted like I broke the law."

Manny Ramirez

Another present-day player of note is Manny Ramirez, who doesn't just march to the beat of a different drummer. He is often the only one in the parade. During the 2005 season, while Red Sox pitching coach Dave Wallace was visiting the mound, the Boston left fielder walked off the field and through the left-field wall, disappearing from view. Fenway Park was abuzz with conjecture about where the slugger had gone and why. When he returned with all the drama of Shoeless Joe Jackson emerging from a cornfield, to cheers, he gave the fans a thumbs-up.

Conjecture grew as to what Manny was doing in the bowels of the Green Monster. Did he go there to pee or not to pee, that was the question.

His absence—is the term "desertion" applicable to these particular men in uniform?—raised the eyebrows of Red Sox management and players, since he barely got back in time for relief pitcher Wade Miller's next delivery. The delivery was not offered at, but on

Manny Ramirez definitely walks to the beat of a different drummer. In this case he walked into the Green Monster to relieve himself during a pitching change.

the very next pitch the batter, Tampa Bay's Joey Gathright, singled to left. What if Manny had still been AWOL in the Wall? It could have been the first uncontested inside-the-park homer in history.

After the game, Miller was asked if he'd thought to check left field before pitching to Gathright. "Why would I check?" he responded. And he had a point. Pitchers shouldn't have to do a roll call before every pitch.

As for Manny's activities inside the Wall, they give new meaning to the term "relief pitcher." "I [peed] in a cup," he said. Bosox manager Terry Francona was philosophical about the incident. "I'm just glad he came back," he said.

Speaking of urine, Willie Horton had a goal to pee in every left field in the American League. A man has to have dreams. Rick Bosetti, a good field–no hit player for the Philadelphia Phillies, St. Louis Cardinals, Toronto Blue Jays, and Oakland A's in the mid-'70s and early '80s, was much more of a visionary. Before he retired, he wanted to urinate in the outfield of *every major league ballpark*. It must have been a great relief when he finally reached his goal.

Kevin Millar

We all have had a Kevin Millar in our classroom. He's the guy who made farting sounds with his armpit when the teacher's back was turned. The guy who claimed a dachshund devoured his home-work. The guy who put the fake puke on the floor. He's also the guy who made coming to school bearable even when exams were loom-ing or your book report was unfinished. A tad obnoxious and yet entertaining, he was the class clown who made you realize that life's not all that serious.

Kevin Millar came to national prominence as a member of the Boston Red Sox, but his apprenticeship took place elsewhere. Millar was acquired by the Boston Red Sox, who pirated him away from the Florida Marlins in advance of the 2003 season.

As a member of the Marlins, he toiled in relative obscurity despite impressive offensive numbers.

When he graduated to the Red Sox, he continued to produce on the field, and the level of his class clownery was elevated. Millar became an instant hit in the summer of 2003 as "Rally Karaoke Guy" when the big screen at Fenway showed footage of him lip-synching Bruce Springsteen's "Born in the USA." Millar's frat-house version of the Boss's anthem captured the imagination of the Boston public. Millar is shown, sleeves rolled up and biceps rippling a la Bruce. His choreography needed work and he wasn't quite ready to appear on *American Idol*, but the performance was inspirational nonetheless.

Steve Sax is one of several players who suffered from a sudden inexplicable inability to throw the ball accurately. No, we're not talking about the occasional errant throw, we're talking about a kind of throwing dyslexia that's painful to watch. Practically overnight the National League Rookie of the Year for the Dodgers in 1982 lost his ability to throw the ball to first base. He was to the first base throw what Shaquille is to the free throw. This is a major drawback for a second baseman. If you're scoring this at home, the 4-3 play became the fourth-row–seat-3 play. The joke was: with Steve Sax, everyone can get to first base. Fans in opposing ballparks, and sometimes at Dodger Stadium, used to don batting helmets for self-preservation.

After bottoming out with 30 errors in 1983, the courageous Sax triumphed over the phobia, and actually led American League second basemen in double-plays in 1989.

The phenomenon began when the Red Sox visited the Texas Rangers in July. One of Millar's classmates at Los Angeles City Junior College decided to deliver the tape to the Red Sox dressing room. It didn't take long for Millar's teammates to know they were in possession of pure gold. At first they just screened it in the clubhouse before games to have some fun at Millar's expense. The first time it was shown, the Red Sox exploded for 14 runs. That was enough to ensure a long and successful run. When the Red Sox went into a slump in the midst of their divisional pennant race with the Yankees, and with ace Pedro Martinez ailing, the Red Sox players decided it was time to break out their secret weapon and featured it on the Jumbotron. In the sixth inning of a game against Oakland, the film had its debut.

The reviews were boffo. The Fenway Park crowd responded as if the Boss himself had walked into center field. And the Red Sox responded by beating up on the Athletics 14–5. The momentum began to build as the Red Sox offense came alive. The Sox went on a five-game winning streak.

Millar also coined one of the most effective New England rallying cries since "the British are coming" rang through the air. He implored his Red Sox teammates to "cowboy up." The rough translation of this cryptic phrase is to step up your performance when it's needed—to come through in the clutch.

Sure, Millar contributed on the field. He batted .276 with 25 homers and 96 RBIs. But it was his intangibles that made the biggest impact. It is easy to dismiss Millar as *just* a clown. But don't do it. Ask anyone on the Boston Red Sox of 2004 and they'll tell you he was he was a leader in the truest sense of the word. Most significantly he brought Manny Ramirez into the Red Sox circle and made him part of a winning unit.

During the historic 2004 ALCS with the Yankees, he was the instigator of a pregame ritual in which Millar and several of his teammates had a sip of Jack Daniels before the final two games. This would be the class clown equivalent of smoking in the bathroom.

Millar is great with names. He has a nickname for everybody and made the Red Sox roster sound like the cast of *The Little Rascals*. This is the major league version of the class clown's Stinky. He also described the 2004 Red Sox as "a bunch of idiots having fun."

Millar was and is a leader in the clubhouse. Leadership takes many forms, and it isn't always the guy with the highest batting average or lowest ERA who takes command. Sometimes it's the guy who provides comic relief and instills a team ethic. When Edgar Renteria came to Boston in 2005 to replace Orlando Cabrera (who had replaced Nomar Garciaparra), he had a horrible year. Fans at Fenway booed him mercilessly. It was the slumping Millar, who was also getting heat from fans, who came to his aid. "I feel it's my right to stand up, because I'm not a very good player, but I bring some intangibles and it's my job to speak about the way I feel about Edgar Renteria," said Millar. "He's my teammate, my family member, and I think he's a great player." Loyalty is something I admire in a ballplayer. I got in trouble twice in my career because I questioned the lack of loyalty by ownership in Boston and Montreal. I paid a huge price for it. Millar brings intangibles that don't show up in the box scores.

Kevin Millar has brought his infectious attitude to teams across both leagues, but don't expect him to reunite with BoSox manager Terry Francona any time soon.

In 2003 he convinced teammates to shave their heads in a show of solidarity. Since then, he has inspired more hair colors and styles than Vidal Sassoon. He also was front and center as some members of the World Champion 2004 Boston Red Sox appeared on *Queer Eye for the Straight Guy.*

Kevin, now a Baltimore Oriole, left a special gift for Terry Francona in the visiting manager's office in Minnesota. It was a bag of dog crap with the note: "Here's to Francona." Francona was not all that appreciative: "I opened it and reached in, I didn't realize what it was. I just called him back and said, 'Any chance you had of ever coming back here just went right down the toilet with that bag.'"

D ave Concepcion, shortstop for the legendary Big Red Machine Cincinnati teams of the 1970s, once tried to end a slump by being tumbled dry in the team's laundry dryer.

Curt Schilling

Kevin Millar is an obvious clown, but sometimes even the most straitlaced players are funny, albeit unintentionally. Curt Schilling is a case in point. Schilling is the no-nonsense, fiercely conservative pitcher who helped bring World Series championships to Arizona and Boston. Politically, he is slightly to the right of Attila the Hun and so far right of me that I can't even see him on the horizon. That's why it's tough to reconcile *that* Schilling with *this* one:

Schilling: "My first foray into Lower Guk was a lot of fun… Completing the Robe of the Lost Circle quest was a blast. Camping raster was a nightmare, but I got stupidly lucky. I had pretty much resigned myself to camping Scythehands in the Mino room, logging in, seeing another monk already there camping, and waiting. One night I log in and there's a 55 level monk there. Great guy. He's been there for, like, 12 hours. No Raster—pop, despawn, pop, despawn—still no Raster." Explanation: Schilling was a devotee of *EverQuest*, an online strategy game. To someone, somewhere, somehow, this all makes sense.

David Letterman tried to spice up Schilling's image when Curt appeared on his show. He produced the following "Top Ten Curt Schilling Pre-Game Rituals" (by David Letterman, copyright May 14, 1999):

10. Sit naked for an hour in a giant tub of Philadelphia Cream Cheese

9. Caress old Mike Schmidt mustache clippings
8. Call Pete Rose—see what the line is on the game
7. Kiss all 200 of my cuddly, adorable Beanie Babies
6. Smoke one of those weird cigarettes that Allen Iverson gave me
5. Wolf down burritos I shoplifted from local Wawa
4. Sing Boyz II Men "I'll Make Love to You" over stadium PA system
3. Run through the stadium parking lot snapping off antennas
2. Learn what not to do while watching tape of Mets game
1. Go rough up some snotty-nosed Swarthmore punks

Any one of those items would have qualified Schill for status as an eccentric—except for the cream cheese thing, which I find perfectly normal and actually quite refreshing.

Corey Koskie

Corey Koskie, now of the Milwaukee Brewers, is one crazy Canuck. Just ask David "Big Papi" Ortiz of the Boston Red Sox. When they were teammates on the Minnesota Twins, the well-traveled third baseman once "allegedly" filled Ortiz's underwear with peanut butter. Crude, you say? Not when you're a perfectionist like this refugee from the Great White North. It is the meticulous detail and degree of specificity that separates him from the crowd. "It was the chunky stuff, not the smooth kind," he recalls, as if the other would have been the work of a dullard. It gets better: Ortiz put the underwear on without noticing and was leaving the clubhouse when someone finally clued him in. The prank brought the team to their knees, not in prayer, but in spasms of laughter. "I don't know what's in that dude's underwear the rest of the time but not to notice you have chunky peanut butter in there…," Koskie told Mike Ganter of the *Toronto Sun*. Of course, like any genius of dirty tricks, he denies all responsibility for the incident.

Corey is no one-trick pony. His other specialties are burning, cutting, or hiding various items of teammates' clothing. A tribute to his ruthlessness is the fact that teammates live in constant fear of him. That's a sign of a true professional.

Dutch Leonard

Another embarrassing incident, this one of the physiological variety, took place on August 1, 1945. It starred Dutch Leonard, a pitcher for the Washington Senators. In the eighth inning of a game against the Philadelphia Athletics, Leonard was pitching a two-hit shutout when Irvin Hall hit a hard comebacker right at the pitcher. The ball struck Leonard in the midsection, and he thought he had the ball trapped between stomach and glove. When he reached for the elusive sphere, he couldn't find it. He checked the usual places, the mound, the infield, but to no avail. Finally he realized there was (presumably) a third ball in his pants—and this one had stitches and a cork center. The hidden ball trick was straightforward, compared to the sleight of hand it took to extricate the horsehide from Leonard's pants. When he reached in to retrieve it, it slipped to the bottom of his pant leg, causing him to fumble around like Pee Wee Herman at a porno flick. By the time the ball was extricated, Hall was safe at first base and the entire ballpark was in hysterics.

Lou Piniella

Lou Piniella, also known as Leapin' Lou, was passionate about baseball as a player and he is so as a manager. In July 2005 he was frustrated by the inability of his Tampa Bay Devil Rays relievers to protect a lead, so he used his relievers as starters and starters as relievers. "People are going to think I'm crazy, but that's what I'm going to do," he said. "I'll bring in whatever reliever I feel like starting the game with, and I'll bring my starter in—in the third inning—and we'll play nine innings of baseball that way. I'm serious."

If his idea had caught on—it didn't—we'd have DHs playing center field, infielders in the outfield, and vice versa. For that matter, why not have pitchers catch, and catchers pitch? It could be like George Costanza's "do the opposite" theory.

As a player, Lou went all out. He went to the plate aggressively and liked to be challenged with fastballs. When he got something else, the future manager was quick to analyze what went wrong.

B obo Holloman pitched a no-hitter in his first major league start on May 6, 1953. He also drove in three runs as Bill Veeck's St. Louis Browns defeated the Philadelphia Athletics 6–0. *Bad* move! Bobo had no place to go but down. And he plummeted. He never pitched another complete game, and by the end of the season he was gone from the major leagues for good. His final line in *Total Baseball* records that he appeared in 22 games, had a career record of 3–7, and an ERA of 5.23. But they can never take that no-no away from Bobo.

After whiffing on a change-up from Geoff Zahn, he explained: "It's like being bitten by a stuffed panda." With these communication powers, it's easy to see why he was born to manage.

When he was managing at Tampa Bay, Lou tripped over the top step of the dugout while charging onto the field to argue a call. He landed face-first on the grass. He later explained, "I just don't have that first-step explosion anymore."

Leapin' Lou and I may be opposites but we are in complete agreement on one thing: the length of a ballplayer's hair has nothing to do with his ability to play the game. When he was with the Yankees, the IBM of baseball teams, he arrived at spring training with the hairstyle of the day—i.e., long. He was ordered to trim his hair. Piniella objected. "What's that got to do with anything?" he argued. Boss Steinbrenner was adamant: "It's a discipline issue. You have to respect the Yankees uniform." Piniella brought out the heavy artillery. "Come on, George," he said, "are you saying that if Jesus Christ returned to earth with his long hair, you wouldn't let him play for the Yankees?"

Georgey-Porgy marched his employee across the street to the hotel pool and said, "I'll make a deal with you. If you walk across that water, I'll make an exception in your case." Of course, Steinbrenner's the kind of guy who would have seen Jesus walk on water and then questioned his ability to swim.

Sources

Allen, Maury. *Bo*. The Dial Press: New York, 1973.

Bouton, Jim with Neil Offen. *"I Managed Good, But Boy Did They Play Bad."* Playboy Press: Chicago, 1973.

Broeg, Bob. *Super Stars of Baseball*. The Sporting News, 1971.

Coffin, Thomas P. *The Old Ball Game*. Herder and Herder, 1971.

Creamer, Robert W. *Babe: The Legend Comes to Life*. Simon and Schuster: New York, 1974.

Daley, Arthur. *Inside Baseball*. Grosset and Dunlap, 1950.

Durant, John. *The Story of Baseball*. Hastings House, 1949.

Ford, Whitey; Mickey Mantle; and Joe Durso. *Whitey and Mickey*. Viking Press: New York, 1977.

Gleason, Paul. *Uleta Blues & Haikus: Songs, Poetry, Sketches*. Skuwampas Press: Palm Desert, California, 2006.

Honig, Donald. *Baseball Between the Lines*. Coward, McCann & Geoghegan, 1976.

Johnstone, Jay, and Rick Talley. *Over the Edge*. Contemporary Books: Chicago, 1987.

Johnstone, Jay, with Rick Talley. *Temporary Insanity*. Contemporary Books: Chicago, 1985.

Kiersh, Edward. *Where Have You Gone, Vince DiMaggio?* Bantam Books: New York. 1983.

Lyle, Sparky, and Peter Golenbock. *The Bronx Zoo*. Triumph Books: Chicago, 2005.

McDermott, Mickey, and Howard Eisenberg. *A Funny Thing Happened on the Way to Cooperstown*. Triumph Books: Chicago, 2003.

Meany, Tom. *Baseball's Greatest Pitchers*. A.S. Barnes, 1951.

Nash, Bernie, and Allan Zullo. *The Baseball Hall of Shame*. Pocket Books/Simon and Schuster: New York, 1987.

Nash, Bruce; Allan Zullo; and Bernie Ward. *The Sports Hall of Shame*. Archway Paperbacks, 1990.

Nettles, Graig, and Peter Golenbock. *Balls*. G.P. Putnam's Sons: New York, 1984.

Paige, Leroy. *Maybe I'll Pitch Forever*. Doubleday: New York, 1962.

Schacht, Al. *Clowning Through Baseball*. A.S. Barnes: New York, 1941.

Smith, Red. *Red Smith's Favorite Sports Stories*. W.W. Norton, 1975.

Thorn, John; Phil Birnbaum; and Bill Deane. *Total Baseball*. Sport Classic Books: Wilmington, Delaware, 2004.